The Churchillians

JOHN COLVILLE

The Churchillians

Weidenfeld and Nicolson
London

ISBN 0 297 78955 4

Printed in Great Britain by
Butler & Tanner Ltd, Frome and London

Contents

Illustrations

Preface

A few months before he ceased to be Prime Minister, Winston Churchill said to me, 'One day you must write about all these things we have seen together'. Many others have written and will continue to write about those 'things', with varying degrees of accuracy and no less varied interpretations. The stage on which Churchill was the leading actor was a crowded one and my present endeavour is to paint portraits of others in the cast. Some I knew well, some were only acquaintances and some, whose association with Churchill was ancient history to me, are depicted as contemporaries saw them or as he and Lady Churchill described them. I have done my best to tell the whole truth as I saw it, noting the blemishes as well as the bloom, but I have tried to distinguish criticism from malice, an objective Churchill would have approved. I have not distilled more than a few bare facts from published sources and do not therefore offer a bibliography. The contents of this book are based on my own observation, on a still vivid memory and yet more, since memory is fallible, on detailed diaries I kept during most of the time I served Churchill.

In writing about those surrounding Churchill it is natural that I should make constant references to him personally and to his views on events and policies. I have not, however, sought to describe him in isolation.

My warm thanks are due to Miss Josephine Butler and Mrs Eileen Old, both of whom painfully but uncomplainingly typed my handwritten manuscript. My delightful family, who can be counted on to produce the maximum disturbance when I am writing a book, were on this occasion a trifle less distracting than usual.

John Colville 1980

CHAPTER ONE

Early Friends

When Winston Churchill became Prime Minister of the United Kingdom on 10 May 1940, he was over sixty-five years old, already qualified for an old-age pension. His energy was undiminished and the flame of his eloquence was undimmed, but many of his fellow countrymen, whatever their politics, considered him notorious rather than famous and regarded him more favourably as a writer than as a politician. For the remaining twenty-five years of his life his fame was spread throughout the world and that fame was matched by reverence and affection.

It is with his associates in his last quarter of a century that this book is principally concerned, but he had been elected to Parliament in Queen Victoria's reign and in the intervening forty years he did not hide his light under a bushel. The offices he held were numerous, diverse and challenging. They included the Admiralty at the outbreak of the First World War. Finally, in 1939, after eleven years in the political wilderness, his voice raised in warning of the coming danger, he became once again First Lord of the Admiralty on the day the Second World War erupted on a continent gripped by fear and foreboding.

During the forty years before he became Prime Minister there were many Churchillians and still more anti-Churchillians. This chapter is concerned with some of the former. Only one of Churchill's friends from before the First World War was at his side in the Second. That was Max Aitken, Lord Beaverbrook, and his relationship with Churchill commands a chapter to itself.

There were a few older men for whom Churchill, in his youth, had regard. The headmaster of Harrow, Dr Welldon, took trouble with an apparently incorrigible boy. That Churchill thought well of him is proved by his invitation to give the address at his wedding. He also respected Sir Bindon Blood, under whose command he fought on the Indian north-west frontier. He was impressed by the advice and philosophy of the American Congressman Bourke Cockran. He liked Sir Ian Hamilton, who befriended him in the Boer War, and there were several of his mother's associates to whom he paid attention. By and large, however, Churchill entered the House of Commons and the twentieth century with many acquaintances but fewer friends than is normal for a young man of twenty-six. Churchillians were rare birds and, apart from his relations, there were none under thirty.

Some men make their way by patience, industry and a long, uncomplaining climb. Others, in politics as in business, thrive on flamboyance. They ensure that their names are in the newspapers and that they are the subject of discussion, even if it be critical, in the widest circles that can be reached. It is more, no doubt, a matter of temperament than of design, for some are in a hurry all their lives while others are content to advance slowly towards a chosen goal, securing each position before they move forward to the next.

Winston Churchill was a young man in a hurry, with no reticence about publicity and no fear of opposition. He was consumed by personal ambition, but he sincerely longed to serve his country and he believed passionately in the causes he espoused. He was prepared to risk his political future rather than abandon a purpose to which he had pledged himself. He was hard-working, but he was certainly flamboyant.

When he was elected to Parliament he did not even know many of his contemporaries in the House of Commons. His parents' friends found him an interesting phenomenon; men of his own age thought him brash, offensive and arrogant. None, however, disregarded his energy and enthusiasm, or failed to recognize his mastery of the written and the spoken word. By his early books, *The Malakand Field Force* and *The River War*, he acquired a reading public. His escape from the Boers in Pretoria and his charge with the Twenty-first Lancers at Omdurman were blazoned across the world's press. He had far to go, but his name was already known. In those days it was still easier to get in by the door marked 'Pull' than by that marked 'Push', though there was always a list of triumphant pushers. Churchill made use of both doors.

Throughout the ages, not least in the twentieth century, there have been politicians who preached compassion but practised spite. Churchill was not among them. I thought it remarkable that, disliked by so many in his youth and presumably both snubbed and thwarted, he never spoke ill of his critics in later days. He remembered kindnesses he had received and opportunities he had been given. Whether deliberately or not, he seemed to have obliterated the other side of the coin from his memory altogether. One day, during the Second World War, he said to me, 'I hate nobody except Hitler – and that is professional'.

In 1900 the Conservatives were in power, Lord Salisbury being about to yield the Prime Ministership to his nephew, Arthur Balfour, to whose urbane, imperturbable intelligence Churchill paid tribute. In due course he became aware of Balfour's dislike of decisive action and accused him of preferring office to principle; but he acknowledged his brain-power and political cunning.

There was on the Government back benches a group of four young Conservatives who aimed to enliven an administration that seemed lacking in drive and purpose. A forceful speech by Churchill tearing to pieces his own Government's defence policy won their approval. Always influenced by his father's example, he remembered that Lord Randolph himself had led a small group of four, the Tory Democrats, in rebellion against Salisbury and the powerful House of Cecil. So he joined forces with his four dissatisfied contemporaries. They were known as the Hooligans, or more often the Hughligans as a pun on the name of their leader who was, strangely enough, Lord Hugh Cecil, one of Salisbury's younger sons.

As a pressure group they made little impact, but at their fortnightly dinners they tended to entertain leading Liberals rather than the members of their own party. They fell beneath the spell of the former Liberal Prime Minister, Lord Rosebery, who had left the field of active party strife but was still a formidable figure in the country. His palace in Buckinghamshire, Mentmore, his London house in Berkeley Square, and his Scottish home at Dalmeny, were open to them, for Rosebery was attracted by their youthful enthusiasm and their sentiments were nearer to the Liberal Imperialists, Asquith, Crewe, Grey and Haldane, as well as Rosebery himself, than to their own party. On the other hand, they stood far from the radical Liberals, including David Lloyd George, who were opposed to fighting the Boer War.

The four other Hughligans, in addition to Churchill, all sprang from eminent backgrounds. There was Lord Hugh; there was Arthur Stanley, son of the great magnate Lord Derby; there was Ian Malcolm, who married Lily Langtry's daughter by Prince Louis of Battenberg; there was Lord Percy, eldest son of the Duke of Northumberland. Stanley and Malcolm later performed many good deeds, but never won a political reputation. Percy, whom Churchill believed to have great promise, held under-secretary-ships at the India Office and the Foreign Office, but died in mysterious circumstances all alone in a second-class hotel in Paris. There remained Lord Hugh.

He was unlike Churchill in almost every respect except for a passionate belief in liberty and the merits of the British Constitution. He was a devout Anglican, austere in his principles, temperate in his habits and erudite in his tastes, and he was a confirmed bachelor. Nevertheless the two men were mutually attracted and Churchill bared his soul to Cecil as he seldom did to others. 'As the Free Trade issue subsides,' he wrote on one occasion, 'it leaves my personal ambitions naked and stranded on the beach, and they are an ugly and unsatisfactory spectacle by themselves though nothing but an advantage when borne forward with the flood of a great outsize cause.' In another letter, written in 1904, he said, 'You are the only person who has any real influence on my mind'. That was why, four years later, he asked Lord Hugh, by then sitting on the opposite side of the House of Commons to him, to be best man at his wedding. Lord Hugh accepted and characteristically wrote to explain the implications of the marriage service.

Lord Hugh Cecil never held office, using his acute intelligence for the next forty years more in the service of the Church than in that of the State; but he remained in the House of Commons till 1936, a representative of Oxford University, a stern censor of conduct, a man of whom Churchill never ceased to be fond. By 1941 he was established as Provost of Eton, much as he had disliked his own schooldays there and unattractive as he thought most schoolboys. Fortunately the Provost is not obliged to be closely concerned with them. Churchill wrote offering him a seat in the

House of Lords 'to repel the onset of the Adolf Hitler schools, to sustain the aristocratic morale and to chide the bishops when they err; and now that the Eton flogging block is destroyed by enemy action, you may have more leisure and strength. Anyhow, I should like to see a brother Hughligan again in the legislature.' A great deal had happened since 1904, but there was one friend of those days who still meant much to Churchill.

Churchill apart, the Hughligans melted away, making no contribution to political history. Their significance is as Churchill's earliest associates in Parliament and perhaps the first friends of his own generation that he ever had. His contemporaries at Harrow and Sandhurst had not found him congenial; those in the wider world had been deterred by his cavalier attitude and his disregard of all who were not in a position to serve an ambition which was, as he had confessed to Lord Hugh Cecil, an ugly and unsatisfactory spectacle by itself. He was, moreover, prone to fits of unreasonable and apparently ungovernable bad temper.

He was the only one of the Hughligans to cross the floor of the House and become a Liberal. He did so just in time to benefit from the political landslide of 1905. By push even more than by pull, and because of his proved abilities, he was at once given office as Parliamentary Under-Secretary at the Colonial Office. When the new Parliament met early in 1906, there were few unfamiliar faces on the Opposition benches, for a comfortable Conservative majority of 130 had been translated into an overwhelming Liberal one of more than 350.

There was, however, one interesting new face: that of the Conservative Member for the Walton division of Liverpool. He was soon to become more intimate with Churchill than anyone on the Liberal side. He was a barrister whose glittering performances as an advocate, whose exceptional intellectual power and mastery of language, and whose forensic skill with both rapier thrust and sabre cut amazed the legal profession. He was the grandson of a coal-miner, and his name was Frederick Edwin Smith, generally known as 'F.E.'. In course of time he became Lord Chancellor and Earl of Birkenhead. Like Churchill he could not resist being wittily offensive; indeed he had the sharper tongue of the two. He could give an answer, Churchill wrote, 'which turned the laugh, if it did not turn the company too, against his assailant'. So they shared a capacity for collecting more detractors than admirers, at any rate in their social relationships.

Already by March 1907 their mutual esteem was such that F.E., who had won academic laurels at Oxford, took Churchill to the University for a debate at the Union in which, with hostility assumed for the occasion, they attacked each other across the debating floor. A few months later Churchill returned the compli-. ment when he took his friend from the Opposition back benches on a ministerial visit to the French army manœuvres, and again, when he had become Home Secretary, he and F.E. paid a joint visit to Constantinople. They served together as yeomanry officers in the Oxfordshire Light Hussars, they dined together, they gambled together, they were happy in each other's company.

They were usually poles apart politically, for Churchill was a convinced Free Trader and F.E. was a staunch Protectionist; but in private they were inseparable. Apart from the gambling, the drinking and the verbal fencing matches, Churchill was increasingly influenced by F.E.'s wisdom. He wrote, after his death, that he had always found 'his counsel invaluable whether in public broil or private embarrassment'. When F.E. made the acquaintance of the newly arrived Canadian meteorite, Max Aitken, he introduced him to Churchill. Churchill, for his part, was working closely with his Cabinet colleague, Lloyd George, and brought him and F.E. together.

From 1910 to the outbreak of war in 1914, party politics in Britain assumed a bitterness which has seldom, if ever, been equalled. The old, almost casual, good personal feeling between Government and Opposition vanished in the wake of the House of Lords throwing out Lloyd George's radical budget and the Liberal Government attempting to provide Ireland with Home Rule against the violent opposition of Ulster. The Government, determined to hamstring the House of Lords, introduced the Parliament Bill, which curtailed the powers of the Upper House. In London society the great Tory houses were barred to Liberals, however distinguished or nobly born, and Conservatives refused to cross the threshold of 10 Downing Street, of Crewe House, or of Lord Carrington's hospitable Liberal home in Princes Gate.

The relationship of Winston and F.E. was unaffected by the general rancour. However, unpleasant incidents occurred.

Churchill told me how ashamed he was on an occasion he had never forgotten. He was driving with F.E. near Harrow on the Hill. He told the chauffeur to take them up to the school. He wanted to show his old seat of learning (at least of modified learning) to F.E., who had failed to win a Harrow scholarship two years before Churchill entered the school. The boys were in the 'Bill Yard' for the daily roll-call. They recognized Churchill and with one accord they booed the well-known supporter of the Parliament Bill and Home Rule for Ireland. He turned his back, humiliated in the presence of his friend, and vowed never to go back to Harrow. He broke that vow many times in later years; but he put his son, Randolph, down for Eton.

From 1911 onwards Churchill's delight was to dine with F.E., Max Aitken and sometimes Lloyd George. He would telephone to say that he was bringing them all back to dinner and it would be pleasant to have some lobsters and roast duck. The problems of housekeeping on a comparatively small budget were something he never grasped. His wife, Clementine, would do her best, for she did not wish to jeopardize her husband's political career or snub his friends; but she resented the late nights, the excessive consumption of brandy, the noise and the rowdiness which were inseparable from the garrulous evenings either in her own house or in that of one of the others. She had a sympathizer and fellow sufferer in Margaret Smith, F.E.'s wife, but they were both too fond of their husbands to do more than remonstrate. Their remonstrances were ineffective, for as Churchill and F.E. did not shrink from hard and intensive work, they saw no reason to be deprived of the kind of relaxation they enjoyed.

They found this form of social intercourse pleasant and politically invigorating, with sharpening of wits by argument and the exchange of well-informed views. Churchill and Aitken had strong constitutions and withstood the large alcoholic intake with impunity. F.E. was less fortunate. Perhaps he consumed more, or had a weaker head. He gained the reputation of being an excessively heavy drinker, and, though it seemed to make no difference to the quality of his performance at the Bar or in Parliament, he did at one moment feel constrained to restrict himself to cider, a self-denying ordinance that filled Churchill with horror.

Throughout the war F.E. stood firm by Churchill in adversity, just as Churchill in prosperity had stood by him. Against the wishes of the Tory leader, Balfour, Churchill persuaded Asquith to make him a Privy Councillor in King George v's Coronation Honours List. Four years later, after the disaster at Gallipoli, Churchill left the Government under a dark cloud of public reproach and personal misery. He went off to fight on the Western Front. The Conservatives, who had never forgiven him for deserting them in 1904, were determined he should not be invited to join the Coalition Government formed by Lloyd George at the end of 1916. It was then that F.E. championed his cause and argued insistently for his restoration to office. Churchill did eventually return, despite Conservative animosity, and worked his passage home as a dynamic Minister of Munitions. He and F.E. were as close as ever, and on Armistice Day they both dined with Lloyd George. It is noteworthy that on the very night the most terrible of all wars ended, with nearly a million British soldiers and sailors dead, the diners at Downing Street praised the courage and endurance of the German army and agreed that it would be impossible to rebuild Europe unless Germany participated.

After the war F.E. was loyal to Lloyd George, encouraging him against Churchill in his wish to recognize the Soviet Union and also, this time with Churchill in accord, in his support of the Greeks against the Turks, an issue which nearly led to war with Turkey and was a principal factor in breaking the post-war Coalition Government. No differences of opinion about Lloyd George's policy disturbed F.E.'s friendship with Churchill; nor did the fact that after the General Strike of 1926 he was, despite his coal-mining grandfather, intransigent in the hard line he favoured taking against the still-striking miners, whereas Churchill thought the coal-owners should make a worthwhile contribution to a fair settlement.

F.E., who had been Lord Chancellor under Lloyd George, was from 1924 Secretary of State for India under Stanley Baldwin. The Viceroy, Lord Irwin, thought him unsympathetic to those Indians who came to London, and it seems probable that, had he not died in 1930, he would have been Churchill's ally in the struggle against Baldwin on the issue of Dominion status for India. Churchill loved the India of the British Raj he had known in his youth. He could not accustom himself to the thought that sooner rather than later that great sub-continent must be self-governing. He believed that if British rule ended so would Indian unity; and in that prophecy he was not proved wrong. F.E., whose high Toryism was in stark contrast to Churchill's instinctive radicalism on almost all issues apart from those relating to India and the Soviet Union, could scarcely have failed to support him in opposition to Indian Home Rule.

Churchill deeply mourned the death of his friend. Several times during the Second World War, when storms were threatening, he told me how much he missed F.E.'s wise counsel. Birkenhead had, like Beaverbrook, a vivid personality, a full-blooded presence, a gaiety of spirit and a mind that was constantly active. These were the qualities that appealed to Churchill. They appealed much less to his wife, whose affection for Lady Birkenhead was warm, but who could not bring herself to like or approve of F.E. She conquered her dislike of Brendan Bracken; she eventually became reconciled to Beaverbrook, whose attentions to her and generosity to her husband wore down her animosity; but F.E. was never in her good graces though she could do nothing to change her husband's immutable regard for him. She thought him a vulgarian, which perhaps he was; she disliked his drinking habits, which sometimes made him insolent and overbearing; she was sure he encouraged Winston's inclination to gamble; and she objected to the thoughtless encouragement he gave to his godchild, her already turbulent and outspoken son, Randolph. Whatever the justice of her complaints, the fact remained that her husband never had a truer, cleverer or more congenial friend.

Lloyd George, with whom Churchill was once so anxious to stand well, and with whom he had dined, conversed and corresponded so avidly, was in a different category from Birkenhead. His charm was irresistible, but he was a political rather than a personal friend. He was a man whose achievements Churchill allowed nobody to denigrate in his presence. For his part Lloyd George was far from being equally loyal to Churchill. Indeed, as the diaries of his second wife and of his secretary, A.J. Sylvester, show, he criticized him frequently behind his back and was jealous of him. Churchill knew nothing of that. For him Lloyd George remained the colleague who had shared the work of introducing a national insurance scheme, and above all the great national leader who had brought victory out of stagnation. He thought of the days when as a member of the Coalition Cabinet he had basked in the favour of a great Prime Minister, returned to power with full popular support in the Khaki Election of 1919. Such were his memories of past glories that even in 1940, when Lloyd George was long past his prime, and even potentially disaffected, he had a longing to bring the ancient giant back into active politics. He toyed with the idea of making him a ministerial overlord of agriculture and was encouraged to do so by Beaverbrook and Brendan Bracken.

When in December of that year the embassy in Washington fell vacant, he telegraphed to President Roosevelt to enquire if Lloyd George would be acceptable. At Chequers that day he asked me if I had any other ideas about a successor to Lord Lothian, the Ambassador who had unexpectedly died. I suggested Lord Cranborne or Sir Robert Vansittart. Churchill replied that he had thought of both, but that Lloyd George's knowledge of munitions problems and his fiery personality marked him out. In order to sweeten the pill of serving under Lord Halifax as Foreign Secretary, he would make him a member of the War Cabinet. He believed he could trust him. And this was the man who had wanted to make a compromise peace with Hitler and whom many thought willing to assume the role of a British Marshal Pétain. It was astonishing how far Churchill's loyalty would go and how susceptible he was to the magic of the past. The President's answer was yes, but fortunately Lloyd George's was no.

There was a cousin of Churchill whom Clementine disliked as much as Birkenhead and Beaverbrook. That was the Chief Liberal Whip in Lloyd George's post-war Coalition Government, Frederick Guest, brother of the, to Clementine, equally odious Lord Wimborne. He was not devoid of merit, and his abilities were recognized by men as diverse as Mr Asquith, Field Marshal Sir John French and General Smuts. He rose to be Secretary of State for Air. He was, however, bad-mannered to the point of boorishness and, though devoted to his country, almost equally devoted to the pursuit of pleasure. More than anybody else he was responsible for organizing the notorious Lloyd George Fund which was partly endowed by the sale of political honours. Churchill liked him, for he had a tendency to disregard failings that less tolerant people found objectionable. Provided a man was brave and patriotic and had a sense of duty, his other defects were easily overlooked. On such matters Winston and Clementine Churchill did not see eye to eye.

A friend in a category all his own was the second Duke of Westminster, called by his family and friends Bendor after a heraldically named Derby winner which had belonged to his grandfather. In Edward VII's reign nobody with a disposition much less saintly than St Francis of Assisi could have been Duke of Westminster and remained unspoilt. Bendor had no inclination to saintly austerity; he denied himself nothing. He even had four wives, all women with fine qualities and notable intelligence. His large estates and vast fortune were competently and imaginatively administered by well-chosen agents, and he was renowned for his generosity. He had much to offer in addition to his fortune: self-centred he might be, but he combined charm of manner with a capacity for friendship and he had both a good brain and personal courage.

Churchill was not reluctant to profit from the luxuries of Eaton Hall or the excitement of hunting wild boars on horseback in Normandy; but he was not solely attracted by the amenities provided. The Duke had a personality to which men and women seldom failed to succumb and his intelligence, though inadequately used for most of his life, was easily recognizable. Early in the First World War he commanded a squadron of armoured cars in the Royal Naval Division and escorted Churchill to British GHQ in France and to the front line. It was as his guest, in a gathering of armoured-car experts, that Churchill first discussed the conception of that momentous new weapon, the tank. Later he took the Duke on a number of visits to France and together they watched the last German bid for victory in the massive Ludendorff offensive of March 1918.

The Duke of Westminster was not a man to expect any reward for services rendered or hospitality given. All he wanted in return was friendship and stimulating company. However, in November 1940 he did ask Churchill a favour. His French mistress, arriving in the British Isles, was seized by MI5 as an alien who must be investigated. The Prime Minister was requested, through his private secretary, to intervene and secure her immediate, unconditional release. He would not; at any rate until the proper formalities had been concluded. But friendship was unimpaired, and in due course the ineffectual private secretarial intermediary was asked to dine to meet the injured lady.

There is an ancient political dining society called, quite simply, 'The Club'. It was founded by Sir Joshua Reynolds and Dr Johnson in 1764 and the list of its past members is a roll-call of the eminent. In 1910, although many friends of Churchill, including Lord Hugh Cecil, Mr Asquith and A. J. Balfour belonged, the members decided they did not wish to elect two such controversial politicians as Mr Winston Churchill, the Liberal Home Secretary, or Mr F. E. Smith, the Conservative MP and prominent barrister. So Mr Churchill and Mr Smith decided to establish a dining club of their own, to be called 'The Other Club'.

They enlisted the support of an equally rejected rogue elephant, David Lloyd George, Chancellor of the Exchequer. They resolved to elect twelve Liberal MPs, twelve Conservatives and twelve 'distinguished outsiders' who were not politicians. They would dine in a private room at the Savoy Hotel once a fortnight when Parliament was in session. The two Chief Whips should be co-secretaries so that the pairing of members might be conveniently arranged and the dinners interrupted as little as possible by the necessity of trooping back to Westminster to take part in divisions of the House.

They drew up the rules of the club which were, and still are, read aloud at every dinner. They were mostly written by F.E., with the lucidity to be expected of a King's Counsel. The last rule declares that 'nothing in the rules or intercourse of the Club shall interfere with the rancour or asperity of party politics'. Churchill told me that this was his composition; but there is a Birkenhead school which ascribes it to F.E.

The first dinner of the Other Club was on 18 May 1911, with the King's private secretary, Lord Knollys, in the chair. The names of the members as the years went by read like an index to a contemporary English history book. Leaders of the armed forces, such as Kitchener, Jellicoe and Trenchard, Alexander and Montgomery, Gort, Alanbrooke and Portal; authors, such as H. G. Wells, Arnold Bennett, A. E. W. Mason and P. G. Wodehouse; artists, several of whom have illustrated the club's record of dinners, such as Orpen, Munnings, Lavery and Lutyens; actors, such as Beerbohm Tree and Laurence Olivier; Dominion statesmen, such as Smuts, Menzies and R.B. Bennett; the rulers of Fleet Street, Camrose, Beaverbrook and Rothermere; several Trade Union leaders; seven or eight British Prime Ministers; and a long list of Cabinet Ministers from all political parties.

There are notable exceptions. Anthony Eden declined an invitation to join because he disliked dining clubs. The names of others are missing because Churchill and F.E. did not consider them men with whom it was agreeable to dine. After F.E.'s death Churchill was, in effect, the sole arbiter of election to the club and dining at the Other Club took second place to nothing in his catalogue of pleasures. Election therefore became the greatest honour he could confer on those he considered estimable and entertaining. Both adjectives were essential: there were many worthy men, members of his Government, like Lord Woolton, Mr Attlee, Sir John Anderson and Lord Halifax, whom he considered estimable; but, whatever others might think, to him they were not men with whom it was agreeable to dine. That was the hallmark required for election to his own special dining club, the meetings of which he insisted on attending even at the height of the blitz in 1940 and 1941.

Politics were the main topic of conversation and there was, at times, both rancour and asperity. There was also wit, much of it provided by the two founders. There was heavy consumption of champagne and brandy, which were provided by benevolent members, in particular Lord Camrose and the Duke of Sutherland. There was also a betting book, with wagers varying from the serious to the ridiculous. There were bets on political developments; Lord Beaverbrook was so unwise as to stake a hundred pounds on Lord Northcliffe, the newspaper magnate, becoming Prime Minister. More heavily, and equally rashly, he laid five hundred pounds against a thousand that he would beat F.E. in the best of three sets of tennis, receiving 15 points in each game. There is no record of the result.

Among the non-political members of the Other Club was Churchill's constant companion over many years, Sir Edward Marsh. A Civil Servant by profession, he became Churchill's Private Secretary in 1906 and accompanied him on his African journey through Uganda. Almost every time Churchill switched office, Eddie Marsh switched too. He was the most useful myrmidon and one of the dearest friends that Churchill ever had. He was much more than a mere Private Secretary. He was an aesthete with a high-pitched, squeaky voice and an endearing if effeminate manner. He had access not only to that high society of the 'Souls', prominent in the social and political life of Edwardian times, but also to the Georgian group of poets, too often neglected in more prosaic days. He was a friend and patron of Rupert Brooke, to whom he introduced Churchill, and he was abreast of the whole intellectual movement of the age. He joyfully performed the most menial duties for Churchill while being, at the same time, a trustworthy pillar who supplied support in adversity and restored confidence when it was in danger of wavering. In the best tradition of the Civil Service he believed in moderation, bringing a restraining influence to bear on his master when he found him in impetuous mood. Throughout his political career Churchill was well served by his staff and his advisers. Eddie Marsh's name is close to the top of the list.

Lastly, among the Churchillians before the 1939 war, must be counted the Duke of Windsor. Only once did Churchill flinch in his resolve to help his former sovereign. That was when, in the summer of 1940, it seemed that the Duke might be flirting with plotters in Spain and Portugal who, on orders from Ribbentrop, were trying to prevent his leaving Lisbon to become the Governor of the Bahamas. The Germans doubtless thought that after the conquest of the British Isles, the Windsors, who had been impressed by Hitler on a pre-war visit to Germany, would be suitable to replace the staunchly belligerent King George VI on the throne. Churchill sent Sir Walter Monckton to persuade the Duke and Duchess to leave the dangerous environment in which they were living, but their demands and procrastination annoyed the Prime Minister, who had more important matters on his mind, almost beyond endurance. They annoyed King George VI just as much.

At all other times, both before and after the war, Churchill had warm feelings for the Duke. He considered that loyalty to the sovereign was axiomatic. He had not known Queen Victoria, but for his first twenty-six years he lived in a world spellbound by

her indestructible prestige and matriarchal grandeur. She represented the British Empire at its apogee. Then, as a young Cabinet
Minister, Home Secretary in 1910, he had been awe-struck by the
charm and experience of Edward VII, near to death though the
King was. George V, a sailor of great goodness but also with a
gruff exterior, was no admirer of Churchill and he espoused that
element of senior naval officers who viewed their former First
Lord with suspicion and in many cases dislike. They were the men
who revered Jellicoe and thought less well of Churchill's disciple,
Beatty. They held Admiral Lord Fisher, who had been Churchill's
First Sea Lord, to be Satan in naval uniform. As George V was
the King, he could do no wrong; but privately Churchill was critical of the way he brought up his children, in particular the bright,
attractive and universally loved Prince of Wales.

Although twenty years older than the Prince, Churchill found
him a shining example of all that youth should be. He seemed,
from his boyhood onwards, to have the makings of an imaginative
sovereign, energetic, full of ideas and yet well versed in the constitutional proprieties. His private life was his own affair, and
Churchill had not been brought up to be censorious about other
people's sexual extravagances. It was sufficient for him that he
and his own wife led blameless lives untainted by scandal of any
kind.

When the Prince of Wales became King Edward VIII, and
almost immediately brought consternation to Britain and to the
peoples of the British Dominions by insisting on marrying the
twice divorced Mrs Simpson, Churchill's instinctive reaction was
to stand by his friend, above all when that friend was the King.
In so doing he came near to the irreparable destruction of his own
political career.

He told me, many years afterwards, that it never for one moment
crossed his mind that Mrs Simpson would be acceptable as Queen.
He had believed, wrongly as he later saw, that this was a passing
infatuation, such as the King had previously had for Lady Furness
and others.

Churchill's analysis was wrong. It may be argued that, for
reasons other than the unsuitability of the woman Edward VIII
loved – his headstrong obstinacy, ingrained self-centredness,
marked preference for pleasure when it clashed with duty,

and admiration for the new German system of government – the abdication was a blessing for Great Britain and her Empire. Certainly Churchill became even more attached to Edward VIII's successor, a King who always put duty first and whom Churchill found a strength and stay in all that arose during the war years, especially in matters affecting the armed forces. In a letter to George VI written in January 1941, he said, 'Your Majesties are more loved by all classes and conditions than any of the princes of the past.'

However, much as he loved George VI, he did not falter in friendship with the Duke of Windsor. Whenever he went to Paris he called on the Duke; whenever the Duke came to London to see his mother, Queen Mary, he called on Churchill. He had lost his country and most of his friends; but there was one who was constant and who was much displeased if the former King Edward VIII was criticized in his presence.

These were the fellow countrymen whose friendship Churchill had enjoyed by the time that, in September 1939, he was once again called upon to take a prominent part in the leadership of the nation. Few of them had influenced his thought, for his independence of judgment was all but immovable. He was sufficiently self-assured to require assistance rather than guidance. He was grateful for help, for explanation, for the intelligent discussion of problems; but decisions were for him alone. The man who came closest to influencing his decisions in that long preparatory stage before he was leader of his country (and, it may be said without exaggeration, of half the world) was F. E. Smith, Lord Birkenhead. When F. E. died, long before his due time, Churchill followed a lonely path, often veering from it with all but disastrous effect, but never doubting his own purpose or questioning his ability to perform.

The later Churchillians, to whom the rest of this book relates, were with him at a time when his policy and his actions were of greater significance than they had ever been before. They plied him with advice; they provided efficient support; they usually kept their tempers, for they loved him truly in spite of disturbing and inconsiderate whims; they quite often succeeded in convincing him to alter his designs, especially in the military scene. He had learned much by experience, and his career after 10 May 1940 strengthens the thesis that responsibility instils caution in the impetuous and decelerates the over-hasty. In essence, however, Winston Churchill remained what he always had been: a man sure of his cause, firm in his convictions and confident of his destiny.

CHAPTER TWO

The Family

Lord and Lady Randolph Churchill were selfish and neglectful parents. Lord Randolph, immersed in his own brand of rebellious Tory politics, seldom spoke or wrote to his elder son except to chide him. Indeed, Winston, who was thrilled by politics and longed to talk to Lord Randolph about them, could remember only one occasion when he had a serious conversation with his father. Lady Randolph, the former Jennie Jerome, loved clothes, society, glamour and money. Her two daughters-in-law saw through her; but her two sons were spellbound by her beauty and, even when they were hard put to it to maintain their own families (for as young men they were impoverished), they would scrape together more than they could afford in order to sustain their mother's extravagances.

Yet all his life Winston Churchill looked back on his unfeeling parents with pride and affection. His father was a figure of public and political importance in his day. Now, were it not for the interest in him that his son's achievements have awakened, he would be remembered mainly by professional historians, and that as a minor character in the panorama of late Victorian politics. To Winston, however, he was a dashing and romantic hero whose illness and untimely death at the age of forty-six alone prevented his rise to the supreme heights of power.

It is not, perhaps, irrelevant that in his old age Winston wrote a short story, called 'The Dream', which contains an account of a discussion between himself and the ghost of Lord Randolph. His father asks him many questions and makes a number of pertinent comments on political matters. It reflects the kind of discussion he would so much have liked to have with his father in the flesh sixty years before, and there is no doubt that nostalgic regret at not having known Lord Randolph better, and basked in his approval, remained with Winston Churchill all his life. An uncanny incident in my own association with him occurred in the early 1950s. I went to his bedroom to talk to him about some business matter while he was shaving. 'Today,' he said to me, 'is the twenty-fourth of January. It is the day my father died. It is the day that I shall die too.' And on 24 January 1965, he did.

It did not occur to Winston, as it has to others, that Lord Randolph's early departure from the scene, when his son was only twenty, freed him from an overshadowing and disapproving influence which might well have had a clouding effect on his political career. As for Lady Randolph, her frivolities, her love-affairs, her injudicious marriages and her self-centredness were overlooked or forgotten. 'She shone for me like the Evening Star,' he wrote; and she continued to do so all his life.

The two closest relations of his own age, to both of whom he was strongly attached from his childhood onwards, were his younger brother, Jack, and his first cousin, 'Sunny', ninth Duke of Marlborough. The Duke was clever but arrogant. His tenants liked him; most of his social equals did not. He was the best of landlords, and had expert agricultural knowledge. In the wider world he was proud, off-hand and frequently offensive. But Winston, three years younger than his cousin, described him with deep emotion as his 'oldest and dearest friend'. They played together at the Viceregal Lodge when their grandfather was Lord Lieutenant of Ireland. They travelled together, they hunted together with the Bicester and Pytchley hounds, they campaigned together in the Boer War, driving side by side from Bloemfontein to Pretoria in Winston's four-horse wagon. They were both yeomanry officers in the Oxfordshire Hussars. They stimulated each other's intellect.

On two matters the cousins differed. The Duke was no pauper, but he was absorbed by his desire to maintain and restore Blenheim Palace as he deemed it should be. Improvements and embellishments were beyond his means, and so he made a loveless match with the American heiress Consuelo Vanderbilt, who was forced to the altar by her socially ambitious parents. Winston found Consuelo beautiful and intelligent. He was therefore grieved that the marriage was an unhappy one, ending in divorce after twenty-five years of incompatibility and several separations. Since the Duke had a mystic side and desired spiritual comfort, he became a Roman Catholic when the Church of England refused him its sacraments. He was thus able to maintain that his first, Anglican, marriage had been invalid, and to marry again. He did so with even less success than on the first occasion, and Winston made his disapproval clear.

There was also political antipathy. The Duke held office before Winston, being first Paymaster General and then Under-Secretary for the Colonies in Lord Salisbury's and Mr Balfour's Governments at the turn of the century. He was an unbending Tory and a devotee of Imperial Preference. Winston, always by conviction a Free Trader, became a member of a Liberal Government which his cousin Sunny abominated and, worse still, a friend of that anti-ducal arch-fiend, Lloyd George. The Duke did little more than bicker with Winston on political matters, but he tried to bully Winston's wife, Clementine. Among the sins which he held against her was that she had dared to write to Lloyd George on Blenheim writing-paper. She disliked him and she never forgave his truculence.

Winston not only loved his cousin Sunny as a man; he revered him as head of the family and bearer of what he considered the proudest name in the land. For most of his early manhood Blenheim was his constant shelter and spiritual home. Once, many years later, I was with him when he leaped with surprising agility over a steel girder and landed in a pool of liquid cement. 'You have,' I said rather impertinently, 'met your Waterloo.' 'Certainly not,' he replied, 'my Blenheim.'

The character of Jack Churchill was strikingly different. Loyal, affectionate and scrupulously honourable, he was also endowed with that most endearing of qualities, natural humility. He did not share his brother's restless energy, consuming ambition, gift of eloquence or quickness of mind. He was always proud to be referred to as 'Winston's brother' and he laboriously pursued his career as an only moderately successful stockbroker. Yet his beautiful wife, Lady Gwendeline Bertie, to whose charms Winston had succumbed before he met Clementine, preferred to marry the younger brother. She produced three gifted children totally unlike each other in their respective abilities.

Winston and Jack loved each other all their lives and the two sisters-in-law were scarcely less devoted. They rejoiced in each other's company; they shared a house during the First World War; during the Second, everywhere that Winston went Jack was almost sure to go, though he was not invited to share in journeys abroad. In September 1941, he and I drove together through devastated Coventry in a car following that of the Prime Minister. The crowd, which had been cheering Winston loudly, renewed their applause as we drove by in the conviction that Jack was the Soviet Ambassador, Maisky. The Russians were popular at that time and Jack, unwilling to disappoint anybody, acknowledged the cheers graciously. I wondered whether they took me for Molotov. Jack lived at 10 Downing Street throughout the blitz. He contrived to be loved by all and was never in the way.

No woman would have found it easy to be married to Winston Churchill, despite his devotion and his affectionate nature. The one he did choose was not only radiantly beautiful, with features that withstood the ravages of age, well educated and with all but infallible good taste: she was also sufficiently self-assured to be able to cope with his demands and his idiosyncrasies. While usually satisfying his frequently immoderate requirements and sometimes rather quaint whims, she supplied the cold douche of realism and common sense that brought domestic order into a home that would otherwise have been chaotic. She furnished and decorated her houses exquisitely. She had no trace of priggishness or pomposity, but her standards were consistently high and her husband, her children, her friends and her domestic staff often fell short of them. She could then display an acidity of tongue before which the tallest trees would bend, and she would occasionally give vent to uncontrollable temper. The storms were terrifying in their violence, but the more usual calms were beautiful and serene.

Her judgment, given after careful reflection, often saved her husband from unwise acts on which he had impetuously determined. There were frequent partings, for the life of an active politician leads him far afield, and in addition Clementine disliked the holidays in the South of France which provided Winston with the sunshine, the carefree society and the painting opportunities which he craved. The claims on her energies were incessant; the trials imposed, albeit with every display of affection, by so restive a husband were hard and exhausting. So it is not surprising that she used to quote with a trace of nostalgia a line of Swinburne's poetry: 'even the weariest river winds somewhere safe to sea'. When her nerves were stretched she sometimes turned on Winston with vitriol in her voice and the flashing eyes of a Fury. But theirs was a marriage, fifty-six years long, which was replete with conjugal happiness and fidelity, she supplying the qualities Winston lacked and he ensuring that their life was never for a moment dull.

They had four daughters of whom three survived childhood. Perhaps Sarah, with her tresses of Titian-red hair, 'the Mule' as Winston called her, was her father's favourite child; but he loved Mary, too, with ever growing affection, and he missed no opportunity to take one or the other of them to his wartime conferences.

It was a different and, in the end, a much sadder story where his only son, Randolph, was concerned. Pugnacious by disposition, forceful in his views, an excellent writer and, at his best, a bewitching companion, Randolph inherited his mother's startling good looks. Laszlo painted him in his youth: the intelligent grey eyes, the light hair brushed back, the splendid bone structure of his face portray a young man destined, it seemed, to make a notable mark in the life of his country. Winston, determined that there should be no repetition of the neglect he himself suffered as a child, and from which only his nanny, Mrs Everest, had done something to rescue him, eagerly associated his son, when still a schoolboy, with his own activities and his own political friends. It is not surprising that Randolph, allowed in his early teens to dine with Lord Birkenhead, Lloyd George or Lord Beaverbrook, and encouraged not merely to listen to them but to argue and debate with them, found his schoolfellows uninteresting companions by comparison. His eyes were firmly fixed on the glitter of high office at a time when his attention should more appropriately have been directed to algebra, French grammar and Latin proses. He once said to me, with quiet disappointment, 'If anybody had disputed my belief that I should enter the House of Commons at twenty-one and hold office by the time I was twenty-three, I should not have bothered to argue. For I regarded it as a certainty'.

Randolph's mother soon recognized the danger. So did

Winston's friends Professor Lindemann and Brendan Bracken. Despite their warnings, Winston himself was incorrigible. He continued to spoil Randolph and to encourage his high aspirations. It was a folly for which both father and son paid dearly in later years.

At an early age Randolph made a successful lecture tour of the United States, where his good looks, his speaking ability and his dynamic qualities were acclaimed. Shortly after he came down from Oxford he fought a by-election, at Wavertree, without consulting his father. He split the Conservative vote and as a result of his intervention the Socialist candidate won. Later on he espoused Winston's Indian policy, which was diametrically opposed to that of Mr Baldwin's Government, but he also flung his energies, against Winston's wishes and with total lack of success, into supporting Duncan Sandys' opponent at another by-election. Some years before war broke out he was already unacceptable to the Conservatives as a parliamentary candidate and, though he had a number of friends who enjoyed drinking and gambling with him, the bright prospects of yesteryear were dimmed. His war record was above reproach, for he joined the SAS in the Western Desert and was later parachuted into Yugoslavia to join the staff of Brigadier Fitzroy Maclean, the Prime Minister's brilliantly successful personal representative with Marshal Tito. Moreover, since in wartime by-elections were not officially contested, he was able to enter the House of Commons as Member for South Preston, a seat he lost immediately it was contested in the 1945 General Election.

Meanwhile Randolph's relations with his father were no longer what they had once been. Whenever he came home, he would complain, all too stridently, about the Government's policy, the strategy of the generals and the quality of members of the Government. At luncheon at Chequers he would start an argument with his father and speak in terms by which those present, often visiting generals or ministers, would be shocked and embarrassed. He would arrive in combative mood and, as one of the Prime Minister's secretaries, John Peck, put it, 'he waged a preventive war'. The meaning of this was that before a man had opened his mouth, Randolph would attack him vigorously for what he thought he might perhaps be going to say.

His father reacted angrily. He loved Randolph, because it was in his nature to love his children, but he liked him less and less, and it seemed that, whenever they met, they quarrelled. Had Randolph realized the unhappiness this brought his father he would have been distraught, for his love and admiration for him (though not for his less forgiving mother) were deep and genuine. As the years went by, the worm turned, and when Randolph arrived, resolved to be good and peaceful, it would be Winston who launched an attack. It ended as a sad and sorry relationship, and yet Winston hoped, almost to the end, that Randolph might successfully re-enter Parliament and make a political career for himself; and he was delighted by the quality of his writing and his journalistic success. He deliberated long and carefully whether to meet Randolph's wish that he should in due course be his father's official biographer, as he himself had been Lord Randolph's. Finally, despite all the differences and difficulties between them, he decided to entrust Randolph with the task, the main reasons being family loyalty and the favourable impression made on him by Randolph's biography of Lord Derby.

With all his faults Randolph had a generous spirit and, although he was often gratuitously offensive, he could, when sober and in the mood, exercise such charm that those who had sworn to have no more to do with him, and never to ask him inside their houses again, forgot their rancour and were won back to their earlier friendship.

Even at his most arrogant his abuse was often original. At one dinner party he engaged in an acrimonious argument with his host. A fellow guest, who was an executive of British Petroleum, joined in the argument. Randolph turned on him. 'You have nothing to contribute to this,' he shouted, 'you are only a clerk in an oil store.' Towards the end of his life, it was feared that, chain cigarette smoker that he was, he had developed lung cancer. Some tissues of a lung were removed and found to contain no malignancy at all. Randolph's friend, Lord Stanley of Alderley, heard the diagnosis as he stood at the bar of White's Club. 'It must,' he said, 'be the only part of Randolph that is not malignant.' Yet, in spite of everything, Lord Stanley and many others loved Randolph. No doubt part of the trouble was that he had grown up under the branches of a great spreading tree, soil in which it is difficult for a young plant to thrive and blossom. It was a fate from which Lord Randolph's early death had saved his father.

Winston found in two of his sons-in-law what he had lost in Randolph. Diana, his eldest daughter, married Duncan Sandys, who after some years in the Diplomatic Service became a Member of Parliament. In 1938 Duncan fell foul of the Secretary of State for War, Leslie Hore Belisha, when he threatened to expose in Parliament the inadequacy of the country's anti-aircraft defences, an inadequacy of which he had become aware from information reaching him as a second lieutenant in a Territorial anti-aircraft battery. Hore Belisha handled the matter with ineptitude; Winston Churchill rallied to the support of his son-in-law; a Select Committee, a Court of Inquiry, a Committee of Privileges were all established; and the Sandys molehill was converted into a sizeable mountain, almost monopolizing the headlines in the newspapers and diverting the General Staff from their efforts to prepare the country for war.

The 'Sandys case' cemented a relationship which would in any event have been close, for Duncan Sandys impressed his father-in-law by his intelligence and supported him in his uphill struggle to awaken Parliament and the people to the Nazi danger. When Winston became Prime Minister, Duncan, whose military career had been cut short by a motor accident that crippled him for life, became temporarily involved with the Cabinet Office, and indirectly with Professor Lindemann and the Ministry of Supply in the promotion of secret weapons. He was soon appointed Financial Secretary at the War Office and thenceforward he climbed the political slopes with ease and rapidity, holding a succession of Cabinet posts under a succession of Prime Ministers.

During the war Duncan Sandys was a frequent visitor to Chequers at weekends. His point of view on a number of matters differed from that of his father-in-law, and still more from that of Lindemann, but he at least had opportunities which all other Ministers would have coveted of making his opinions heard in the highest quarter. All the same, he was not, during the war, one of the most intimate members of the Prime Ministerial entourage, no doubt because, being a hard and conscientious worker, he stuck to his departmental last. After 1945, when Churchill was Leader of the Opposition, Sandys became his European bearleader.

Churchill's crusade for European unity, when he made resounding speeches at Zurich, Luxembourg and the Hague, was largely generated by Sandys' enthusiasm for the European cause. It was an enthusiasm that Churchill shared, but, as is explained elsewhere in this book, Churchill's was based on a concept in some respects closer to that of Charles de Gaulle than of Monnet, Schumann, Spaak – or Duncan Sandys.

In 1960, after a marriage lasting twenty-five years, Duncan and Diana Sandys, who had parted a few years earlier, were divorced. Diana had not, at least for many years, meant nearly as much to her father as her two sisters, and Clementine had little personal regard for Duncan Sandys. So he, though not his children, effectively vanished from the Churchill scene. Even during the early 1950s, when he was first Minister of Supply and then Minister of Housing in Churchill's second administration, Sandys' appearances at No. 10, Chartwell and Chequers were rare and his relationship with his father-in-law, though in no way antagonistic, was less close than before. Yet a few years before Churchill's death, and after Duncan and Diana Sandys were divorced, Churchill said to me one day, 'I wish you would ask Duncan to come to the next dinner of the Other Club. I should so much like to see him again, but if I asked him to luncheon or dinner, Clemmie would be upset.' With Winston Churchill loyalties did not evaporate.

A more significant relationship began when in 1947 Mary Churchill married Christopher Soames. The bridegroom, an officer in the Coldstream Guards, was assistant Military Attaché in Paris and thus well known to the Ambassador, Duff Cooper, and to Lady Diana. There was, however, an age gap of forty-six years between Winston and his new son-in-law. So it was not surprising that Winston had never heard of Christopher and was anxious to be sure that his youngest, greatly cherished daughter was marrying the right man. In fact, Mary Churchill was showing deeper insight than most people, for Christopher Soames undoubtedly was the right man for her, and indeed for her father, although he was at that time disliked by many of his contemporaries. So, forty-six years earlier, her father had been.

Churchill did not hesitate in welcoming the newcomer. He installed the bride and bridegroom at Chartwell Farm, only a few hundred yards from Chartwell itself. Thus Mary, who drew year by year still closer to her mother, and Christopher, who was not only a good conversationalist but was quite prepared to gamble at gin rummy with Winston, were continuously present on the Chartwell scene and the arrival of five children in fairly rapid succession strengthened the relationship between the generations.

It was, however, Christopher Soames's own conduct and abilities that were the principal element in endearing him to his father-in-law. He managed the farm, in which Winston took an enthusiastic if unknowledgeable interest. He was consulted about private and financial affairs. He was soon an indispensable companion. Then, in 1949, came the horses. Winston knew nothing about racing, but he did love a gamble, sometimes greater than he could afford, and with his pathetic reverence for his father, it thrilled him to revive Lord Randolph's racing colours.

To Clementine's horror and indignation, Christopher persuaded Winston to buy a racehorse. With the help of a canny friend, Christopher enabled him to acquire for fifteen hundred pounds a grey, Colonist II, which proceeded to win eleven races, to the loud plaudits of the crowd, to an increase in the popularity of the Leader of the Opposition and to its owner's immense satisfaction. With a deft touch Christopher then bought a few brood mares and, when the opportunity arose, a stud farm which increased greatly in value. Several good horses, such as Vienna and High Hat, were bred there and Winston was elected a member of the Jockey Club. He was fascinated by everything that affected the prospects of his own horses, even if he had no wish to study the form or to become a racing expert. Success on the turf was an unexpected addition to the pleasures of life. It had not figured in his youthful or middle-aged dreams, but he now had an enterprising son-in-law who understood how to awaken and sustain his enthusiasm.

Christopher was never devoid of self-confidence in the presence of his father-in-law who had, in any event, mellowed greatly with advancing age and was a less alarming figure than in former years. The successful racing initiative consolidated the relationship and since Winston loved the company of young people and treated them as if they were his contemporaries, there were by the end of 1951, when he formed a Conservative Government, no barriers at all between him and this new member of the family circle. Randolph, jealous of the influence his brother-in-law had acquired, referred to him scornfully as 'The Master of the Horse'.

In the General Election of February 1950, Christopher Soames was elected Member of Parliament for Bedford, a seat he held with an increased majority when, at a second attempt in October 1951, the Conservatives obtained a working majority. Winston had never been disturbed by accusations of nepotism. During the war he gave Duncan Sandys office, because he justifiably considered him worthy of it, and Randolph had undoubtedly been chosen for South Preston because he was his father's son. There had even been a cry in the House, 'What about Vic Oliver?', in reference to Sarah's husband.

However, in the 1951–5 Government he was careful not to advance Christopher Soames's claims too soon. He contented himself with appointing him his Parliamentary Private Secretary, a position which he would certainly have been loth to confer on anyone he did not know well. Yet I believe that, with the strange perceptiveness, almost bordering on prophecy, that was his, he saw Christopher as a statesman in the making, and that it was not just family affection which moved him to think and speak so highly of his son-in-law.

Winston was by no means always swayed by Christopher's views or inclined to accept his advice. He retained the independence of judgment which was one of his dominant characteristics. But, as he grew older, he tended to concentrate his attention on the few matters that really interested him. Thus Ministers suffered less interference in departmental affairs than had been the lot of their predecessors in the wartime Coalition and, more than ever before, heavy responsibilities fell on to the shoulders of the Secretary to the Cabinet. However, there is much that a Prime Minister must do and decide which is not within the sphere or competence of a departmental Minister, even those as alert, intelligent and experienced as were, for instance, Anthony Eden, R. A. Butler, Lord Swinton and Lord Chandos. After Churchill's all but fatal stroke in June 1953, he confined his remaining energies to what he believed to be the issues of overriding significance: the maintenance of a special relationship with the United States, a new deal with the Soviet Union and the perennial problems of Egypt, the Canal zone and the Middle East. So it was that the suggestions of those closest to him, in particular Christopher Soames, Sir Norman Brook (the Secretary to the Cabinet) and even, to some extent, myself, acquired increasing weight.

Christopher, though suspect to a few of Churchill's colleagues, and in particular to Anthony Eden, acted with discretion. No effort was too great where the comfort, happiness and public image of his father-in-law were concerned, and he had among his qualities one which was of special value. He could study a complicated paper, in which the pros and cons of an intricate proposal were examined in detail, and put his finger on the one or two points of real significance that required a decision. He could discard the reams of largely immaterial argument: he could apply the basic judgment of common sense. He did not use his position to excite the Prime Minister in favour of rash proposals; he did not exercise his influence on behalf of his friends or against those he disliked; he quickly acquired an understanding of 'the sense' of back-bench Conservatives in the House; and he kept Churchill dispassionately briefed about political sentiment.

Without Christopher Soames, Churchill's last administration might have been less stable and successful than in the event it was. It may even not be fanciful to suggest that Christopher's handling of his father-in-law made some contribution to the greatly increased Conservative majority with which Churchill's successor, Anthony Eden, won the General Election of May 1955. If so, it was ironical that, in forming his new Government, Eden was persuaded only by the earnest recommendation of Norman Brook, and against his own prejudice, to offer Christopher Soames junior office at the Air Ministry. He realized that not to do so would give pain to Winston Churchill in his retirement and, although he had so long been deprived of the highest office by Churchill's disinclination to leave the scene, he retained for him an affection inspired by many years of co-operation. It was for Soames a stepping-stone on the way to far greater responsibilities and, in due course, to international fame. To achieve that goal he had, without malice or intrigue or indeed intention on his own part, stepped into the shoes so long destined for Randolph.

CHAPTER THREE

The Prof and Brendan

If he were writing fiction an author might reasonably be criticized for creating and presenting as friendly associates two such improbable characters as Professor F.A. Lindemann, first and last Viscount Cherwell, commonly known as 'the Prof', and Brendan, first and last Viscount Bracken. Yet from shortly after the First World War until Churchill's second administration in 1951, they were jointly and severally his firmest supporters and most intimate friends. Others might waver; they did not. Discordant in temperament, distinct in their interests and abilities, often diametrically opposed on economic policy, the Prof and Brendan were nevertheless faithful friends to each other as they were to the man they worshipped and glorified. One of them might, and quite often did, criticize the other behind his back, but it was done with tolerant good humour. This was not the invariable rule or practice for either of them when other colleagues and associates were discussed. They were the most loyal disciples Churchill ever had, in a class apart from his other friends and boon-companions, so that despite the evident dissimilarities, it seems appropriate to write of them in the same chapter.

Lindemann had a distinguished presence. His deep-set eyes looked out beneath gently arching brows and a curving, well-developed forehead. His nose was of noble Roman shape, his moustache was flat and neatly trimmed, his mouth suggested refinement. His complexion was grey, but not unhealthy, and his hair, well smoothed down, was never ruffled or untidy. He wore beautifully cut clothes, out of date in design, and it was impossible to imagine him dressed in anything else. He and his clothes were spotlessly clean, almost clinically so. I used to wonder idly what he looked like in pyjamas, or a dressing-gown, or a bathing suit.

I never knew, for he declined to spend a night at Chequers, always returning after dinner to his own bed at Oxford; and I doubt if he was often tempted to enter a swimming-pool.

If the Prof looked distinguished, though at first sight forbidding, Brendan looked neither. He was tall and well built, with broad shoulders, and he walked with a swinging stride. His lips, which he used to brush with his fingers when in pensive mood, were thick, and his teeth were bad. His nose was straight and his short-sighted eyes were permanently encased in thick spectacles. On top of it all was a huge mop of wiry red hair, thick and spreading, protruding above his ears and sometimes straying down across his wide, deeply lined and slightly receding brow. He was ugly, but there were few men with livelier and more expressive faces. When Brendan came into a room, people instinctively moved in his direction.

There is no doubt that Lindemann had, as Churchill frequently said, 'a beautiful brain'. His rival and enemy, Sir Henry Tizard, placed him on a par intellectually with Lord Rutherford, the original splitter of the atom and father of modern nuclear physics in Britain. By personal effort he transformed the Clarendon Laboratory at Oxford from a run-down, all but perishing scientific institution into one of international fame, the foremost centre of low temperature research in physics and almost the equal of its more renowned Cambridge rival, the Cavendish. There were few physicists to surpass him in knowledge, though as the years went by he grew lazy about research. There was certainly nobody with a more photographic memory for facts and figures.

The Prof was not just a highly distinguished scientist. His range of interest stretched far beyond his laboratory. Indeed, although he was apt to speak with disrespect of classicists, and had no love or understanding of the visual arts, he was convinced that scientists were not the people to direct or even influence national and international policy. Breadth of education was vital to the complete man or woman.

Like many mathematicians, the Prof had an ear for music and he is said to have been a skilled pianist, though such was his modesty that few heard him play. He was a tennis player of professional quality so that high among the least likely achievements in his astonishing career is the fact that he was once the tennis champion of Sweden. He could quote long passages from the Bible by heart and his knowledge of almost all periods of history was impressive. He did indeed have 'a beautiful brain'.

His personality was thought by many to be less beautiful; but among his laudable characteristics was his refusal ever to boast of his successes. It was difficult to draw him out on the subject of the resurrection of the Clarendon Laboratory. He would not give a straight answer, at any rate to me, when asked if it was true that he had risked his life, without a parachute, to prove a theory about the recovery of aircraft from spins which he had developed on paper to his own mathematical satisfaction. The story is that in 1916, when working at the Royal Aircraft Establishment at Farnborough as one of a brilliant team of scientists engaged in aeronautical research, he deliberately put an aeroplane into a spin and pulled it out again by using the formula he had devised. This formula then became the standard drill learned by every pilot. If the story be true – and there were serious witnesses who vouched for it – there can have been few acts of higher courage. The Prof himself made no such claim.

There are many examples of Lindemann's kindness. He took trouble to further the interests of those he approved and to defend their words or actions. He was not afraid to stand up for them against the most powerful opposition, for he was morally as well as physically courageous. He performed numerous charitable deeds by stealth. Just as striking, and the reason that many found his personality less beautiful than his brain, was the all but inexhaustible venom with which he pursued those who had ever opposed him. His memory was not just comprehensive; in recording past slights it was elephantine. Woe betide his enemies and detractors once he was in a position to obtain revenge, however distant in time their hostility might have been. He had no trace of that readiness to forgive and forget so characteristic of Churchill. He was a faithful friend, but he was a dedicated hater.

There were whole categories of men and women whom the Prof disliked. He was basically anti-Semitic, though he was moved by the plight of the Jews forced to leave Germany by Hitler from 1933 onwards and did all he could to find them employment, especially if they happened to be clever scientists who might have something to contribute to the quality of the Clarendon Laboratory. He had a distaste for coloured races whom he thought inferior and repulsive. Above all he developed a cold hatred for the Germans. In all these respects he differed profoundly from Churchill, who was a Zionist sympathizer, with many Jewish friends, who had no colour prejudice, and who thought it essential to make a distinction between the Nazi leaders and the people they had so shamefully misled. Like Edmund Burke, Churchill knew no way of indicting a whole nation.

Lindemann's anti-German obsession was a curious phenomenon. Though brought up in Devonshire, he was himself of recent German or at least Alsatian origin. His father, born in the German Palatinate, was an immigrant to Britain who had built, and still owned, water-works in Germany, thus adding to a considerable inherited fortune. His mother was American by birth, born of a British father; but it was his scientific, German father whom he loved. Moreover his gifts as a scientist had been developed first at Darmstadt and then in Berlin where he was the star pupil of the famous physicist, Dr Nernst. There, too, he became a friend of Einstein. He was deeply indebted to German scientific genius.

In the 1930s Lindemann was quick to see the advancing German menace, particularly in the field of aerial warfare by which, ever since his years at the Farnborough experimental establishment, he had been enthralled. It was probably then, when he and Churchill found themselves impotent to rouse the British from their slumbers, and when men like his friend Einstein were being hounded out of Germany, that the seed, perhaps sown at Farnborough twenty years before, sprouted and grew. Once a hatred was established, the Prof had no understanding of half measures. I will describe two pertinent examples of which I was myself a witness.

In September 1944 he attended the Second Quebec Conference. The American Secretary of the Treasury, Henry J. Morgenthau Jr, was also there, and he had a simple, dramatic plan which he discussed with the Prof. It was to pastoralize Germany, so that she ceased altogether to be an industrial nation. Since the Conference had met to discuss, among other things, the treatment of Germany when victory was won, this seemed to Morgenthau an ideal occasion to spring his plan on the two heads of Government.

I was not in the room when Churchill, at Roosevelt's request, initialled the short document. I do not know how Morgenthau had presented it to the President, nor whether Lindemann spoke at all. However, he showed me a copy with clear approval and I think he shared Morgenthau's disappointment when, on the following day, the two Secretaries of State, Anthony Eden and Cordell Hull, joined forces to trample on the scheme. As for Churchill, I never heard him mention the incident, either on the day the plan was initialled, or on our journey home by sea (when post-mortems on all the conference discussions were held), or afterwards. It represented a policy which Churchill abhorred, and I can only surmise that he added his initials, after the President had appended his, because his thoughts were on other things and he did not want to have a dispute on something that seemed irrelevant to the larger matters, and in particular the equal sharing of atomic weapons, which were the main occupants of his thoughts. It was unlike Churchill, but I can think of no other reason; nor, when specifically asked many years later, did he provide any explanation.

The Prof, however, had not abandoned the idea. As late as February 1945, with victory well in sight, he reverted to the subject during an afternoon walk at Chequers. He was depressed by the economic and financial future as he saw it and I noted that 'he is very much a Jeremiah these days'. He was convinced that Britain could survive only if she seized the pre-war markets of Germany and Japan; and 'as for Germany,' he continued, 'she must not be allowed to export, but must live with an autarchic system and accept a low standard of living.' Perhaps Morgenthau was saying the same kind of thing in Washington and that equally little attention was being paid to his views. It is strange that two clever men of German origin, one of them without a drop of Jewish blood in his veins, should have been so ardent in planning for the impoverishment of their ancestral homeland.

On leaving the Farnborough experimental establishment at the end of the First World War, his valuable contribution generally acknowledged, the rich Lindemann procured a Rolls Royce and chauffeur and decided on an academic career. He was elected to a professorial chair at Oxford, going first to Wadham College and then to Christ Church. Most of the dons disliked him. He was fastidious, he was sarcastic, his wit and rapid repartee seemed spiced with a malice unacceptable even at College High Tables. He was arrogant and overbearing; and he was bored by the middle classes.

He preferred dukes, especially those of Westminster and Marlborough who were both intelligent. He thus met Winston Churchill, first at Eaton Hall, Chester, and then at Blenheim Palace. Churchill, fascinated by the professor's intellect, established a relationship which led to discussions on defence matters, and in particular the future of aerial warfare, and included scientific aid in the construction of a chain of ponds and pools at Chartwell. Much as Clementine disliked the majority of her husband's men friends, the Prof was an exception. He loved children and took trouble with hers, he played her favourite game, tennis, outstandingly well, and he knew how to charm women by courtesy and attention. In addition to Clementine's approval, it was a happy chance that two of Lindemann's friends, Lords Birkenhead and Camrose, were as close or even closer to Churchill. The sparkling brilliance of the former and the serene wisdom of the latter were magnets to both the Prof and his new-found master.

In the 1930s Lindemann was among the most assiduous of Churchill's small band of followers who were vainly striving to warn the Government and the people of the wrath to come. In pressing for more urgent and effective measures of air defence, the Prof, largely by his overbearing tactlessness in the Air Research Defence Committee, made an enemy of the Chairman, the eminent scientist Sir Henry Tizard, who had been one of his oldest friends and whose son was his godchild. He also antagonized all three Service Departments. Thus by 3 September 1939, when war was declared, there was no more unpopular figure in Whitehall than Professor F. A. Lindemann, known to have been retained on an important Defence Committee against the wishes of Tizard and solely because Ministers were alarmed and over-awed by Churchill. In later years Tizard would have been glad to bury the hatchet, but Lindemann, by then riding high in official favour, saw no reason for so doing.

With the outbreak of war he entered the promised land, and once Churchill became Prime Minister it indeed began to flow with milk and honey for him. He became the great interpreter, a man who did more to ease the load and illumine the dark corners than anybody other than General Ismay. He had already, during those locust-eaten years of the 1920s and '30s, explained and simplified for Churchill important scientific developments such as radar and the anti-submarine Asdic device. Now, with a new, powerfully staffed statistical office behind him, and with his own superb capacity to translate complicated jargon into clear, comprehensible English, he became an indispensable contributor to Churchill's method of conducting the war effort. As early as June 1940, with invasion threatening, he was the Prime Minister's right-hand man at the anxious meetings to solve supply problems held each morning at 10 Downing Street. His lucid charts of aircraft production, ship-building, food supplies and almost every other facet of the war effort were brought up to date weekly and were in constant demand by the Prime Minister.

The Prof was addicted to unorthodox weapons. Some of them, such as an aerial minefield suspended between heaven and earth to trap raiding aircraft (of which he still had high hopes as late as October 1940), were bones of contention in the pre-war Tizard Committee and do indeed seem to have been impractical conceptions. Others, which he influenced the Prime Minister to support against the obstruction of those devoted only to standard weapon production, were in due course successful. He championed and cherished a special research department, established in the country under the direction of Colonel Millis Jefferis. It explored new inventions, experimented with them and proved them. Jefferis was often brought to the notice of the Prime Minister whose encouragement was solicited and readily given. He was among the Prof's bluest-eyed boys. In August 1940 Churchill demanded that the Ministry of Supply should provide hugely increased facilities for scientists since 'the whole character of the war both by sea and land in 1941 may be affected by the development of these weapons'.

There was the Sticky Bomb, the Blacker Bombard, the U.P.-weapon and a dozen other ingenious devices which the Prof promoted with zest. There was also the proximity fuse and a photo-electric cell causing shells to explode as they passed close to their objective. The Prof thought this might render aircraft obsolete as weapons of war. It took months to develop and was then handed over to the Americans, who mass-produced it. It proved its value, but it did not render military aircraft obsolete. There were times when Lindemann, alternating between soaring optimism and querulous pessimism, came near to despairing of these new developments reaching fruition; but persistence was as much one of his virtues as obstinacy was one of his defects, and in the end a number of apparently fantastic inventions, offered by ingenious people, were proved and produced.

It was because Lindemann was an analyst, critic and interpreter rather than a creator that Churchill seldom did more than listen politely to his political views and judgment of people. He did, however, like to have the Prof near at hand, almost whatever subjects were under discussion. So rooms were provided for him and his statistical section in the Prime Minister's own wartime offices, and from 1951 onwards he was lodged on the top floor of 11 Downing Street. He was part of almost every scenario, wearing his long dark overcoat and bowler hat even on board battleships and in aeroplanes, his devoted valet and secretary, Harvey, also wearing a bowler hat as he walked beside him.

His ability to entertain was invaluable and when he was in the right mood, none of Churchill's entourage could be better company. He replied to Churchill's banter with good humour and an equal facility for repartee. I remember one dinner-party conversation at Chequers just after the death in December 1940 of Lord Lothian, British Ambassador in Washington.

Churchill: What a monstrous thing that Philip Lothian should not have allowed a doctor to be called. He might have been saved. Is anyone here a Christian Scientist?
Lindemann: Well, I am, if you divide the two words.
Churchill: I am willing to admit that you have some claim to be the latter.
Lindemann: Which is the only one of which, under my tuition, you have the smallest qualification to judge.

Lindemann was a vegetarian, living largely on the white of eggs. He was also a non-smoker and a total abstainer, except in respect of a statutory 32 cubic centimetres of brandy which he was regularly commanded to consume when dining with Churchill. The Prime Minister was uneasy about the strict austerity measures imposed on the British people in wartime. He told Lord Woolton, the Minister of Food, that almost all the food faddists he had ever known, nut-eaters and the like, had died young after a long period of senile decay. 'The British soldier is much more likely to be right than the scientist. He cares about beef.' But in these matters he recognized that the Prof was a law unto himself. He was capable of taking much trouble over simple things for unimportant people. In the late summer of 1941 I was preparing, with Churchill's connivance, to escape from Whitehall and become a pilot in the RAF. To do so I had to pass examinations in navigation and mathematics and I had long forgotten all my school 'maths'. So I bought a book entitled *Teach Yourself Mathematics*, which was inadvertently left lying on top of the Prof's celebrated aircraft production charts. He was pained by this invasion of his own erudite papers, but on discovering who was the owner of the book, he postponed his intended departure to Oxford and spent an hour explaining to me in simple terms and with carefully drawn sketches the navigational theory of the triangle of velocities.

Although Lindemann quarrelled with many scientists, who resented his arrogance and his unhesitating use of Churchill's favour and authority, there were some who respected his determination to obtain results. In conversation, during the early months of the war, he used to say that the man he admired most was Watson Watt, inventor of radar. Had he been willing to bow the knee to cumbersome bureaucratic processes, in such vogue before the war, the timely radar installations which contributed so much to Britain's salvation in 1940 would have been fatally delayed. The Prof also pushed the claims and sang the praises of R.V. Jones, a former pupil at the Clarendon Laboratory, who discovered the secret of the German directional beam for raiding bombers, helped to bend it so as to lead the raiders astray, collaborated with the Prof in obtaining approval for the aluminium strips called 'window' which confused the German radar defences, and was a tower of strength in the struggle to identify and defeat the German v-weapons.

It was not only in scientific matters that the Prof acted as an interpreter. He was not a professional economist or experienced in finance, but his fertile brain easily comprehended intricate problems which Churchill had neither the time nor the inclination to study in detail. He threw himself ardently into the fray relating to the vexed question of Article VII of the Anglo-American Mutual Aid Agreement. The Americans, in return for demanding no material repayment by Britain of the goods and services supplied under the Lease-Lend Act, wanted Britain to accept foreign imports free of tariffs and to dismantle the system of Imperial Preference. Lord Beaverbrook, Brendan Bracken, Leopold Amery and many others were up in arms. Britain, they pointed out, had bled herself white, selling her investments in the USA in a bargain basement until she had practically nothing left; and now the Americans were demanding a pound of flesh in payment of sacrifices uncomplainingly made in a common cause.

Lindemann took the opposite view, for he believed that Britain's future was tied to the United States. He once said to me that if Roosevelt and Churchill had both been in power after 1945, he had no doubt there would have been an economic union of the English-speaking world, followed one day by common citizenship. Just as centuries ago the Scots complained of union with England, but ended by dominating the country, so the British would eventually dominate America. The Prof was nothing if not an outspoken patriot, though not always a realistic one.

Battle raged between the Prof and the Beaverbrook-Bracken school. They fought lustily for the soul of the Prime Minister, whose attitude to the American demands would decide the issue. I went for a walk with the Prof who spoke like the famous Gloomy Dean of St Paul's. The Conservatives would, he declared, be crushingly defeated at the post-war election. Beaverbrook and Brendan were using their influence with Churchill in an endeavour to sabotage important measures, such as the new National Health proposals, of which they were hopelessly ignorant. Above all he objected to Beaverbrook's scheming against Article VII and the serious effort being made to regulate the international trade cycle, just to please the farmers. Churchill at first tended to lean to the Beaverbrook side, but by pertinacity, and with support from the Treasury and the Foreign Office (neither of which were often on his side), the Prof won the battle. 'It is,' Churchill remarked, 'no use arguing with a prophet: you can only disbelieve him.' In the end he did not disbelieve him.

In 1944 the Prof went to war with Duncan Sandys, then at the Ministry of Supply, about the size of the warheads to be expected

on the German v-weapons and the damage they would be likely
to cause. He was right in some of his assertions, but wrong in
others. Feelings ran high and Duncan Sandys, in spite of being
Churchill's son-in-law, was placed firmly on the Prof's black-list.
The Prof for his part found a niche in Beaverbrook's. One day
in 1945 I had a mild argument with Beaverbrook when I asserted
that over the v-weapons the Prof had been more often right than
wrong. That afternoon a messenger came to No. 10 from Beaverbrook. He brought a brown-paper parcel and insisted on standing
by while I opened it, presumably to ensure I did not make a copy
of the contents. Inside was a black loose-leaf dossier. Successive
pages each contained a record of one instance where the Prof had
made an erroneous forecast.

In 1951 Lindemann, against his professed wish, was conscripted
by Churchill as a member of his new Cabinet. During the two
years he stayed there, he fought two single-handed battles and won
them both. The Bank of England, with the support of the Treasury, decided that the best way to stanch the near-mortal drain of
the country's life blood through a continuing decline in gold and
dollar reserves was to let the pound go free. It was a most secret
plan which included taking revolutionary steps without first informing the United States or the rest of the sterling area. Lindemann called it 'the bankers' ramp' and he stimulated first Churchill
and then the Cabinet to oppose what might well have been an economic Suez crisis, with perhaps longer term and more disastrous
results.

His second victory was over his new foe, Duncan Sandys, once
again at the Ministry of Supply. The Prof was the Prime Minister's
adviser on atomic energy and, by reason of his personal friendship
and co-operation with Admiral Strauss, Chairman of the American Energy Commission, he had a leading part to play in Anglo-
American discussions. He was determined to wrest the control of
atomic energy from the civil servants in the Ministry of Supply
and place it in the specialized grasp of an independent organization
such as the Americans had established. The battle was fierce and
long. At times it seemed to be lost, for Churchill's patience was
not inexhaustible and by March 1953 he was angry, almost to
breaking point, with Lindemann. However, the Prof marshalled
his arguments well and, since in this instance he could not rely

on Churchill's support against Sandys, he brought his case before the Cabinet and won the day. He was thus the founding father of a new Atomic Energy Commission.

Shortly afterwards he retired to Christ Church, Oxford, his only home. He discovered that Duncan Sandys, transferred from the Ministry of Supply to that of Works, held the ultimate responsibility for a plan to drive a road through Christ Church Meadow, under the Prof's very window. This was a proposal of the Ministry and not a plot by Sandys to avenge his recent defeat; but the Prof thought otherwise and he immediately sought the help of everybody of importance, from the Prime Minister downwards. He lived long enough to see the vandal proposal shelved.

His last contribution was in the field of technological education, for he was acutely aware that Britain was falling far behind the United States which, in turn, seemed to be losing the race to the Soviet Union. Statistics had always been his armoury and he produced startling figures to prove his contention. The Ministers primarily concerned had taken no action and Churchill did not have the time to give the matter full consideration until he took Lindemann and me on a holiday to Sicily immediately after his retirement from office in April 1955. Then, after dinner one evening, he listened attentively to the Prof on the subject, said that he felt guilty of having taken no action while he still had the power, and fully endorsed the Prof's conviction that something equivalent to the Massachusetts Institute of Technology or the California Institute of Technology should be built in England. I offered to raise the money, using Churchill's name, and the offer was accepted. The result was not a new technological university, as the Prof had wished, for there were neither the funds nor the teachers available without robbing existing organizations.

However, Churchill College, Cambridge, emerged from this Sicilian conversation, and the ardent Oxford scientist was the first to agree both that the technologists should be leavened by a minority studying the arts and humanities, and that Cambridge, with its great engineering school, was a more appropriate site than Oxford.

Lindemann died in July 1957. He had made scores of enemies in his life. Few of them were as persistent in their rancour as he was himself. He had also made many friends, to whom he offered the best of companionship, witty conversation and an affection which, with his deep personal shyness, he did his best to disguise. Black was black and white was white: for him there was no such shade as grey. Alone, on an elevated pillar, he placed Winston Churchill whom he served with unwavering fidelity for thirty years and whose path through dark and tangled thickets he did as much as any man to smooth and illuminate.

One year after Lindemann, Brendan Bracken died, at the early age of fifty-seven. He was not, like Lindemann, expensively and selectively educated. He was largely self-taught, with results that were much to his credit. He shared with Lindemann the gift of an extraordinary memory. It was not a photographic memory for figures; but details of people, houses, dates and historic characters were stored in a granary that was continually replenished. When Bracken was present, no books of reference were required.

Buoyant and expansive in his lifetime, he had no wish to be recorded or remembered. He left instructions that all his papers should be burned. Yet such was his personality, and so strange was the mystery of his background and of his jet-propelled rise from nothing to eminence, that two able writers, neither of whom knew him, were impelled to write his biography and disentangle the long-suppressed story of his turbulent childhood in Ireland, his experiences as an adolescent in Australia, his brash determination to enter a public school at Sedbergh when he was well past the age of a schoolboy, his entry into a well-known firm of publishers and his rise, while still in his twenties, to prominence in journalism and, a little later, to significance in South African gold-mining. Founder of the *Banker*, purchaser of *The Economist*, Chairman of the *Financial News*, all before his twenty-eighth birthday, he was a Member of Parliament by the time he was twenty-nine. All this he achieved with little political help. He had attached himself like a limpet to Churchill when he was only twenty-two, and had been of energetic assistance to him in several by-elections, but Clementine Churchill, who was later to become a devoted friend, at first regarded him as an outlandish and potentially malign influence on her husband. So although he stimulated and amused Churchill, he was not always welcome at Chartwell and during the years of upward struggle he received no sustained encouragement in his political aspirations.

'There is,' said the Minister of Agriculture in reply to a Parliamentary Question, 'no known method of suppressing bracken.' There was laughter on both sides of the House of Commons, but, wittingly or unwittingly, the Minister had hit the nail on the head. Brendan Bracken was totally irrepressible and therein lay much of his strength.

Cheerful though he nearly always seemed to be, he was a realist, and there were two faces he could show. When the clouds were dark with menace, he was not oblivious of the fact. I have many memories of his forebodings. In April 1941 he warned that the Coalition Government was losing popular appeal. 'The honeymoon is over,' he said, 'the grim realities of marriage must now be faced.' The House of Commons might accept Income Tax at ten shillings in the pound with masochistic pleasure, 'like self-flagellating friars', but it was false bravado to pretend that the country was revelling in austerity. Later in the war he frequently pointed out the dangers of complacency, declaring that the Home Front was seriously war-weary. The risks of the 1944 landing in Normandy worried him for months in advance. Unlike Lord Beaverbrook and most of the leading Tories, he prophesied election defeat in 1945; and in 1953, just before the coronation of the Queen, when all the world seemed to be smiling, Brendan told me he thought little of the Government's prospects, he doubted Churchill's ability to continue, and he was strongly critical of Mr R.A. Butler's financial policy.

All this, and much more, was for private consumption. With Churchill he was invariably in high spirits, bursting with optimism and discounting bad news or depressing forecasts. Indeed there was nobody better able to dispel Prime Ministerial gloom and induce good temper. He loathed Chequers and seldom went there, disappearing for the week-end with an air of mystery and declining to let anyone know where he had gone. But during the week, at No. 10, or its annexe in Storey's Gate, the ebullient Brendan was ever at hand to calm, soothe and invigorate, though his irruptions when political appointments were under discussion were usually distracting and unhelpful.

He was unfailingly thoughtful for Churchill. When the Prime Minister was in a bad temper, unreasonable or inconsiderate, Brendan was the only man who could laugh him out of the mood. 'You are,' he would say, 'behaving like Mr Sparrow.' Mr Sparrow was a disgruntled and objectionable bird who appeared on Sundays in a column written by Nat Gubbins for the *Sunday Express*. The feature was a weekly joy to Churchill. Mr Sparrow would smile, the ill-temper would vanish and Brendan's simple but determined strategy worked. He was considerate when the news was bad, applying his fertile imagination to the discovery of something good and cheering. One evening in February 1941 the Admiralty telephoned an agonizing account of the destruction of a convoy in the Western Approaches. It was by no means the first. Brendan begged me not to tell Churchill that night, for the news would prevent the sound sleep on which depended his strength to carry the heavy burden. The distress must be postponed till the morning and meanwhile Brendan flung open the door, contrived to put on a happy smile and invented a string of amusing, if untrue, political gossip to send Churchill to bed unworried and relaxed.

In June 1953 Churchill had a serious stroke. Brendan was not a frequent visitor, for he had become an observer of the political scene and no longer a participant. I sent a letter to him by car from Chartwell. Within two hours of receiving it he was standing anxiously at the front door. Discovering that Churchill was temporarily paralysed, he came back next day with the most convenient invalid chair that could be purchased. He stayed to preach recovery and his confident predictions were so convincing that he restored Churchill's spirits and helped to raise him from what his doctor feared was a deathbed. He galvanized his will and convinced him that as the world did not have the smallest inkling of the seriousness of his illness, he had plenty of time to recuperate and must continue in office. He mobilized the support of Beaverbrook and Camrose and between them they managed to gag the Press, to the subsequent indignation of many Members of Parliament.

He was considerate to others also, especially those in a humbler station than his own. One late autumn night in 1940 a bomb hit the old Treasury building. Brendan and I emerged from the Downing Street air-raid shelter, wearing dressing-gowns and tin hats, to survey the damage. A Treasury messenger had been killed. Brendan took pains to discover his name and, without telling anybody in official circles, sent the widow money to supplement the inadequate pension she received. On a pleasanter occasion, in 1941, Brendan arranged at the Ministry of Information a display of films of the Atlantic Charter meeting between Roosevelt and Churchill which had arrived by air from Newfoundland that very day. He invited the Cabinet and all the grandees of Whitehall. It was typical of him that he also invited all Churchill's domestic servants, provided transport, met them himself at the door, and insisted that the film should not begin until they had arrived and were seated.

Brendan never stopped talking except when Churchill was present. In the time of the nightly air-raids which began in September 1940, he organized a 'mess' for the Private Office and its ancillaries in the reasonably safe offices at Storey's Gate where iron shutters had been attached to the windows. He presided over the dinner parties, prepared by an excellent Swedish cook whom he imported from the *Financial Times*, while orderlies of the Royal Marines waited at the table. He invited Members of Parliament, visiting Americans, writers and businessmen as fancy took him, and he encouraged the rest of us to do the same. He dominated the conversation. His flow of invective was powerful and he welcomed argument. He had an armoury of nicknames that sounded pejorative, but were more often than not affectionate. It did not take me long, after his arrival at No. 10, to discover that the Coroner was Neville Chamberlain, the Parachutist was the Tory Chief Whip, David Margesson, and the Film Star at the War Office (or alternatively Robert Taylor) was Anthony Eden. Yet he respected Chamberlain, was devoted to Margesson and liked Eden personally, though he was not one of his political admirers. The Desiccated Undertaker was Sir Samuel Hoare and God's Butler was Sir John Anderson. Those who loved Brendan, and they were many, quickly saw through the façade of ruthlessness and the pretence of callousness with which he tried to disguise an ingrained good nature devoid of bitterness. In this he was the antithesis of Lindemann.

His incessant conversation sometimes palled, especially when he had ceased to take an active part in politics; but more often it compelled attention, for his vocabulary was wide, his imagery original and his theories, whether or not his audience accepted them, were neither tame nor commonplace. He told prodigious lies, without the smallest qualm. This was often just to help him prove a point, for he had no dishonest purpose and once the dross had been washed away he was the soul of honour. The lies were also told from sheer exuberance, from his Celtic love of exaggeration and to disguise the carefully guarded secret of his own background and origin. They were exclusively white lies: he liked to impress and he usually succeeded.

Sometimes the banter would vanish and there would be genuine emotion, for he was a romantic who was not very good at hiding the fact beneath a transparent veil of cynicism. He pretended to be an atheist, or at least an agnostic, and yet his frequently blasphemous exterior concealed a persistent care for religion. Two men whom he loved, and whose influence on him he admitted, were the Archbishop of York, Cyril Garbett, and the Roman Catholic Bishop Mathew. One evening in the mess a Brendan I hardly recognized emerged when an Irish man of letters whom he had invited to dinner declared himself an atheist and made a vicious attack on the Christian religion. Brendan went into vehement action. In a display of inspired eloquence, mingled with abuse of his guest, he produced an apologia for Christianity which would have enthused any congregation in Westminster Abbey.

He liked and respected the United States, but nothing irritated him more than self-satisfaction, whether British or American. If he scented it, he would take counter measures. I remember him embarrassing some over-confident Americans in the autumn of 1944 by proclaiming that President Roosevelt was more interested in his own re-election than in a contribution to the common struggle. He spoke no foreign language and knew little about Europe. Europeans for their part were mystified by him. Desmond Morton declared that at some gathering where Brendan was present he was approached by one of the leading Free French representatives who said: 'Ah, so that is Bracken. I have heard of him. He has the vocabulary of Mr Churchill but of the left.' How, Morton asked, did Brendan interpret that?

Brendan became Minister of Information in July 1941. He succeeded three men, Lord Macmillan, Sir John Reith and Duff Cooper, all famous for their previous achievements and all a failure at the Ministry. He did not want the post, for he preferred the corridors of Downing Street; but he could not say no to

Churchill. He continued, however, to spend his evenings at the Storey's Gate annexe, to drop casually in on the Prime Minister without appointment and to behave as largely as before. He was scathing about his new office. After only one day in charge he christened it 'Bloomersbury'. However, he was admitted by all, politicians, civil servants and journalists, British and Allied, to be an instantaneous success in 'Bloomersbury'. He remained at his post until the end of the Coalition Government in May 1945, and he left with well earned plaudits from all with whom he had dealt.

His knowledge of people and his encyclopedic memory were in frequent demand when appointments in Church or State were under discussion. Grave attention was paid to his views. His opinion carried less weight than might have been expected when political appointments were under discussion. Churchill formed his Coalition Government in the days after he became Prime Minister partly, where the major offices were concerned, on his own initiative, partly in consultation with Mr Attlee and Sir Archibald Sinclair, but mainly in close co-operation with Captain David Margesson, the Chief Whip and, to a lesser extent, Sir Edward Bridges, the Secretary to the Cabinet. Three men who ardently desired to influence the choice were Beaverbrook, Bracken and Randolph Churchill. The new Prime Minister listened to their opinions but was not guided by them. So it continued when in due course James Stuart succeeded Margesson as Chief Whip. Brendan, who excelled as a 'fixer' where outside appointments and financial deals were concerned, and was a lusty fighter in any fray he chose to enter, did not hold the post of *éminence grise*, which the outside world believed was his, when ministerial appointments were under discussion.

This was true in 1940 and at later stages in the war. In March 1945 I noted that when Churchill and James Stuart had reached agreement on a number of undersecretarial appointments, Brendan arrived and tried to upset the whole apple-cart. Finally, in order to check Brendan's flow, the Prime Minister turned to me and, quite out of the blue, diverted the conversation by giving me a blow-by-blow account of the great German attack of 21 March 1918 as he himself had witnessed it from ten thousand yards behind the Fifth Army front.

A few days later I wrote, 'Brendan's advice becomes less sound as Lord Beaverbrook's influence grows more enveloping'. And in May 1945, just after the German surrender, when the policy for a General Election campaign was under discussion, Brendan was not invited to dine at No. 10 with the others principally concerned. He was, I observed, 'offended with the Prime Minister over a number of minor slights and, like Achilles, is sulking in his tent'. The reason for all this was the new Beaverbrook-Bracken axis which became a factor in politics during the last year of the war.

It is hard to determine which of the two was the leader. Beaverbrook had much the longer experience of political intrigue, but perhaps Brendan was the tougher character. Certainly Beaverbrook claimed that this was so. Their alliance was complicated by the fact that, although Beaverbrook was sincerely devoted to Churchill, he thought it fun to intrigue against his Government and his advisers, whereas Brendan, charmed, entertained and often influenced by Beaverbrook, was nevertheless unshakably Churchill's man. In the last analysis, what Churchill decided was law for Brendan.

Undermining Ernest Bevin, the Minister of Labour, and supporting Herbert Morrison, the Home Secretary, was among their favourite intrigues. It was the more exciting because Churchill had great respect for Bevin and much less for Morrison, a sentiment shared by the leader of the two ministers' own party, Clement Attlee. The anti-Bevin theme dated from 1940 when Beaverbrook, justifiably obsessed by urgency, saw no reason why the workers in the aircraft factories should not disregard established working hours, safety regulations, air-raid warnings and restrictive practices as readily as he did himself. Bevin, the embodiment of trade union authority, was no supporter of sluggards in days of national emergency, but he was not prepared to let Beaverbrook drive a horse and cart through accepted union practises. In an almost Prof-like vendetta, Beaverbrook persisted with attacks on Bevin long after he himself had ceased to be Minister of either Aircraft Production or Supply; and Brendan, for no obvious reason apart from the fun of political intrigue, marched eagerly beside him. In the event, their combined efforts made no impact at all.

A commentary on their judgment of the two Labour rivals is to be found in post-war history. Bevin was a resolute Foreign Secretary who stood boldly up to Molotov and did not hesitate to face Stalin's challenge to the West in blockading Berlin. Morrison was held by many impartial judges to be as incompetent a minister as ever sat in the Foreign Secretary's chair. It is perhaps a digression worth making that when Churchill was Leader of the Opposition after the war, I asked him which of his wartime Labour colleagues he thought the best. I expected him to say 'Bevin', but without hesitation he replied 'Attlee'.

Bracken and Beaverbrook did not restrict their mischievous activities to the relationship of Bevin and Morrison. They extolled each other, Beaverbrook even suggesting that Brendan, who would have been totally unsuitable, should replace Lord Halifax as Ambassador in Washington. That was at a time when Halifax had already won golden opinions at the White House and was in the process of becoming as widely acclaimed in America as any British Ambassador could hope to be. Harry Hopkins, reflecting Roosevelt's opinion, spoke loudly in his favour to Churchill.

They donned the mantle of unbending conservatism and inflexible capitalist orthodoxy, two doctrines that were foreign to Churchill's old-fashioned liberal instincts. Brendan had long been saying, perhaps with perspicacity, that the only hope of stabilizing prices lay in preventing an all-round rise in wages and that inflation would be the main post-war hazard. He then set himself the task of undermining the proposals in the Beveridge Report and in particular those for a national health service. Beaverbrook, no longer in the Cabinet, supported him wholeheartedly. Unfortunately for them the establishment of a Welfare State, for which they felt such distaste, was strongly approved not only by the Labour ministers, but by Eden and Lord Woolton and with only occasional lapses by Churchill himself. Thus when Bracken spoke in Cabinet against the proposals, he was almost a lone voice. I remember thinking this ironical when in October 1944 I listened to him begging Churchill to show more interest in the Home Front. The prospect of post-war social benefits had an important effect on the morale of the Home Front. The Welfare State was a policy of the wartime coalition which the Labour party later succeeded in presenting as its very own.

On 26 July 1945 Churchill sat in his map-room with Brendan and Beaverbrook, watching the results of the General Election as seat after seat fell to Labour. I was there too, and it was impossible not to reflect how fundamentally they had all misjudged the temper of the electorate, Brendan and Beaverbrook in promoting High-Tory, pre-war policies, Churchill in fighting the campaign with the bellicose tactics he had found so effective on the hustings in 1905. No doubt the country wanted a change after fourteen years of Conservative majority in Parliament. No doubt many people who voted Labour were sufficiently untutored politically to believe, after years of coalition government, that Churchill, who was almost universally adored, would continue to lead them whichever way they voted. No doubt, too, the line so ardently pursued by Brendan and Beaverbrook had little effect on the result.

During that last year of the war, and for ten years after it ended, the Beaverbrook-Bracken axis was so strong that it seemed as if Brendan had been weaned away from his primary loyalty. It was not so, even though he was more often in Beaverbrook's company than in Churchill's. He may in his innermost thoughts have felt that his fidelity had been inadequately recognized. His name did momentarily appear as Secretary of State for the Dominions in a list for the reconstruction of the Cabinet drawn up, but at the last moment discarded, in April 1944. A year later, when Churchill formed his Caretaker Government to serve during the two months of party strife before the General Election, Beaverbrook encouraged Brendan to think that Churchill should have offered him the Chancellorship of the Exchequer rather than the lowlier Admiralty portfolio.

Brendan was defeated at the General Election and then returned with an alarmingly reduced majority in a by-election for the safe Conservative seat at Bournemouth. He began by taking an active part in the deliberations of the Shadow Cabinet and it was he who, seeing the need for drastic reorganization in the Conservative party, advised Churchill to appoint Lord Woolton ('the Draper', as he irreverently called him) chairman of the party. However, little by little he lowered the tempo of his political activities, dedicating himself to the affairs of the *Financial Times* and the South African mining company, Union Corporation. He was again closer to Churchill than he had been before the General Election and he did much to restore a serene relationship between him and Beaverbrook. When the Tories returned to power in 1951, Brendan refused office, accepted a viscountcy but never set foot in the

House of Lords, which he disparagingly nick-named 'the Morgue'.

He kept away from Downing Street, but at his own house in Lord North Street his talk was of Churchill. There were reminiscences that grew longer and longer; there were criticisms, intended to be constructive, of the new Government's policy and members; but above all there were anxious enquiries about Churchill's health and welfare. The natural affection of one who had deliberately cast off his own family, and had never found a wife, was concentrated on the man who really mattered to him. It was the man whom he had selected as his hero when, at the age of twenty-two and until recently only a lowly-paid assistant schoolmaster, he forced himself on Churchill's attention at the Westminster by-election and won an approval which lasted till his death. In the process he made friends of all ages and both sexes, and he did so because pushing, tactless and even offensive as he could sometimes be, he cast a spell with many ingredients, of which the strongest were a warm heart, a generous nature and an often unselfish regard for others which mingled unexpectedly with strands of egocentricity.

It would be invidious to compare the qualities of the Prof and Brendan. Perhaps it is fair to say that the first achieved more and the second gave more.

CHAPTER FOUR

The Private Office

At 10 Downing Street, before Churchill arrived on the scene, there were three male Private Secretaries, of varying departmental origin, and one lady, Miss Watson. If she had a departmental origin, nobody could remember what it was, for she had sat in Downing Street since the days of Lloyd George and Bonar Law. Her main function was to amass the frequently scattered information required for answers to Parliamentary Questions and to reply to letters from the general public. She was a kind and thoughtful spinster in her late fifties who was, however, a little longwindedly alarmist about the nation's morale, the dastardly intentions of Mr Churchill's clique, the insidious spread of bolshevism and the telephonic message *Air Raid Warning Yellow* which was received every time some solitary enemy aircraft was spotted cruising twenty miles off Sheerness.

There was a Press Officer, housed in a distant part of the building, and there were a dozen competent secretaries, commanded and galvanized by the admirable Miss Stenhouse who had been on the scene almost as long as Miss Watson. There were also four grave, trustworthy and soberly attired messengers who kept the downstairs part of the house in polished and spotless perfection.

The two senior Private Secretaries sat in the room immediately next to the Cabinet Room, and there was another equally well furnished office, darkened by the adjoining wall of the Treasury, in which sat the junior male Private Secretary, Miss Watson and the Parliamentary Private Secretary, Lord Dunglass. In a separate room, opening out of the Cabinet Room at its far end, was Sir Horace Wilson, Chamberlain's intimate adviser on all matters, whose own secretary was the efficient, and at first rather alarming, Miss Gwen Davies, a contemporary of Miss Stenhouse and a woman whose heart of pure gold was matched by a fearless, Welsh loyalty. The mere thought of Winston Churchill made her shudder; but she ended by being one of his most stalwart partisans. She and Miss Stenhouse embodied the tradition of unquestioning (though by no means uncommenting) service to successive prime ministers.

Working at No. 10, even after the outbreak of war, was a gentlemanly occupation in a well-established private house of pre-war comfort. Coal fires glowed in every grate, at the tinkle of a bell one of the grave messengers appeared to seek instructions, there were ivory hairbrushes and clean towels in the cloakroom; and everything reminded the inhabitants that they were working at the very heart of a great empire, in which haste was undignified and any quiver of the upper lip unacceptable.

The work was efficiently partitioned. In addition to wider and more general activities each Private Secretary had his own special responsibility (in my case the Ecclesiastical Patronage of the Crown and such appointments as Regius Professorships), and there was a middle-aged lady with years of experience and a long, specialized memory for each of the different sectors. They comprised Civil List Pensions, the Church, the Honours List and the appointment of Lords-Lieutenant. It was a system more reliable than modern mechanical memory-machines can offer.

On the other side of Horse Guards Parade, the First Lord of the Admiralty, Winston Churchill, had a less dignified establishment, but it was doubtless a more physically active and fast-moving one. It was called 'the Private Office', a service department term which had never been used in No. 10, the Foreign Office or other civilian departments. In May 1940 when Churchill came down to his new abode, like a wolf on the fold, he brought with him not only the name, Private Office, but also two of its highly intelligent and, at that moment, also highly geared members, Eric Seal and John Peck.

Chamberlain went off to be Lord President of the Council, taking his sound and sensible Principal Private Secretary, Arthur Rucker, with him. Miss Watson was, by common consent, immovable; but Sir Horace Wilson was sent away to concentrate on being Head of the Treasury and Lord Dunglass retired to the back benches of the House of Commons, none but Miss Watson having recognized him as a future Prime Minister. That left, in addition to the indispensable ladies, Anthony Bevir, a scholarly Old Etonian newly arrived on the scene from the staff of the Cabinet Office, and myself. Churchill was far too busy to look closely at either of us and so we were absorbed automatically and unprotestingly into the immigrant Private Office. Anthony Bevir had been badly wounded at the end of the First World War, through the whole of which he fought meritoriously (itself a strong recommendation in Churchill's eyes), and he was a man who put other people's interests before his own. A dedicated snuff-taker, with literary taste and wide historical knowledge, he readily assumed responsibility for all the dull but necessary ploys such as air-raid precautions and negotiations with the Ministry of Works and the Treasury. He was ill at ease in the speed and clatter of Churchillian life and temperamentally unsuited to serve an unpredictable master. So he was relegated to handle the ecclesiastical patronage on the grounds that I, who had become acquainted with all the characters in Trollope's Barchester novels during the previous nine months, was too juvenile to deal with bishops. 'On the other hand,' said Eric Seal when he broke the news to me, 'I think you might be better than Tony Bevir at dealing with the Prime Minister.'

Bevir took infinite pains to help anybody in trouble and often thought of original ways to do so. Indeed he was one of the kindest and least self-seeking of men. He continued to serve Church and State, to the benefit of both, under Attlee after 1945, under Churchill once again and under Anthony Eden. In 1952, Churchill, who had developed an affection for him, decided that his faithful service merited a reward. He proposed to recommend him for a KCB in the new Queen's Birthday Honours List. He was, it appeared, of the wrong seniority in the Civil Service for a knighthood of any kind and the Secretary to the Treasury, Sir Edward Bridges, descended in wrath on No. 10. He had a blazing row with the Prime Minister: at least Bridges blazed, but to my surprise Churchill remained icily calm. Fortunately the Queen, quite independently, had decided that Bevir's long and helpful connection with Buckingham Palace on episcopal matters deserved a KCVO. The Prime Minister at once concluded that a personal gift of this kind from the Queen was even more distinguished than the Order of the Bath. So with a mischievous smile he told me to let Bridges know he would withdraw his proposal.

By an unhappy chance Bevir then proceeded to lose his key chain in a taxi. Attached to it were all the important box-keys in Whitehall and that of the garden entrance to 10 Downing Street. So the locks had to be changed with great speed and at great expense.

When the Honours List was published a few days later, the Treasury were dumbfounded. They had been outwitted by their own First Lord and their Sovereign. However, they had the last word. On the morning the list appeared my telephone rang. It was Sir Burke Trend, future Secretary to the Cabinet. 'Do you know,' he asked, 'what KCVO stands for? Keys Can Vanish Overnight.'

Eric Seal, who arrived with Churchill from the Admiralty, became Principal Private Secretary, but did not last a year. His wits were sharp, he was hard-working and he was efficient, but Churchill treated his secretaries as part of the family, especially during weekends at Chequers, and he was embarrassed if they were not entirely congenial to him. Seal, for all his qualities, was not.

The other arrival from the Admiralty was John Peck, an estimable and entertaining product of Corpus Christi College, Oxford. He had an irrepressible and iconoclastic sense of fun, a gift for writing light verse, a likeable personality and an attractive Hungarian wife. He was the only member of the Private Office to remain in it, without interruption, throughout the war. I began and ended in it, but in the interim I made two excursions into the Royal Air Force, with Churchill's undiluted approval, but much to the inconvenience of both the Private Office and the Air Ministry.

Two new men entered the fold. Shortly after the change of government John Martin arrived from the Colonial Office and in the spring of 1941 Leslie Rowan came to No. 10 from the Treasury. Mercifully they both had as rippling a sense of humour as John Peck, so that laughter echoed through the building at the gloomiest times; and they found Churchill's eccentricities, and sometimes even his chronic lack of consideration for those attending him, entertaining, especially as his inconsiderate behaviour was combined with generosity and affection to all who served him. He did, however, require constant attendance by his Private Secretaries, and one of them had to remain up, even when there was nothing to do, until he went to bed at two, three or even four a.m. When, at Christmas 1940, Seal suggested that all the Private Office might be allowed a few days' leave, he replied that the most he would allow was one and a half hours off for Divine Service, and that continuity of work never harmed anyone. As he left for Chequers on Christmas Eve, he wished us all a busy Christmas and a frantic New Year.

At Brendan Bracken's suggestion, the Prime Minister promoted John Martin to be Principal Private Secretary when Seal departed to other fields. He was, and is, a good scholar and efficient administrator, but he has confessed that at first he did not find it easy to work for Churchill, whose outbursts in those hectic days could indeed make the foundations tremble. Highly though Churchill thought of his merit and many as were the important foreign journeys on which he accompanied the Prime Minister, his Scottish reserve, modesty and innate shyness prevented him from developing the easy relationship with Churchill which came naturally over the years to his eventual successor, Leslie Rowan.

Churchill did not entrust his Principal Private Secretaries during the war with the delegated power which he had bestowed on Eddie Marsh and P. J. Grigg in days gone by, or as he sometimes did after his return to office in 1951. Martin for his part did not aspire to the role of adviser which Arthur Rucker had assumed with Chamberlain and Seal had sought, with scant success, to assume with Churchill. He was content to ensure that the Private Office performed the duty of bringing to the Prime Minister's attention, clearly presented but seldom predigested, all that it was necessary for him to see, and excluding the vast amount of material that it was not. Under Martin's leadership, which lasted four years, the Private Office was both cheerful and effective. It was so well attuned to Churchill's personal predilections and his unusual methods of work that none of its members succumbed, though they may occasionally have wilted, beneath the stresses and anxieties of war.

Leslie Rowan, whom Martin extracted from the reluctant Treasury in 1941 to fill the vacancy left by his own promotion to

Principal Private Secretary, suited Churchill perfectly. He was outgoing and outgiving, with the readiest of smiles, a first-class memory for detail and the pleasantest of social graces. Churchill delighted in his company and kept his friendship alive even when, after the war, Rowan returned to the Treasury and worked for that austere Chancellor Sir Stafford Cripps. He was, Churchill considered, a man with whom it was agreeable to dine; and he elected him a member of the Other Club.

Most Prime Ministers put much reliance on their Parliamentary Private Secretary and their Press Secretary. Churchill saw no good reason to have either. He believed that as he had been a journalist, he could handle the Press himself. If he wanted to explain his policy on a particular issue, he would send for a newspaper proprietor or an editor. The Ministry of Information, in due course under Brendan Bracken, was responsible for the general guidance of the newspapers and one of the Private Secretaries could deal with the parliamentary lobby correspondents. John Peck did so, and the lobby correspondents were entirely satisfied. Since they were trustworthy men, it was possible to give them a great deal of background information which was not for publication. They never betrayed the trust. In Churchill's second administration he declined to have anything at all to do with the existing Press Secretary whom Attlee had left behind. The poor man left in dudgeon. However, Churchill was persuaded to accept the services of Mr Fife Clark, whom he at first viewed as an unwanted encumbrance, but ended by trusting and, which is much more remarkable, using.

The post of Parliamentary Private Secretary involves an intimate and uninhibited relationship with the Minister. Churchill was prepared to accept such a relationship only with a man he knew well and thought an agreeable companion. In 1940 Brendan Bracken performed the duties of the post, but firmly declined the title. When he became Minister of Information, Churchill made no move at all to find a replacement. It seemed to him that James Stuart, who had succeeded David Margesson as Chief Whip, could well perform the function if necessary. James Stuart thought this would be a deplorable arrangement and with the utmost difficulty he persuaded Churchill to accept the Member for Richmond, George Harvie Watt. The Prime Minister began by ignoring his existence, as politely as possible; but Harvie Watt had a secret weapon. In the turmoil of war Churchill could find time to attend the House of Commons only at question time and for full-dress debates in which he was taking part. However, the House was his spiritual home and its activities were of absorbing interest to him. Harvie Watt, of his own accord, started to write short, pungent and informative weekly résumés of events in the House, and presently the Prime Minister looked forward to their arrival with positive impatience. The sturdy PPS, with his Scottish accent and Dickensian appearance, won first Churchill's attention and then his esteem. They were never close friends, for their backgrounds and interests were far apart, but for the Prime Minister, as for many other people, Harvie Watt had a part to play in what Churchill used to call 'the scheme of things'.

Churchill had a naval ADC, Commander Thompson, who was his Flag Lieutenant at the Admiralty before being brought to No. 10. He took no part in the work of the office, but he performed a useful service in arranging the Prime Minister's journeys, plans for which were liable to be whimsically altered at short notice. Thompson accompanied him on all his travels, though he was never consulted on matters of business or policy. Churchill was fond of him and treated him rather like a slightly spoilt spaniel. There was also another Thompson, the Inspector, who had been Churchill's detective for many years, who knew all his foibles and could, at appropriate moments of crisis, be an effective substitute as valet, secretary, friend and nanny. Both Thompsons had an indispensable role in 'the scheme of things'. Last, but by no means least in the Private Office, was the chief clerk, Charles Barker, who kept both the papers and the Private Secretaries in order, was an expert on old silver, cheered up the doleful and was cynically destructive of pomposity. Life at 10 Downing Street would have been less efficient and less enjoyable without him.

Churchill had few secrets that he withheld from the members of his Private Office. So it was cause for some perplexity when in the summer of 1940 yellow boxes stamped VRI began arriving at No. 10. They were brought, usually personally, by 'C', head of the Secret Intelligence Service, who when not shrouded in his professional mystery was known as Brigadier Stewart Menzies, a member of White's Club and a former officer in the Life Guards. Stranger still was the fact that only the Prime Minister had a key to open those faded relics of Queen Victoria's reign: not even the Principal Private Secretary was entrusted with one. They were made of wood covered in tattered yellow leather and were so old that when John Peck was handling one the bottom fell out. The papers were scattered on the floor, to the consternation of MI6 when this untoward event was reported to them. The contents, as we discovered (for Churchill was occasionally disposed to show them to one or other of us), were intercepted German signals which formed the most vital source of intelligence received during the war. The code name was 'Boniface', perhaps chosen by a Roman Catholic friend of mine who worked at Bletchley where the signals were deciphered. It seems that the Air Ministry and the Admiralty called them 'Ultra', the name by which they have become famous; but in central government circles the few who knew of their existence referred to them as 'Boniface'. So well was the secret kept that at the end of the war even General Ismay's personal assistant believed 'Boniface' to be the pseudonym of a spy planted in the German General Staff.

These most secret documents were the sole form of intelligence, or indeed of spying, in which Churchill was constantly interested. The activities of the Ministry of Economic Warfare, whose Minister, Dr Hugh Dalton, he much disliked, were of but slight significance to him. The Special Operation Executive and other clandestine organizations, however effective, did not attract his attention. He knew less than he should of the gallantry and initiative of British agents working in Europe under the direct threat of the Gestapo. This was partly because he saw as little as possible of Dalton, under whose broad authority most of them came, and there was no direct contact with No. 10 on these matters. The only Resistance Movement on the Continent in which he took more than passing interest was that of Marshal Tito in Yugoslavia. His son Randolph was there, serving under Brigadier Fitzroy Maclean, and also Bill Deakin who had spent many months at Chartwell before the war, helping him with his composition of *Marlborough* and the *History of the English Speaking Peoples*, and whose personality was as pleasing as his scholarship. His other links with the British intelligence and security services were mainly through Menzies, who came regularly to No. 10 with the yellow boxes, and one of his specialized advisers, Desmond

Morton. Lindemann kept him informed of scientific developments to which he did give careful attention, and jointly with
Sir John Anderson reported the progress of 'Tube Alloys', the
code name for the atomic bomb programmes.

Excitement has been aroused by spy stories, by the confessions
of defectors and by television serials on the subject. It may be that,
'Boniface' apart, the importance of the intelligence services has
been overstated, except in such vital scientific areas as the detection of the wireless directional beam and the v-bombs. There were
exceptions, by no means least the system organized by J.C. Mas-
terman for the detection and subsequent utilization of enemy
agents in the Allied cause. There were also the ingenious decep-
tion plans devised to mislead the Germans. However, as far as
British espionage itself went, it is permissible to doubt whether
the results justified the effort. In July 1940 Desmond Morton told
me that 'c' had received notice of an imminent invasion of the
British Isles from no less than 260 sources. The appetite for this
kind of information soon became jaded.

Perhaps, too, at a later stage the treasonable iniquities of Burgess
and Maclean, of Philby and others, on behalf of our former Russian allies, have been given rather more significance than they
warrant. The purveyors of nuclear secrets to the Soviet Union
after the war – Fuchs, Nunn May, Pontecorvo – did, of course,
make a notable contribution to the knowledge and power of those
who rule on the other side of the Iron Curtain; but mere spying,
in war and peace, is more often a literary and televisual entertainment than an actual menace. When in 1951 I suggested to
Churchill that he ask for all the known facts about the Maclean/
Burgess episode, he said that he regarded them as two squalid
traitors of no material interest. However that may be, for commercial purposes a great deal of melodramatic misinformation has
been offered to the gullible public and has been believed.

Among the short stories Churchill wrote there is only one spy
story, and that is about a dramatic raid he and some senior naval
officers made during the First World War on a house in the High-
lands where they had noticed a searchlight installed on the tower.
The searchlight turned out to be one used for spotting deer on
the hill, and its owner a man of undoubted integrity. All the same,
in 1914 spies did give some cause for alarm, for there was no radar

and the methods of communication were less sophisticated than twenty-five years later. By 1939 they were no longer a serious threat, at any rate in the United Kingdom. In some of the exaggerated accounts, more fictional than factual, which have been written or televised, Churchill's name appears; but in my own experience at Downing Street, spies made scarcely any impact on our affairs. It may therefore be wholesome to discredit at least one of the more widely accepted and more fundamentally inaccurate stories that have been told.

I never heard Churchill speak of Sir William Stephenson. Nor, among living witnesses, did John Martin, John Peck or General Sir Ian Jacob. Since Sir William played an important part in British intelligence in North America, and was much admired as an exponent of his art, his name may have been mentioned to Churchill. It was probably known to Roosevelt also, because Stephenson directed British intelligence on American soil. In a much publicized book about Stephenson it is alleged that Churchill asked him to dinner at Beaverbrook's house in May or June 1940. The alleged letter of invitation, printed in the book, is a clear invention, for Churchill, who was punctilious in such matters, never referred to Lord Beaverbrook as 'the beaver' and never, for obvious reasons, signed himself W.C. There is indeed nothing to confirm such a meeting in either Churchill's or Beaverbrook's papers. On the way to the dinner party, at which Churchill apparently took the place of the butler and let Stephenson in by the front door, we are asked to believe that Stephenson invented the famous morse 'v' signal. We are also told that a fellow guest was Lord Trenchard, who talked about his fighter aircraft and his capacity to resist a German attack as if he were still holding an RAF command. It was ten years since he had done so. It is quite a relief to find that Admiral Jellicoe, Marshal Foch and General Pershing were not also present at the dinner party.

Foremost among the inventions in this book, *A Man Called Intrepid,* by the American author William Stevenson, is the allegation that Sir William provided a secret liaison between the Prime Minister and the President and was in constant communication with Churchill on intelligence and military matters. In reality, as is well known, Churchill and Roosevelt provided their own liaison: they were in uninterrupted communication with each other for over

six years. It is more than doubtful whether Stephenson ever set
foot in 10 Downing Street: none of those who were there in the
war can recollect his so doing. Yet his fictional relationship with
Churchill has been so widely believed since the publication of
Stevenson's book that when Sir John Martin visited the Central
War Room in Storey's Gate, now open to public view, the guide
pointed to a chair in the room used for Cabinet meetings as being
the one in which 'Intrepid' used to sit. In sober fact this so-called
'Intrepid' never entered that room, at least when Churchill was
occupying it. The flavour of the book was given in an illustrated
brochure advertising it. There was a photograph of Churchill
standing in the ruins of the bombed House of Commons. The man
with his back to the camera, announced the caption, is 'Intrepid'.
It is, unmistakably, Brendan Bracken. It seems that the more
brazen and indeed idiotic the assertions, the more readily they are
believed.

Included in a book called *The Ultra Secret* by Group Captain
Winterbotham is a story that Churchill, learning of the intended
raid on Coventry well in advance, deliberately sacrificed the city
and its inhabitants in order to preserve the 'Boniface' secret. The
truth is this. All concerned with the information gleaned from the
intercepted German signals were conscious that German suspicions must not be aroused for the sake of ephemeral advantages.
In the case of the Coventry raid no dilemma arose, for until the
German directional beam was turned on the doomed city nobody
knew where the great raid would be. Certainly the Prime Minister
did not. The German signals referred to a major operation with
the code name 'Moonlight Sonata'. The usual 'Boniface' secrecy
in the Private Office had been lifted on this occasion and during
the afternoon before the raid I wrote in my diary (kept under lock
and key at 10 Downing Street), 'It is obviously some major air
operation, but its exact destination the Air Ministry find it difficult
to determine'.

That same afternoon, Thursday 14 November 1940, Churchill
set off with John Martin for Ditchley, Mr and Mrs Ronald Tree's
house in Oxfordshire generously made available to the Prime
Minister once a month when the moon was full and Chequers was
vulnerable. Just before Churchill left, word was received that
'Moonlight Sonata' was likely to take place that night. In the car

he opened his most recent yellow box and read the German signals in full. He told the chauffeur to turn round, and went back to Downing Street.

On arrival he decided that due precautions must be taken, for he assumed the operation to be aimed at London and to be a more massive assault than had ever been made before. He ordered that the female staff be sent home before darkness fell. He packed John Peck and me off to dine and sleep in a sumptuous air-raid shelter prepared and equipped in Down Street underground station by the London Passenger Transport Board. They made it available to the Prime Minister as well as to their own executive. Churchill called it 'the burrow', but used it himself on only a few occasions.

'John Peck and I dined apolaustically in "the burrow".' I commented, with a blend of gratification and disapproval, 'Caviar (almost unobtainable in these days of restricted imports); Perrier Jouet 1928; 1865 brandy and excellent Havana cigars.' Meanwhile Churchill, impatient for the fireworks to start, made his way to the Air Ministry roof with John Martin and saw nothing. For on their way to Coventry the raiders dropped no bombs on London.

There is not even the thinnest shred of truth in Group Captain Winterbotham's story of Coventry. It is to be hoped that neither this incident nor a score of others with which Mr Stevenson's book about 'Intrepid' is gaudily bedizened are ever used for the purpose of historical reference. To dispel such an unacceptable hazard is my excuse for this long digression.

Churchill trusted all who worked for and with him, and in those whom he grew to know well he was prepared to confide even his innermost thoughts. Some of his Private Secretaries became his lifelong friends and all of them formed part of that secret circle to which he would often refer, glaring round the dining-room at wartime meals, when he was about to launch into a confidential discussion of military operations or foreign policy. They never let him down: there were sometimes leakages from the Cabinet, but never from the officials whose duties, on social as well as on ordinary working occasions, gave them access to views, information and items of gossip for which the Press would have been willing to pay a small fortune and the enemy a vast one.

However anxious the times, however arduous his labours, dinner was for Churchill a meal never to be skimped or hurried. When it began his temper might be short and his mind preoccupied, so that as he fell voraciously on his soup (and the first course, of at least four, must always be soup) he was often less than attentive to his neighbours and might glower disapprovingly at the company in general. The clouds soon lifted and he became both loquacious and benign. Business might be done, politics and strategy discussed and relevant papers demanded, but more often than not the occasion was one for carefree relaxation between the long day's effort and the meetings or paperwork that would occupy the late night and early morning hours. When the time came for the brandy to circulate on the candle-lit table, Churchill's wit prolonged the sparkle of the champagne that had preceded it. Loth to join the ladies and allow the long-suffering servants to clear away, he would replenish his glass, relight his cigar (which was always going out) and quote the words of Dr Faustus, 'Let us command the moment to remain.'

When Churchill returned as Prime Minister in 1951, he had long since reached the age at which new faces are unpalatable. He inherited Mr Attlee's Private Secretaries. Arriving at 10 Downing Street with Sir Norman Brook he flung open the door connecting the Cabinet Room to the Private Secretaries' offices. Four men were nervously awaiting inspection by their formidable and by now legendary new master.

He gazed at them, closed the door without saying a word, shook his head and proclaimed to Norman Brook: 'Drenched in Socialism'. This remark was not only unfair, but also inaccurate. Civil Servants, even at No. 10, have no overt political association. 'Send for Leslie Rowan,' he continued. That, Brook explained, was impracticable. 'Then send for Jock Colville.' That was practicable, and I was duly sent for.

His new Private Office in fact contained intelligent and hardworking men drenched in neither Socialism nor Conservatism. Two off them, David Pitblado and David Hunt, Churchill soon grew to trust and respect. Familiar though the surroundings were – for the old, original 10 Downing Street had not yet been demolished and reconstructed – the urgency and the close companionship forged in war were missing. His habits had scarcely changed, but he was slower, less impetuous, much less irascible and much more inclined to delegate. Family ties and Auld Lang Syne were high on his list of desirable amenities. So Christopher Soames and I, each representing one of those amenities, were the main repositories of his confidence. Anthony Bevir, the lapels of his black coat brown with snuff, would emerge from time to time to recommend the solution of some episcopal imbroglio. Brendan Bracken seldom presented himself, Randolph was treated with caution on account of his journalistic indiscretions, Lord Beaverbrook was only an occasional telephonic intruder. Memories of the hectic, exciting nights of 1940 and 1941 had receded to become part of the old house's atmospheric history, merging with the shades of Pitt and Palmerston, of Gladstone, Disraeli, Lloyd George and Baldwin.

Yet there was no sadness and only a trace of nostalgia. Churchill's eightieth birthday was celebrated with nationwide enthusiasm, Government and Opposition combining in their display of affection. Chartwell had replaced Chequers as the usual scene of weekend activities, and there, as at No. 10, the Private Office continued to perform its duties punctually and efficiently. It was no mere gesture of obligation when on finally resigning Churchill gave each of its members a silver v to remind them of a great past and to signal his hope of a bright future for all of them.

CHAPTER FIVE

Beaverbrook

The thesis is a man of superhuman drive, of ingenuity and imagination, of generosity to friends and adversaries alike, especially when they were in distress or in disgrace, and a zealous champion of the unorthodox. The antithesis is a juggler with men and money, an incorrigible intriguer, a prodigious liar, a dedicated mischief-maker and a politician of unsound judgment. The synthesis is Lord Beaverbrook.

He was quick and he was daring. In the first decade of the twentieth century, Max Aitken, impecunious son of a Presbyterian manse in New Brunswick, built himself a fortune by deals and mergers that moved favourably with the fair tide of growing Canadian prosperity and a consistent 'bull market'. The methods he used are said to have been within the law as it then stood. They bore some resemblance to those of the great American tycoons at the turn of the century. Perhaps they were less ruthless, perhaps they were less dishonest; but a rapid rise to riches breeds rumour and feeds envy. So Max Aitken left Canada in the summer of 1910 with a reputation by no means unsullied. There was, in particular, a cement deal which, rightly or wrongly, was long held to his discredit.

He brought with him to London a beautiful wife, Gladys, whom he loved but did not cherish. Her happiness and convenience were always subordinated to his own. He took an influential sector of British political society by storm, for his charm, exuberant good humour and eagerness to bestow financial benefits on new-found friends opened important doors with a speed that has never been equalled. Six months after his arrival in England, this unknown Canadian parvenu was a Conservative Member of Parliament and the political protégé of a leading Conservative, his fellow Canadian

Andrew Bonar Law. He was already in process of becoming a close acquaintance of David Lloyd George, of the Conservative paladin F.E. Smith, and through him of the Home Secretary, Winston Churchill. He even succeeded in buying control of that proud British company, Rolls-Royce, which he subsequently sold at a handsome profit.

Bonar Law was a worthy and intelligent man who led the Conservative contingent in the wartime Coalition Government. He was eventually Prime Minister for a brief, sad period at the end of which he died. Beaverbrook, throughout his own long life, always sang Bonar Law's praises, and since he owed his early political opportunity to Law, the theme was a laudable one. In fact, though not in the saga Beaverbrook recited, his hero was indecisive and rarely impressive. Law was profoundly unhappy when, in 1916, he found himself a key figure in the struggle which brought down Asquith, the Liberal Prime Minister, and replaced him by the dynamic Lloyd George who forthwith became the supreme British War Lord.

Churchill sometimes quoted lines composed by Hilaire Belloc when they drove to London together after a week-end visit in the country. Belloc's verse began:

> *Of all Prime Ministers I ever saw*
> *The least remarkable was Bonar Law....*

Be that as it may, the Aitken standard remained nailed to Bonar Law's mast. What King David was to Jonathan, Law was to Aitken, who was able to make better use of this early, influential contact than could poor Jonathan. Law might have written of Aitken, as David did of Jonathan, 'Very pleasant hast thou been unto me: thy love to me was wonderful, passing the love of women'. The last five words would, however, have been an exaggeration, and quite possibly misinterpreted.

Towards the end of the First World War Lloyd George temporarily won Aitken's allegiance and, much against the wishes of King George v (indeed behind his back), made him Minister of Information. Before long the new minister gave his first display of a practice he was to develop to a fine art in the Second World War: he resigned. Meanwhile he became principal shareholder in the dull and stagnant *Daily Express*, which he offered to build up as an organ of the Conservative party, but which, in due course, he converted into a vigorous journal bearing the stamp of his genius and originality. He was made a peer of the realm, with the title Beaverbrook. He once said to me, 'The morning after I became a Lord, I cut myself shaving. The blood ran blue.'

Blue blood was not his favourite product. As with much else his attitude was ambiguous. He enjoyed the company of the nobly born provided they were either decadently amusing or socially outrageous. Lord Castlerosse, the talented gossip writer, was his boon companion; he had, for a time, a soft spot for his daughter's first two husbands, Drogo Montagu and the Duke of Argyll; he felt no resentment at Churchill's ducal ancestry, doubtless concluding that it was balanced by strong, red American blood; and he admired Lady Diana Cooper for her beauty and her wit. The mistress he truly loved was Mrs Richard Norton, daughter of a baronet and wife of the elder son of a peer. Deep down, however, he respected only self-made men, looking with a mixture of scorn and envy on the Cecil family, Lord Halifax, Lord Lothian and the Stanleys, who combined brains and political astuteness with a famous genealogy and an ease of manner bred by social self-confidence. Lord Salisbury, the powerful potentate who paved the way for Stanley Baldwin's premiership, and his son, Lord Cranborne, led the field as stimulators of Beaverbrook's aversion, with Halifax lying a close third.

One evening at Cherkly, Beaverbrook's country house in Surrey, I was part of a small gathering at a dinner party illuminated by his rollicking sense of fun, superb Moët et Chandon and artful guidance of the conversation. However, before he went into the dining-room a cloud had settled on his brow. He launched into a tirade against the Foreign Secretary, Anthony Eden. Then, looking keenly at his guests, his voice suddenly raucous, he turned on the inoffensive Lord Queensberry and made an unprovoked attack on him as a representative of birth and privilege. Those who scale the heights without inherited advantages deserve greater respect than the spoon-fed, provided they reach the summit by honest endeavour; but the scene was embarrassing. Only two years before he had written to Anthony Eden, 'Strange as it may seem, I am listed among your admirers'; and Beaverbrook himself was not one to eschew privilege. The sun broke through as he ushered us into the dining-room, but that brief squall revealed the depth of his disdain for inherited wealth and position. When he extolled the gallantry of his son, Little Max, one of the most celebrated and decorated Battle of Britain pilots, it was not from parental pride alone. His son had proved his right to his inheritance. There was, he could justly boast, nothing spoon-fed about Group Captain Max Aitken, DSO, DFC.

Perhaps it was to make amends for the sparkle of the champagne, and for the company he so often kept but despised himself for enjoying, that he established in his own circle and on the staff of his newspapers a nursery for talented young socialists. Aneurin Bevan, Michael Foot, Frank Owen, Hector McNeil and Tom Driberg were among those who worked or laughed and caroused with the master. They were intelligent and entertaining, free of the inherited self-confidence he found distasteful. He claimed to Brendan Bracken that by introducing Bevan to the pleasures of high living he had diverted him from becoming the British Lenin. Bevan was too honest a man to allow his political opinions to be influenced by the flesh-pots, nor did he have a touch of Lenin's cold ruthlessness; but like all whom Beaverbrook chose to regale and to flatter, he was drawn to that wide smile, that rapid wit and those small, endearing attentions which owed more to good nature than to artifice.

Beaverbrook chose his left-wing associates shrewdly. They mostly rose to high political office and he supported them loyally. This was more than could always be said about those from his own party whose ambitions he decided to encourage. Once they were climbing the ladder, he was sometimes impishly enthusiastic in his efforts to pull them down again. On the other hand when he heard that Tom Driberg, one of his extreme left-wing satellites and the original William Hickey of the *Daily Express*, had been caught by the police committing an illegal homosexual act in a public place, Beaverbrook immediately sent his faithful valet, Albert, with a sheaf of bank-notes and instructions to save the unhappy Driberg from incarceration by hook or by crook.

His whimsical flirtations with left-wing politicians reached a climax in the early months of 1940, during the twilight war period when there were only serious hostilities at sea. He was alleged to have made a private pact with members of the Independent Labour

Party, then at the far left of the political arc, to support them with money and propaganda in an endeavour to procure a compromise peace with Hitler. Two months later he was to be found among the most zealous and effective antagonists of Hitler; but in the summer of 1941, McGovern, one of the ILP Members of Parliament, revealed in the House of Commons that in March 1940 Beaverbrook had offered to finance 'Peace Candidates' to fight by-elections. Churchill, who knew nothing of this, at first accepted Beaverbrook's denial and said so in the House. Thereupon McGovern produced evidence for which his ILP colleague James Maxton, one of the most truthful and respected men in Parliament, was prepared to vouch. Churchill said to me that he feared fewer people would believe Max than Maxton. By then Beaverbrook was disillusioned with the ILP. His new hero was Stalin.

The search and support for unpopular causes was combined with an unswerving loyalty to one which stood in obvious contradiction to most of them: the British Empire. Beaverbrook was a convinced imperialist in his Canadian youth. He remained one for all his active life. He launched and led a crusade for Empire Free Trade which, like the Crusades of medieval times, attracted many supporters and failed to achieve its objective. He wanted tariffs to be raised against foreign goods and he thought Imperial Preference the panacea for all ills. He emblazoned the front page of the *Daily Express* with a crusader in armour, wearing the cross of St George. At one of Churchill's last birthday parties I had an argument with him across the table. 'Ah,' he said, 'you don't believe in the Commonwealth.' Deliberately trailing my coat, I replied, 'Not much; but I did believe in the Empire'. 'That,' he replied, 'is the only sensible remark that has been made here to-night.' Of course, it was not.

He liked to record the political commotions in which he had participated, particularly those of the British Government in the First World War. He wrote with scintillation and his books make enjoyable reading. Yet they give the impression that an element of fantasy is intermingled with historic fact. After reading *Men and Power*, a book containing graphic descriptions of the politicians, the soldiers and the crises in the last years of the First World War, I asked Churchill whether those accounts were true. 'They are Max's interpretation of the truth,' he replied.

One day I went for an afternoon walk with Beaverbrook. He described to me how he brought about the downfall of Lloyd George in 1922. He discovered that Lloyd George had been selling Honours to replenish the Liberal party's funds and perhaps his own as well. So he set off for Wales and arrived, unannounced, at the house of a man who had been offered a peerage. 'How much did you pay?' he enquired. The man indignantly denied that he had paid anything at all: the peerage was in recognition of his great services to the country. Beaverbrook took out his cheque book. 'If you will tell me what you paid, and will give me the Prime Minister's letters, I will write you a cheque for the total amount, and your peerage will have cost you nothing.' After some hesitation, this Liberal stalwart admitted that he had paid a hundred thousand pounds. Beaverbrook wrote out a cheque and received the correspondence with Lloyd George in exchange. He repeated the process with a baronet-to-be – but that cost him only twenty-five thousand pounds.

Returning to London, he went to 10 Downing Street. He found access difficult, because instructions had been given that he was to be barred the door. However, he finally forced his way into the presence of the Prime Minister and said: 'George, you have got to resign.' Lloyd George went red with anger, and asked him how he dared to speak in that way, and ordered him to leave the house at once. Beaverbrook had arranged for a front page of the *Daily Express* to be printed with the headline 'Honours Scandal Exposed', and for the letters from Lloyd George to the peer and the baronet to be reproduced. He took this paper from a brief-case and presented it. 'If your resignation is not in the King's hands by six o'clock to-night,' he said, 'that is the front page of tomorrow morning's *Daily Express*.' Lloyd George resigned.

Whether Beaverbrook expected me to believe this story, I do not know. It does not bear any relation at all to what the history books relate about the fall of Lloyd George, nor would that canny Welshman have committed such delicate and dishonest proposals to writing. I think it was just that Beaverbrook enjoyed story-telling, an art in which he excelled. I remembered that in January 1944 I had stood with him and Clementine Churchill in the medina at Marakech. We had watched the dancers, the snake-charmers and above all the story-tellers who stood surrounded by

a crowd of squatting listeners. What they said was unintelligible
to us, but their eloquence and the gesticulations fascinated Beaverbrook. He said that story-telling was the same the whole world
over, and it was a great art to practise.

The relationship of Churchill and Beaverbrook went through
many vicissitudes, but they could not go for long without each
other's company. They seldom agreed on matters of policy, they
had a different code of morals and behaviour, they sometimes had
blazing rows; but neither was a man of rancour or a bearer of
grudges and each had a warm streak of loyalty and personal affection for the other. Beaverbrook was capable of pursuing a vendetta,
if usually for a comparatively short time, and Churchill was not.
Beaverbrook continued to be at once a romantic and a cynic: Churchill was an unadulterated romantic. The abdication of King
Edward VIII provides an illustration of this. Churchill supported
the King, and risked destroying his political career in the process,
simply because he believed in loyalty to his Sovereign. Beaverbrook told me that he joined Churchill in the fray because 'I
just thought it was a lot of fun'. He did not like kings or queens
anyway, but as he did love the British Empire with all sincerity,
there was no way in which he could show public antagonism to the
Crown.

Jealousy was not among Churchill's failings, and even when
Beaverbrook tried, unsuccessfully, to supplant him as the first
claimant to Brendan Bracken's loyalty, he showed no resentment.
He had, like Beaverbrook, a natural tendency to be both impatient
and impetuous, but he was the wiser, the more responsible and
by far the more truthful of the two. Moreover, he had basic principles in which he genuinely believed, whereas Beaverbrook had
few principles, only a limited number of convictions, no respect
for the truth, and loyalties restricted to a few old friends and
employees and, above all, to Winston Churchill himself. He criticized Churchill behind his back, sometimes quite viciously, and
on occasions he came close to intriguing against him; but that was
part of the incessantly revolving Beaverbrook kaleidoscope. It
was no reflection on the love he felt for an old friend whose policies
frequently disappointed him, but to whom he was personally
devoted and for whose welfare, in sickness and in health, he was
prepared to make greater effort and sacrifice than he was for his

own wife. This affection was so firmly reciprocated that even when Beaverbrook had estranged almost all his Cabinet colleagues, was busily engaged in promoting strife between two stalwarts of the Labour party, Herbert Morrison and Ernest Bevin, and was crying havoc far and wide in every Ministry but his own, Churchill stood up for him against all comers and would listen to no slanders aimed at his friend.

The only occasion on which I heard of Churchill showing open disapproval of Beaverbrook on grounds of principle was long before I knew either of them. The story was told to me by Clementine Churchill. She had a scrupulous regard for the truth and it is therefore difficult to disbelieve the story. The first Lady Beaverbrook was lying ill at Stornoway House, their London home overlooking Green Park. There was an evening party there to which the Churchills were invited. As they entered the hall, Clementine, who had known the butler for many years, asked him how Lady Beaverbrook was. 'Her Ladyship is dying,' replied the butler. Winston and Clementine Churchill turned on their heels and walked out into the night. A day or two later Lady Beaverbrook died. The kindest explanation is that Beaverbrook wanted to block his mind to the imminent tragedy and chose any diversion to enable him to do so.

When Churchill became Prime Minister, on 10 May 1940, he at once turned to Beaverbrook, a close friend of thirty years' standing, for companionship and support. He had no intimate connection with those he must ask to join his government. Indeed many of them had long been his political opponents and only one, Beaverbrook, fell into the important category of 'those with whom it is agreeable to dine'. So although he seldom accepted Beaverbrook's advice on appointments, and still less often on military strategy, he was comforted by his presence during the first challenging days of his new administration. Moreover, Churchill now had bitter experience of the deadly cost of insufficient air support in modern war. He had seen what befell Poland in September 1939, on the outbreak of war; he knew that his own projects in Norway had been brought to disaster only a few weeks before by the superiority of the German Luftwaffe. Even as he was forming his Government, Holland and Belgium were succumbing to a German attack made with overwhelming air support.

He asked Beaverbrook to become Minister of Aircraft Production and to perform a miracle of improvisation. The King was reluctant, as his father had been in 1917, for he knew how widely mistrusted Beaverbrook was in Whitehall, in Parliament and in military circles. Moreover, he told Churchill that such an appointment would be ill received in Canada where, at any rate in Liberal circles, Beaverbrook's reputation did not stand high and his early financial deals were still held against him. With a combination of tact and argument Churchill persuaded the King to withdraw his objections. On 14 May Beaverbrook became head of an as yet non-existent department which was to do much to save the country in its supreme hour of need.

One day in August 1940 he telephoned to ask me to tell the Prime Minister that the Germans had bombed an important aircraft factory at Rochester and had missed with every one of their bombs. The Almighty, he said, was not always against us. 'In fact God is the Minister of Aircraft Production and I am his deputy.' In those whirlwind days Beaverbrook did assume almost divine powers, to which he had no legal or constitutional right whatever, and he produced miraculous results.

He enlisted men of quality like Sir Patrick Hennessy of Fords, Sir Wilfrid Freeman from the Air Ministry, and Sir Archibald Rowlands from the Treasury. They were also men of drive, and many of them shared his own predilection for piracy. They were supported by the staff and resources of the *Daily Express*. They did not, of course, produce aircraft from nothing. The long and slow developing process of designing and building Spitfires and Hurricanes was, by good fortune, approaching the stage of full production. However, speed was the essence. Traditional processes must be discarded, ingrained prejudices must be eliminated, the cumbersome methods of the Air Ministry must be circumvented, raw materials destined for tanks and other less urgent requirements must be seized, if necessary by stealth and duplicity, new records of production and methods of repairing damaged aircraft must become reality rather than targets, and spare parts must be disgorged for immediate use. All this was achieved and more besides; for with the Prime Minister's irresistible strength behind him Beaverbrook overthrew the Air Ministry's fervent faith in the bomber and sacrificed everything to the vital need for fighters.

Even as early as 4 June 1940, three weeks after he took office, I was able to write in my diary, 'Lord Beaverbrook is producing the goods in an astonishing way'.

The only person from whom he sometimes sought advice was Churchill, and that was not because he wanted advice but because he needed support in his piratical activities. Thus, late in June 1940, he came to Chequers to ask whether his ministry should continue to increase production or should concentrate on the improvement of engines and armaments. The views of the Air Ministry on the subject did not worry him. He said to me a few days earlier that the Air Ministry was a rotten ministry and Sir Archibald Sinclair a thoroughly bad minister, who was hood-winked by his subordinates. However, perhaps he knew that it was being said, by no means least by distinguished soldiers working in the office of the Minister of Defence, that Beaverbrook the Minister of Aircraft Production was still Beaverbrook the Press magnate; that he attached supreme importance to the number of aircraft he could produce, as he formerly did to the numbers of the *Daily Express* he could sell; and that 'circulation' had always been his primary objective.

So he wanted reassurance from the Prime Minister. Churchill said that for the next few months quantity was what mattered. Could we improve quality without decreasing the already remarkable level of output? Beaverbrook replied that that could be done and he went away comforted to be able to claim support for his activities from the Prime Minister and Minister of Defence. Powerful though his personality was, there was also a measure of diffidence and he seemed to feel the need of endorsement by the highest authority. In this he was unlike Churchill who loved to bask in approbation, but did not find it a prerequisite for the pursuit of policies of which he had convinced himself. Indeed, he throve on opposition and tended to be more invigorated by disagreement than by meek approval.

With incessant energy the new ministry 'cannibalized' the surviving parts of wrecked and damaged aircraft. In days, perhaps even in hours, a new Spitfire replaced two or three that had been apparently destroyed. Aircraft factories were divided into small sections and dispersed throughout the country so that no amount of concentrated enemy bombardment could destroy the industry's productive capacity. Workers in office and factory were encouraged to disregard the constant air-raid warnings that did so much to dislocate and delay. Working hours were lengthened to an extent that was positively unwholesome, and 'holiday' was a forgotten word. Thus, in one of the most brilliant lightning campaigns ever conducted, the short-term requirements of the Royal Air Force were successfully met and victory in the Battle of Britain was given its foundation. Whatever criticisms may be levelled against Beaverbrook's antics at other times and in other places, he must always be accorded a high place in the ranks of those whose personal efforts saved their country from disaster.

None of Beaverbrook's occasional vendettas were more vigorously sustained than that against the Air Ministry and its Secretary of State, the Liberal leader Sir Archibald Sinclair. Lady Violet Bonham Carter told me one day that she could get nothing out of him. 'Archie,' she said, 'is in a Trappist mood.' I asked her whether he had not, perhaps, been struck dumb by Lord Beaverbrook's blows.

Those blows began to fall in May 1940. They continued to rain on the Minister and his department until Beaverbrook handed over aircraft production in May 1941; and for the rest of the war any damaging stroke that could be aimed at the Air Ministry was joyfully bestowed. The air marshals, as a race, were subjected to as much obloquy as the Secretary of State, with the exception of Sir Wilfred Freeman, who had been hived off into Beaverbrook's own Ministry at its inception. As early as 2 July 1940 with the Battle of Britain pending, Beaverbrook asked to resign because of his difficulties with the Air Ministry and the air marshals. He knew that he would be told not to desert his post in his country's hour of need, but it seemed to him an oblique way of ensuring Prime Ministerial support in his departmental wrangles. A week later I listened to his passionate phillipics against Sinclair, the employment of old men and, thrown in for good measure, Lord Halifax. Churchill was bored by this constant harping on the same themes, but he was so impressed by production results that he was slow to react. Indeed on 10 August he said to me that Beaverbrook had precisely what his task required: genius and brutal ruthlessness. He had never in his life seen such startling results, not even at the Ministry of Munitions during the First World War. Our production of aircraft already exceeded that of the Germans by one-third.

Sometimes Beaverbrook did go too far. At the end of August he attacked the Air Ministry's sensible plan to send air crews abroad for training, to Canada, South Africa and Rhodesia, where they could be instructed without interference by enemy action. Churchill replied to his objection, 'I attach the greatest importance to your opinion, but you must either face the facts and answer them effectively, and with a positive plan, or allow the opinion of those who are responsible to prevail.' Then there was the problem of obedience to air-raid-warnings. Beaverbrook was for none; the air marshals were for a lot. The Cabinet, bearing in mind its responsibility for civilian lives, was left to decide the issue. It found a compromise.

He continued to resign, using asthma as an alternative excuse to the air marshals, and although he complained that Herbert Morrison was useless as Minister of Supply, whose task was to provide tanks and other equipment for the army, he flatly refused an offer to himself of wider responsibility for supply matters. By December he was alleging that he was building so many aeroplanes that the Air Ministry, with its slow and inefficient training programme, would soon be unable to man them. Churchill wearily begged the question by announcing that he preferred 'sharp criticism and counter-criticism between the two departments to their handing each other ceremonial bouquets'. Thus the unceasing battle against the air marshals went merrily on until, at the end of January 1941, Churchill told me that he was heartily sick of it and it must be stopped. It was not stopped, even when Beaverbrook had moved to other spheres, and in June Churchill commented that his friend just did not begin to understand how to get on with military men. At the height of Beaverbrook's vendetta against the Air Ministry I was walking with Churchill out of the Houses of Parliament. We met the Duke of Norfolk. 'What a relief,' said Churchill, 'to be confronted by an Earl Marshal instead of an Air Marshal.'

Beaverbrook's parting salvo was fired at the Air Ministry as late as April 1944. He informed the Prime Minister that the Air Ministry, and indeed the Secretary of State in person, were parties to breaking the law. There was a 'pig scandal'. Under the rationing arrangements those who kept pigs had to surrender their ration-coupons for bacon. Various RAF establishments had enterprisingly decided that rather than throw away the swill at the camp, they would feed it to pigs and thus add ham, sausages, bath-chaps, gammon and pigs' trotters to their existing rations. This sensible plan was strongly encouraged by Group Captain Sir Louis Greig, personal assistant to Sir Archibald Sinclair. He felt that he was helping to increase the nation's food supply. Indeed he was; but it was contrary to the bureaucratic interpretation of the rationing laws. On a visit to an RAF station in company with Sir Louis, Sinclair was proudly presented with some home-made sausages. It would have been ungracious to refuse; but he was, alas, thus made an accessory to crime. Luckily Queen Mary, who was among the most rigorous in conforming with the rationing laws, had a similar experience. On hearing of that, Churchill, to Beaverbrook's disappointment, ruled that no action at all was to be taken. Implicating the entirely innocent Queen Mary would have caused an even greater scandal than failing to punish the illicit RAF pig farmers.

Once the Battle of Britain was over and the excitement, which was Beaverbrook's elixir, had abated, he returned to his less commendable activities. He harried the Prime Minister with almost weekly letters of resignation, giving as an excuse the asthma which was certainly the heaviest cross he had to bear, but which seldom interfered with his activities when his interest was aroused. He received most favoured ministerial treatment. For instance, when Hess unexpectedly arrived, Churchill gave directions that details of the interview with him should be shown only to Attlee, Eden and Beaverbrook. He assumed various offices, all of which displeased him. He became Minister of State, and then Minister of Supply. He ended the war in a non-departmental capacity as Lord Privy Seal. He continued to send the Prime Minister endless minutes, letters and memoranda which distracted Churchill from more urgent occupations. He criticized military strategy, in which he was entirely inexpert, and the time came when even his close friend and admirer, Brendan Bracken, said that he took up more of the Prime Minister's time than did Hitler. He persuaded the Prime Minister to sign an open letter he had drafted to the farmers, urging them to 'stick it and not grumble'. This had a deplorable effect on the agricultural community. He made mischief about the conduct of operations in Crete. He upset the Post Office by a grandiose scheme to make Faraday House in London the seat and centre of Government. He poked his finger into every available pie, whether or not he had any knowledge of the ingredients.

A man who had been so assiduously, and happily, involved in political intrigue at the highest level between 1916 and 1925 could not be expected to renounce all pretension to it when his close friend became Prime Minister in 1940. He was unsuccessful for the most part because Churchill was too independently minded to be influenced in his decisions by Beaverbrook, Bracken, Lindemann or any other close friends. The importance of maintaining an acceptable balance between the parties forming his Coalition Government was never far from the Prime Minister's thoughts, so that he paid more attention to the promptings of Attlee for the Labour party and successive Chief Whips, David Margesson and James Stuart, for the Conservatives than he did to those of his more intimate friends and dining companions.

Beaverbrook went on trying. In August 1940 he was complaining about both Ernest Bevin, the Minister of Labour, and Herbert Morrison, the Minister of Supply, who he said ran his ministry as if it were the London County Council. He persuaded Churchill to invite him to Chequers with Bevin so that he could stir up trouble about Morrison. He flattered Bevin, who was a deplorable performer in Parliament, calling him a natural House of Commons man and the only orator in the Labour party. He made many sly allusions to the competing merits of capitalism and socialism. He supported Bevin's proposal to plough up more acres and increase farm production. He even fell in with his suggestion that there should be a new Ministry of Building. He made it clear that he thought Arthur Greenwood, Attlee's second in command, should leave the War Cabinet, and he hoped Bevin would assume a post still more important than the Ministry of Labour. It was all in vain: the stolid Bevin was unmoved; the no less stolid Churchill was unimpressed. Shortly afterwards Beaverbrook decided that Bevin was no good and began to pull out all the stops in support of his rival, Herbert Morrison. It was years later that somebody remarked to Bevin that Morrison was his own worst enemy and

Bevin made the celebrated reply, 'Not while I'm alive, he ain't.'
However, the disharmony was already there and Beaverbrook
gleefully twanged the strings.

Another opportunity for mischievous meddling came in the following December when Churchill had invited Lord Halifax to replace Lord Lothian in Washington. The consequent remodelling
of the administration was delicate, for the correct proportions
between Conservative, Labour and Liberal must be kept. Just
before Christmas Beaverbrook and Lloyd George lunched with
Churchill. Beaverbrook produced plans to upset the whole delicate
remodelling operation which had already been agreed, and he
pressed that Lloyd George, growing senile and in any case both
jealous and disaffected, should enter the Government as an agricultural overlord. It was feared that Churchill had been swayed
by Beaverbrook's wild proposals. Those whom the fears assailed
underrated Churchill. He was stimulated by Beaverbrook; he
regarded Lloyd George with deference. He might be moved by
their eloquence at the dining-room table, but his second thoughts
were usually his wisest.

It had been expected to be a relief when, his great mission of
1940 gloriously accomplished, Beaverbrook decided to remain for
a year or so out of the Government. The disadvantage was that
his restless mind at once discovered an exciting cause to pursue
with renewed, non-asthmatic vigour. Shortly after Russia was in-
vaded, Churchill sent him to Moscow to discuss with Stalin how
best the British (and indirectly the Americans, who were not yet
at war) could give material support to the Soviet Union. Beaverbrook was captivated by Stalin's insidious charms. Thenceforward
he became as stalwart a supporter of Russia as any member of
the Communist party and, as time went by, a dedicated enemy
of the free Polish Government and its gallant divisions of hard-
fighting soldiers under General Anders. The discovery that the
Russians and not the Germans had murdered more then ten
thousand Polish prisoners of war at Katyn was one of the first
danger signs to alert Churchill to the possibility of a post-war
Russian menace. Beaverbrook affected not to believe it and he
argued strongly in favour of recognizing Russia's seizure of
the Baltic States and part of Finland, acts no less wicked than
Germany's seizure of Czechoslovakia and Western Poland. I have

a letter from him in red ink. As a post-script he added, 'This is not written in the blood of a Pole.' I assume he wished it had been.

Worse still, he aided and abetted Roosevelt and the American Chiefs of Staff in their suicidal wish to help Russia by opening a Second Front in France during 1942. Many hundreds of thousands of lives were saved by the firm resistance which Churchill and the British Chiefs of Staff raised against such blood-soaked folly. The Americans had, at that time, little active experience of war, and Beaverbrook had none. His support of a cross-Channel operation two years before it could be undertaken with a real probability of success was certainly prompted by his desire to help the hard-pressed Russians; but it brought much toil and turmoil to his late colleagues who, while attempting to secure the communications and oil resources of the Middle East in hard-fought campaigns in North Africa, were burdened with the most dangerous and unrealistic proposals put forward in the whole course of the war.

When, under strong pressure to make at least a token assault, British Commandos and a Canadian Division landed at Dieppe in August 1942, they were forced to retire with heavy casualties. Beaverbrook was infuriated by the losses of the Canadian troops who took part. Perhaps it did not cross his mind that those losses were in some degree due to the enthusiasm with which he had encouraged the Americans to call for the wrong action at the wrong time. General Montgomery, whose caution as a commander was more often praiseworthy than the reverse, was not a participant in the operation, but he is on record as having the wisdom to advise its cancellation.

In June 1944 the great invasion of France, so ardently desired by Beaverbrook, Roosevelt and General Marshall in 1942, at last took place. A million Americans and a million troops of the British Empire stood ready to land in Normandy. The Western allies had total command of the skies. Their great battleships lay off shore bombarding the enemy positions with 15-inch guns. An artificial 'Mulberry Harbour' had been ingeniously constructed over many months and an oil supply line called Pluto was laid across the bed of the English Channel. The Germans had been weakened by grave loss of blood in North Africa and Italy, at Stalingrad and in the Ukraine. The cities and factories of Germany had been flattened by the bombers of the RAF and the USAAF. Yet, as those who landed in Normandy well know, it was by no means a walk-over even in the conditions of 1944. They, better than the military critics and historians, can judge what their fate would have been if the protagonists of 'Second Front Now' had had their way in 1942 or even in 1943.

As Beaverbrook did not mind being attacked himself, he saw no reason why others should object to his paper's attacking them. If the *Daily Express* criticized one of his colleagues, Lord Cran-borne for instance, he took refuge in the false pretence that he exerted no control over the paper. However, attacks on Churchill were forbidden and since Churchill was no exception to the rule that all politicians are sensitive to press criticism, however ephemeral, he was grateful to Beaverbrook for this dispensation. He did, however, feel obliged on one occasion to adopt the sub-terfuge of forgetting to ask Beaverbrook to sign his name in the visitors' book at Chequers because a colleague who had been vigorously attacked in the *Evening Standard* was coming on the following day.

Beaverbrook would not tolerate a confusion of identities in his papers. One Sunday after the war, Ephraim Hardcastle, the *Sunday Express* equivalent of William Hickey, made a scurrilous attack on me. He had confused me with a cousin, Richard Colville, a gallant naval officer who had become Press Secretary to the King and had incurred Ephraim Hardcastle's displeasure. I dined with Beaverbrook the next day and complained, expecting a few chuckles, a denial of responsibility and a defence of his employee. However, when he discovered that a mistake had been made in the identity of the target for attack, there was no laughter at all. 'I'll tear his liver out,' he said.

In 1945 Beaverbrook and Bracken joined hands in an energetic campaign. They were longing for party strife to reopen, whereas Churchill shared the hopes of Attlee and Bevin that the Coalition would continue until not only Germany but also Japan had been defeated. High Tory politics were their prescription. In February they made fruitless efforts to persuade Churchill to reverse the Cabinet's decision to accept Lord Woolton's proposals for post-war reconstruction based on the reports of Sir William Beveridge and other eminent men. Attlee was driven to protest in writing against what he wrongly believed to be Churchill's undue attention to his friends' ignorant views, complaining that these were apt to be thrown into the scale against the considered opinion of an expert Cabinet Committee. Bracken was the mouthpiece, for Beaverbrook was no longer in the Cabinet. Churchill was angered by this letter, and he was not pleased when his wife adjudged Attlee's initiative both courageous and justified. He was still more surprised when he showed it, private and personal though it was, to Beaverbrook who said he thought it a very good letter. Beaverbrook's unexpected but not untypical reaction was still rankling that evening when Churchill took me to see a film featuring Edward G. Robinson. 'He looks just like Max,' Churchill said disparagingly.

Early in May 1945, Churchill did protest to Beaverbrook that he was being too high-handed in his machinations, both within the Tory party and in the arrangements for a forthcoming General Election. However, when, by a decision of their Party Conference, the Labour ministers were obliged to break up the long and glorious Coalition, Churchill finally accepted Beaverbrook's advice to omit from a letter to Attlee a laudatory and beautifully worded tribute that he had wished to pay his former Labour colleagues. By the end of May Beaverbrook was already suggesting that Brendan Bracken should be regarded as Churchill's eventual successor rather than Anthony Eden, and though he was not shown in advance Churchill's celebrated 'Gestapo Speech', he let it be widely known, in pursuit of his wider political objectives, that it had been seen and approved by the Conservative Chief Whip, James Stuart. It had not; and I had told him so.

It is no easy task to assess a man with such a mercurial personality, with qualities and defects that were both so great. He was mischievous when he had no urgent task to absorb his vivacious energy. But he was not, as many believed and said, evil. Those who supped with him were wise to supply themselves with a long spoon. Yet the supper was always stimulating and he would have been among the first to advise on the length of the spoon. Perhaps he could be cruel, but I never myself saw or heard an act of cruelty on his part. No doubt he was a hard and demanding task-master to those who worked for him, but although he could

be mean to others, he was generous to his employees. He harassed
them. He would ring a man up day after day, perhaps at hourly
intervals, until he lived in terror of the telephone ringing. Then
the ringing would cease altogether and the wretched victim would
begin to fear that he was discarded, and that he was no longer an
object of interest. But few of his employees deserted him or,
harassed and infuriated though they might be by unreasonable interference, failed to stand up for him when he was criticized and
abused. He could be a bully and a slave-driver. Yet he was to such
an extent a man of contrasts that he performed acts of charity,
in the biblical sense of the word, greater than might be expected
of anyone. The following story illustrates the soft and generous
element in his nature.

On Christmas Eve 1940 one of the hard-pressed Civil Servants
in the Ministry of Aircraft Production was still at his desk at nine
p.m. He had been working six and sometimes seven days a week
for months, arriving while it was still dark in those days of sum-
mer-time in winter, and leaving each night long after the air-raid
sirens had driven most people into their nearest shelter. At last
he rose from his chair and went to wash his hands before making
his weary way home. On returning to his office he found a parcel.
Inside it was a beautiful necklace and a note saying: 'I know what
your wife must be feeling. Please give her this with my regards.
It belonged to *my* wife. B.'

He was capable of carefully thought-out kindness, he provided
unforgettable hospitality and he took great pains to help others
on their way. His judgment was often faulty and his advice could
be unsound; but it was seldom that he failed to arouse affection,
even in those critical of his waywardness. When he died, a few
months before his devoted friend, Churchill, there were many who
found the world a drabber and less exciting planet.

CHAPTER SIX

The Americans

When an angry Member of Parliament called Churchill a 'Yankee mongrel', he was delighted by the insult. He took it as a compliment. He was first and foremost, and proudest to be, a British subject, nor was anybody more characteristically English; but his mother's blood was a potent tie with the United States to which he felt an emotional attachment all his life. He joyfully accepted membership of the Cincinnati Club, which had been close to the heart of his grandfather, Leonard Jerome, and he died with the unique distinction of being at once a British subject and an American citizen. When this last honour, the greatest which the United States could give him, was originally proposed, he misunderstood: he thought the intention was, as it were, to hi-jack him and change his nationality. 'I am,' he said to me, 'a British subject and as that I intend to die.' The true and touching intention was made plain and he then accepted the honour with the pleasure which the promoters of the plan hoped to give him, though he was too frail to go to Washington and himself receive the citizenship from President Kennedy.

Churchill had none of the characteristics which grate on Americans. His voice, with its lisp and deep intonation, attracted them and he easily grasped, if he did not always share, their thoughts and intentions. Nor did Americans grate on him. From time to time he would refer crossly to 'those bloody Yankees', but more often he spoke, with feeling and conviction, of their generosity, their idealism and their unflinching faith in freedom. The State Department came in for frequent criticism, but not much more so than the Foreign Office; the American Chiefs of Staff were sometimes accused of ignorance or obstinacy, as were his own; but by and large he met the Americans more than half-way. He trusted them and he believed in them. It was his ambition to forge and sustain an indissoluble family connection between the English-speaking peoples.

For the most part the Americans gave back as much affection as they received. Churchill was as great a hero in their eyes as in those of his own countrymen. He was, at least until the last year of the war, the most potent force in the alliance that won it. That same alliance, weakened by his departure and Roosevelt's slow decline, lost the peace. It was not without good reason that he called the final volume of his war memoirs *Triumph and Tragedy*.

Churchill's American friendships were almost all political and military. An exception was the financier and presidential adviser Bernard Baruch, six foot five inches tall, with thick white hair and a prominent hearing-aid attached by a long lead to a battery in his pocket. He met Churchill at the end of the First World War when they were both concerned with munitions productions and were involved in the negotiation of the Treaty of Versailles. What might have been a passing acquaintanceship ripened into friendship in strange circumstances.

Churchill went to New York shortly after the Wall Street crash of 1929. The stock markets were in turmoil. Fortunes vanished overnight and punters operated desperately in the hope of recouping their losses whenever a small rally on the Stock Exchange was foreseen. Baruch's immediate reaction had been to tell Churchill that America was 'on the auction block'. He then recovered his confidence and on 15 November 1929 he cabled: 'Financial Storm definitely passed.' A year later he was still convinced of the brighter side, writing to say that the depression had hit the bottom and he did not think profits would decline further. It is surprising that he made so great a fortune. When Churchill arrived in New York, unhampered by his wife's sobering presence, he allowed his gambling instinct to take charge. He went to Baruch's office, sat down before the price indicator and played the markets. He knew nothing of what he was doing: to him it was like playing roulette at Monte Carlo. He plunged deeper and deeper. Finally he stopped, for he had lost more than he possessed. He realized that he must sell Chartwell and all he owned. Baruch came into the room and Churchill told him he was ruined. Baruch explained that, guessing what would happen, he had given instructions that every time Churchill bought Baruch would sell, and every time Churchill sold Baruch would buy. He was therefore all square. Presumably Baruch paid the commissions. Churchill never forgot the debt he owed.

He was much affected by the account Baruch gave of his own rise to fortune. I was present when he told the story which is one he doubtless repeated, with slight variations, on a number of occasions. His mother, whom he adored, was a rigidly professing orthodox Jewess. On the Day of Atonement young Bernie was about to leave for the office in Wall Street where he worked as a junior clerk, when his mother reminded him of his duty to spend the morning with her at the synagogue. This was awkward because on that day a new stock was to be issued at a price of 70 and Bernie had invested all his savings, and a little more, in an order to buy. He had worked out that if, by some misfortune, the price fell to 65, he must immediately sell. His savings would be lost, but he would be solvent. However, his mother's wishes and authority were paramount. He went with her to the synagogue.

Opening at 70, the Stock fell steadily to 65 and even lower. Had Bernie been in Wall Street he would have been obliged to sell. In the late morning there was a rally and when he returned to the office he sold at 82. From that beginning, and with consistent flair as a speculator, he built his fortune. The moral of the tale depends on the reader's view of both religious observances and the capitalist system.

During the war Baruch, who had advised many presidents, thought highly enough of his own political acumen to send long and rambling letters which Churchill did not often have time to read. They would lie for weeks in his special black box reserved for private affairs until he found the energy to dictate a short, appreciative reply which usually failed to take account of what Baruch had written. However, when Baruch came to England in April 1945, he was given a rapturous welcome and asked to Chequers. Thenceforward, whenever Churchill went to New York, whether in or out of office, he stayed with Baruch, who was delighted by the opportunities to invite Eisenhower, Dewey and Dulles, the Harry Luces and the Windsors to meet Churchill at his apartment. He was a host for whom no trouble was too great, and though it became a trial of patience to listen to his views and forecasts, Churchill remained devoted to him and never forgot the gratitude he owed. The last time I saw them together Baruch waxed eloquent on Britain's declining power, making a number of suggestions for the recovery of strength by prescriptions that did not seem entirely practical. Churchill gave an answer which was scarcely easier to interpret. He said, 'It may be better to bear an agonizing period of unsatisfactory time. You may kill yourself in getting strong.'

The relationship of Churchill and Roosevelt can be divided into two periods. The first and, from Churchill's point of view, by far the more fruitful was from the outbreak of war until the summer of 1943. In 1939 the two men did not know each other. They had been introduced briefly at a Gray's Inn dinner when Roosevelt came to London in 1918 as Assistant Secretary of the US navy. In September 1939, already twice elected President, he chose to start a correspondence, not with the Prime Minister, Neville Chamberlain, but with the First Lord of the Admiralty, Winston Churchill. It was almost two years after that before they met in the flesh, but in the meanwhile they became 'pen pals', by letter and by telegram, of the most persistent kind. The correspondence lasted, with the later intervention of many personal meetings, until the President died less than a month before the end of the war in Europe. It consisted in all of some two thousand communications between them.

The first period was one of discovery, daring and venture. It was also one in which Roosevelt's idealism was clear-sighted. He was well aware that at least four out of five Americans were unwilling to be involved in what they saw as the quarrel of European states, the very lands from which their ancestors had fled in search of freedom and prosperity. He was equally aware that the Nazi threat was of greater than local significance and that when Hitler said, 'Today Germany is ours: tomorrow the whole world', America was embraced in the threat. He determined to spare nothing in his endeavours to sustain the West European democracies against the most powerful military machine the world had ever seen, and he had the vision to determine that whatever advice to the contrary he might receive from his Ambassador in London, Joseph P. Kennedy, Churchill was and would remain the standard-bearer of resistance.

By the end of May 1940 the collapse of France was evident and Churchill's resolve to fight on was equally so. Roosevelt sent for the British Ambassador, Lord Lothian, on the very day the Dunkirk evacuation started. He suggested that if the worst came to the worst, the British Empire might continue the struggle from Canada. He added, quaintly as it seemed to Churchill, that the seat of government should be in Bermuda, because it would distress Americans if the British monarchy were established on North American soil. Perhaps he had forgotten that the Governor General of Canada was in all respects the personal representative of the King and exercised the royal powers from Ottawa.

As the year drew anxiously on Roosevelt and Churchill were in almost daily communication. Millions of American rifles and their ammunition were shipped to Britain. A squadron of American fighter pilots joined the RAF, the Neutrality Act was only honoured in the breach and Roosevelt knew that the British were bleeding themselves almost to death, in what he already regarded as a common cause, to pay for the food and arms that must be imported from America. Churchill was not aware that this last embarrassment was nagging at Roosevelt's conscience, for the overt signs were that America expected to be paid on the nail for all services rendered. However, he finally decided to omit from a long letter to the President, about the shipping emergency, a paragraph he had intended to include. It read as follows: 'While we shall do our utmost, and shrink from no proper sacrifice, to make payments across the exchange, I should not myself be willing, even in the height of this struggle, to divest Great Britain of every conceivable saleable asset so that after the victory was won with our blood and sweat, and civilisation saved and the time gained for the United States to be fully armed against all eventualities, we should stand stripped to the bone. Such a course would not be in the moral or economic interest of either of our two countries.'

Had he but known, Churchill need not have bothered even to draft that paragraph, for Roosevelt was already planning the means of obtaining Congressional approval for the generous, all-embracing Lease-Lend Act. Churchill has said to me that, despite his love for the United States, he feared the Americans would always be good businessmen before they were good Samaritans. He discovered that he was wrong.

In January 1941, Roosevelt's intimate friend and adviser, Harry Hopkins, arrived in England. He was the *éminence grise* of the White House, a man of radical, indeed left-wing, convictions whose early life had been dedicated to social welfare, a cause which had brought him together with Roosevelt. His hair was thinning, he walked slowly, stooping as he went, and his grey eyes appraised everybody and everything. He seemed to be a chain smoker and, though he drank with moderation, he excluded neither wine nor women from the desirable pleasures of life. He had a sense of humour, a slow but effective power of repartee and as great a readiness to see virtues as defects, whether in people or in institutions.

Hopkins had long been suspicious of the British, with an old-fashioned fear of the red-coats and a deep-rooted dislike of privilege and class distinction. Yet when he dined with three Cabinet Ministers, two of them Labour stalwarts, Bevin and Morrison, and the third a former captain of industry, Sir Andrew Duncan, he said that the understanding and comradeship had amazed him: nothing of the kind would have been conceivable in the United States. Churchill told him of a sentence quoted in one of the censorship reports on letters sent abroad, which declared, 'there is a warmth pervading England'. It was true, and Hopkins said that he sensed it. That warmth, that readiness for sacrifice and that temporary obliteration of several of the seven deadly sins, including Greed and Envy, is something which writers and television producers of a later generation have often failed to grasp or recapture.

Churchill took to Hopkins at once. He had never heard of him till his visit to London was announced but, apart from the fact that he was the President's special emissary, Churchill found him stimulating, bursting with ideas, sympathetic to what he saw of the British war effort, keen to advise on still greater American help and personally fascinated by the Prime Minister.

During a weekend at Chequers Hopkins provided the assembled company with eloquent encouragement by his descriptions of the American Government's readiness to go to all lengths, short of war, to help Britain in her solitary struggle against the powers of darkness. This was, he said, America's war too, though his Government's aim was to be the arsenal rather than a fellow combatant. They would shrink from nothing, in the last resort not even war, to contribute to the defeat of Nazi Germany. To us, living in a beleaguered island, fighting alone against heavy odds, our ships torpedoed in scores and our cities nightly bombed, this was exhilarating to hear. We had always been sure that we were going to win in the end, but faith was now reinforced by reason.

The President remained unshaken all through the spring and summer of 1941, when first Greece and then Crete were added to the list of British disasters and Rommel's newly landed Afrika Corps drove to the very frontier of Egypt. In August Churchill came back from his Atlantic Charter journey to Newfoundland, his first meeting face to face with Roosevelt since that evening at Gray's Inn twenty-three years before. My colleague, John Martin, who accompanied him, told me he had heard the President say: 'I do not intend to declare war: I intend to wage it.' So the theme Harry Hopkins had expounded was still valid. Nobody was thinking much about Japan, and Pearl Harbor was still a peaceful anchorage for the US navy.

In 1941 two more of Roosevelt's trusted friends arrived in Britain and immediately made their mark with Churchill. One was Averell Harriman, the President's special representative on supply and economic matters. The other was Gil Winant, successor to the discredited Joseph Kennedy as Ambassador to the Court of St James.

Harriman, hard-working, well informed and cosmopolitan in experience, may have been daunted by his first invitation to dine at 10 Downing Street, for after dinner he was given a steel helmet and bidden to follow the Prime Minister on to the Air Ministry roof to watch a sharp and noisy air-raid. His face was long, handsome, but rather heavy, and the general impression was one of almost uniform greyness. He spoke, like Hopkins, slowly and deliberately. He was serious and his smile was the more attractive for being comparatively rare. Everything he did he did well, and he found the second best intolerable. When he took up polo, he became the best polo-player in America. He developed a liking for croquet: he proved almost unbeatable. In politics and diplomacy he was soon to be found near the summit. His judgment

may not have been invariably good, for he was among those mesmerized by the Russians. No doubt he would argue that in this
he was a realist. In all matters relating to the supply and organization of American deliveries he deserved the golden opinions he
won and he soon became a valued addition to Churchill's circle.
Eventually, as a widower, he married Randolph's former wife,
Pamela, to whom both Winston and Clementine Churchill were
devoted. For more than twenty years after the war Averell Harriman was prominent in American public life, whether as Ambassador, Governor of New York or adviser to a series of presidents.
His work in England in the early years of the war was a productive
period in a long and dazzling career of service both to the United
States and to her allies.

Gil Winant was self-effacing, though proud that he was generally said to look like Abraham Lincoln. His modesty disguised the
courage of a lion, physical as well as moral. One night in February
1941 Churchill sent me in an armoured car to the American
Embassy with a draft on which he wanted Winant's comments.
The raid that night was heavy. While I sat with Winant upstairs
at No. 1 Grosvenor Square, the earth shook. I counted the whistles
of four bombs which seemed to fall close and, though I hesitated
to say so, I felt that the basement would provide a more convenient
working place. Winant did not lift his eyes from the document
he was studying.

An ambassador's channel of communication is the Foreign
Office, but Winant became almost an appendage of the Prime
Minister. His wife, from whom he was partially estranged, was
in London for only a short time and so Winant spent week-end
after week-end at Chequers. He was there in June 1941, when
Hitler attacked Russia (saying, to my surprise, that he believed
it to be a feint), and he was there the following December when
the news of Pearl Harbor was received. With his quiet voice, his
courtesy, his liking for people and his willingness to concentrate
on their interests, he became and remained a personal friend of
the Churchills, their children and their whole entourage. Nobody
maligned Winant, but he, if he thought his own Government at
fault, was outspoken in his criticisms of and to them. In his
loyalties he bestrode the Atlantic.

With men such as Hopkins, Harriman and Winant at hand,

Churchill's understanding of United States policy, firmly grounded in his exchanges with Roosevelt personally, was usefully enhanced. The almost unclouded relationship lasted beyond the end of 1942. When Singapore and Hong Kong fell to Japan and when the North African campaign went badly, with the fall of Tobruk in June 1942, Churchill was harassed by serious criticism and discontent at home. Roosevelt's heart warmed to his beleaguered friend and his sympathetic actions in support were the tonic which did as much as anything else to restore Churchill. There was a deep difference of opinion over the American and Communist demand for a Second Front in 1942, which General Marshall ill-advisedly recommended, Harry Hopkins doubted and Lord Beaverbrook mischievously promoted. Churchill's resolute defiance of that display of fantasy, which could only have resulted in incomparable disaster, bred no ill-will in Washington and there was perfect equanimity in the Anglo-American relationship when in November American troops had their somewhat inauspicious baptism of fire in North Africa.

A gradual change occurred in 1943. The British still had many more men in action than the Americans. It was not indeed till 1944, a month after the landing in Normandy, that the American armed forces fighting on all fronts equalled those of the British Empire. But the residual strength, in industry and in manpower, lay with the United States, and as the Americans became more powerful they were less sensitive to British views. When Britain was alone, nothing was spared on her behalf and it was natural that she should have the major say in strategy. It was equally natural that once the United States was at war and American lives were at stake, the White House, the State Department and the armed services should have no intention of playing a subsidiary role to any foreigners even if they spoke the same language and had the same common law.

The established collaboration of the President and the Prime Minister made the transition easier, and so did the presence in Washington of Lord Halifax, an ambassador congenial to both Roosevelt and Hopkins, and Field Marshal Sir John Dill, the British representative with the combined Chiefs of Staff. Dill had commanded a corps under Lord Gort when the British Expeditionary Force went to France in 1939. He had subsequently been a tired and largely ineffective chief of the Imperial General Staff in London. In Washington he blossomed. He looked, and was, distinguished. General Marshall, the most significant of the American Chiefs of Staff, liked him personally and respected his wisdom. His experience of tactics and strategy in two wars was recognized. The American Chiefs of Staff treated him as one of themselves. Nothing he said or did gave offence, and when he died, worn out by care and over-work, the American armed forces displayed their feelings by burying him in Arlington Cemetery with their own hereos. He was not one of the generals closest to Churchill, but he served his country faithfully and well in Washington.

At the Casablanca Conference between the President and the Prime Minister in January 1943, military plans were agreed without undue dispute. It was then that the declaration of unconditional surrender was proposed by Roosevelt and willingly agreed by Churchill. Few decisions have been subjected to more post-war criticism, although it can only be conjecture that the Germans, infatuated as they were with Hitler and more disciplined than any other race in the world, would have overthrown the Nazis if Allied intentions had been more generously phrased. The Germans, and in particular their Generals, are too straightforward to be competent plotters. Be that as it may, the theory that shrewdly stated that war-aims and acceptable terms of surrender would shorten the war had a long history. As early as the autumn of 1939 various German intermediaries suggested that arrangements could be made to dispose of the Nazi leadership if the Allies declared they would not partition or humiliate Germany. Chamberlain and Lord Halifax did not dismiss this idea, but Churchill and his followers did. As far as the United States was concerned, Lord Lothian reported in April 1940 a conversation with Roosevelt, who favoured the idea of an Anglo-French declaration to the heads of neutral states that there was no intention of partitioning Germany or destroying her sovereignty.

By the time of the Casablanca Conference Roosevelt's thoughts were drastically changed. Churchill for his part expressed the view he had always held, one shared by most of those who had memories of 1918 and its aftermath. The Germans, rising phoenix-like from the ashes, persuaded themselves that their army had not been defeated. It had been stabbed in the back by weak-kneed civilians and a revolutionary mob. An armistice had been signed while the army was still intact, still able and willing to defend the Rhine had it not been for the treasonable forces in their rear. Moreover, the German people had, so their apologists declared, believed implicitly the liberal and generous intention of President Wilson's Fourteen Points. That had been their reason for laying down their arms; and they had been deceived. Perhaps they should have listened to the cynical French Prime Minister, Clemenceau, whose comment on Wilson's Fourteen Points was that the Almighty found ten sufficient.

This time no excuse should be given for false interpretation of the facts. The German army must be seen to have been defeated. Peace should be dictated from Berlin on whatever terms the victors chose. Afterwards, as Churchill certainly intended, there would be magnanimity; but first there must be unconditional surrender. On this the President and the Prime Minister thought alike; and so in January 1943 did the majority of their countrymen.

The German and Italian forces in North Africa were at last annihilated. General Marshall now realized that a Second Front in France, which he had so strangely believed possible in 1942, could not be established in 1943. 'Only an undistinguished minority of historians will take the opposite view,' Churchill said to me. To him the strategy was that of a bull-fight. The landings in Sicily and the subsequent invasion of Italy were to be the lances of the picador. The banderillas would be inserted and in 1944 would come the death stroke by the matador, when the bull's head was down and his strength sapped. That stroke would be the invasion of northern France, 'Operation Overlord'.

It was towards the end of 1943 that Anglo-American differences were made plain. They appeared at the Tehran Conference with Stalin in November, for Roosevelt inclined to the Russian rather than the British arguments. They were sharpened by an American proposal to place both the forthcoming operation in Normandy and the entire Mediterranean area under one American commander-in-chief; and that at a time when the British casualty rate was two and a half times greater than the American. Churchill flatly refused. They reached their climax in 1944 and the first few months of 1945, though all the while the decencies were preserved, the Churchill-Roosevelt exchange of views continued and the armies fought victoriously side by side.

On 4 June 1944, two days before the Normandy landing, General Alexander's Anglo-American army captured Rome. It had been agreed at Tehran that once this was accomplished, Alexander would surrender seven of his divisions, almost a quarter of his force, to General Eisenhower for the campaign in France. The American Chiefs of Staff, strongly supported by Eisenhower, proposed that they should be used for a landing in the south of France. Despite Churchill's unrelenting opposition and his argument that circumstances had changed since the plan was put forward, they insisted, and Roosevelt endorsed their obstinate refusal to consider any alternative. The three American divisions removed from Alexander's command were among the best he had and there were four Free French divisions of excellent quality. It was a futile effort, for the troops landing on the Riviera met no resistance and did not force the withdrawal of any German divisions from the main battle in the north. It was mid-November before they were able to bring active support to Eisenhower. Meanwhile the Germans reinforced their army in Italy.

It was the first major strategic error made by the American Chiefs of Staff and it may have prolonged the war. For Churchill had an alternative and imaginative plan. It was to leave four or five of the diverted divisions with Alexander, thus giving him the strength to push the Germans across the River Po and back to the Alps, and to use two or three for an amphibious landing near Trieste. Alexander's forces would then advance through the Ljubljana gap in Yugoslavia, cutting off from their supplies eighteen German divisions fighting Marshal Tito's Partisans. Once through the gap, they would make for Vienna. There was nothing to stop them. Vienna, and perhaps even Budapest, might have fallen to the Anglo-Americans rather than to the Russians; and the Germans, assaulted on three fronts, might have collapsed in the late autumn of 1944, long before the Iron Curtain had fallen across eastern Europe. Whether it would have happened thus can only be a speculation, but Churchill believed it to be worth the attempt. The alternative was the waste, by inactivity, of seven excellent divisions, the prolongation of the war through the winter and the seizure of eastern Europe, from Stettin to Trieste, by the

Soviet armies. Historians may believe that Churchill's strategy was a will-o'-the-wisp. We shall never know, for it was still-born.

At the Second Quebec Conference in September 1944 all appeared serene. Churchill, having lost his battle for the Ljubljana gap, did not revert to the subject and the Americans were co-operative on other matters, such as the British wish to make changes in the proposed zones of occupation in Germany. Churchill was, as always, delighted with General Marshall, whom he recognized as a man of rare quality, even if he judged him more remarkable for his statesmanship than for his gifts as a military strategist. He was also on excellent terms with General Arnold, head of the American air force, who so far reciprocated Churchill's feelings that he gave him a C54 aircraft fitted for the personal use of the British Prime Minister. Of the admirals, he found the reticent, sometimes gruff Leahy sensible and approachable, but he was wary of Admiral King, Chief of the US Naval Staff, whose ambition, thwarted by Roosevelt under constant pressure from Churchill, had been to shift the weight of allied effort from Europe and Africa to the Pacific. Churchill and King were noticeably unforthcoming in each other's presence. After the conference the Churchills spent two days with the Roosevelts *en famille* at their home, Hyde Park. Then as we glided away eastwards on board the *Queen Mary*, Churchill told me he was alarmed by the state of the President's health, cheerful, good-humoured and amenable though he had been.

Thereafter the slide began. America was now demonstrably the senior partner, Montgomery was not seeing eye to eye with either Eisenhower or Bradley, the State Department was developing an inordinate affection for the Russians and the President was at one and the same time winning an election and losing his grip.

First there was Poland. Stalin halted his troops short of Warsaw so that the Germans could massacre the Polish Home Army which had risen to fight in anticipation of the Russian arrival. Churchill was so incensed by the Russian treachery that he proposed to Roosevelt suspending supplies to Russia unless their army moved forward to help the Poles. The answer was no. The Russians brazenly arrested and tried, on trumped-up charges, sixteen Polish emissaries who went under safe conduct to parley with them. Churchill asked permission to use some convenient American air bases to fly in supplies to Warsaw. The Americans, afraid of distressing Stalin, again refused.

He flew to Moscow in October, largely, so he said, to convince Stalin that the Quebec Conference did not mean the Anglo-Saxons were 'ganged up' to the exclusion of Russia. When he was there he was temporarily deluded by the goodwill with which he was received and, on the spur of the moment, he handed Stalin a piece of paper suggesting a division of influence in the various eastern European countries. This was to hold good until the war was over. It was not intended to be a permanent arrangement; but to the Russians temporary influence meant permanent possession and they joyfully accepted a 90 per cent stake in Roumania and 75 per cent in Bulgaria. They did not argue about only 50 per cent in Hungary, for there would be opportunities to rearrange that later. Churchill had been concentrating his mind on Greece and he thought he had done a good deal by obtaining Stalin's agreement that the Anglo-Americans should have 90 per cent in that vital Mediterranean area.

The next source of friction was, in fact, Greece. Single-handed, with only tepid support from his own colleagues, he defeated the Communist take-over tactics and flew to Athens on Christmas Day 1944, to dictate a settlement backed by Alexander's armies. *The Times* and the *Manchester Guardian* were indignant, but their angry reproaches were as nothing beside those from Washington where the Greek Communist guerrillas were regarded as a noble army of liberation. The British troops in Greece, who saw the inhuman atrocities this noble army had committed, were solidly behind Churchill. So, after a visit of investigation, was the British Trades Union Congress.

Shortly before Christmas Gil Winant came to Chequers with a long face. He had been instructed to say that the American Government required certain compensations for Lease-Lend. The principal demand was for overwhelming advantages in the arrangements for post-war Civil Aviation, including rights in parts of the British Empire. They also wished to insist, in pursuit of a quarrel with the Argentine, that the British stop importing Argentine beef. And perhaps, despite Casablanca, it would be a bright idea to make a declaration of good intentions to the Germans, though if the Russians objected that might be difficult.

Winant said he was so ashamed, particularly over the Civil Aviation demand, that he did not have the face to stay to luncheon. Churchill replied that even a declaration of war should not prevent their having a good luncheon together. What Churchill thought, but did not say to Winant, was that none of this would be happening if Roosevelt were still in full command of himself and his Government. He was disturbed at having to oppose his American friends on so many issues at the same time.

There were soon yet graver issues. The State Department, without consultation, published a statement critical of British policy in Greece and in Italy. Then came Yalta. Churchill and Eden said privately, on their return, that Roosevelt was a dying man. At Yalta the Americans, under his ineffective chairmanship, had been weak and had thrown away the cards they held. Matters did not improve when, shortly after Yalta, the State Department suggested that the Russians should be consulted about affairs in Greece. Just at a time when a united front was vital, with the post-war dispositions about to be made, a cloud of misunderstanding enveloped London and Washington and, on 12 April 1945, Roosevelt died. The statesman who, unlike so many people in Europe and America, had taken the threats in Hitler's *Mein Kampf* seriously, made the mistake of believing that the Russian Communists, purified in the furnace of war, would now live peacefully with their Western neighbours and disregard the doctrines they had spent so many years in disseminating.

Roosevelt's successor, Harry Truman, had not been admitted to the inner counsels. Even if he had, his positive intervention at so early a stage could not have been expected. So General Eisenhower, partly in keeping with his own orderly strategic plan and partly in response to the spirit of appeasement which dominated the State Department, forfeited the chance to reach Berlin and Prague before the Soviet troops, and to hold them until Germany surrendered. Then, by tripartite agreement, the troops would in any case retire to their allotted zones provided the Russians held to their undertakings in Poland and elsewhere. Alexander had been ham-strung, so that Tito's Partisans seized the Italian city of Trieste and all Austria was in Russian hands. Eisenhower wilfully declined the opportunity to show eastern Europe who the liberators of Germany and Czechoslovakia had been.

It is tempting to speculate whether history would have been changed if General Douglas MacArthur had stood in Eisenhower's place. There might not, perhaps, have been such a smooth integration of British and American officers as characterized Eisenhower's Supreme Allied Headquarters and made no small contribution to victory. There would have been a more explosive clash of wills between MacArthur and Montgomery than was the case with Eisenhower. Perhaps he would have handled the Free French less tactfully; perhaps he would have had difficulties with Patton. It may, however, be that once the allied armies had crossed the Rhine, MacArthur would have pressed forward, adapting his tactics to the new opportunities arising and disregarding the caution of the State Department and the uncertain instruction received from his own Chiefs of Staff. Churchill did not know MacArthur, but their temperaments were not dissimilar. They might, between them, have so contrived matters that while the Russians were still fighting on the River Oder, the American and British armies thrust their way into Berlin and the Americans, having entered Prague, stayed there. The dismal story of the post-war years in eastern Europe would, perhaps, have been recorded differently if MacArthur had had a hand in the affair.

As it was, Churchill set out to woo Truman and mend fences. But low tide was approaching. He was making good progress with Truman at Potsdam, finding him open and forthcoming, when the Conference was temporarily halted to enable him to return to London for the General Election results. To the astonishment of Truman and still more of Stalin (who had assumed the results were prearranged) the Conservatives were heavily defeated. Mr Attlee, whom Churchill, in contrast to Roosevelt's neglect of Truman, had taken to Potsdam to ensure that he was fully briefed in current developments, thoughtfully placed General Arnold's C54 at his predecessor's disposal and Churchill flew away for a holiday by the Italian lakes.

In nature most of the impurities cleave to the lower ground. The hilltops are bare of undergrowth; the tall trees stretch above the creepers. Human beings obey another law. The higher they climb, the grosser the temptations they meet. Few who reach the summit can be acquitted of vanity or conceit, whatever other vices they are strong enough to resist. I make a distinction between the two. Vanity is a failing suffered by those who care too much what others think of them. Conceit is self-satisfaction, the mark of people sufficiently sure of themselves to hold the opinion of others as of little account except in so far as it favours or impedes their progress. Both vanity and conceit are defects, but neither need be destructive of personal charm or of zeal to serve the community. They are seldom fatal and they do not necessarily strangle virtues. They are more exasperating in some than in others.

Roosevelt was vain: Churchill was conceited. Their two successors, Harry Truman and Clement Attlee, were neither. Dragged to the top by chains of unlikely circumstances, their ambition was to serve their fellow men. Neither of them knew much of any country beyond his own national horizon. There may be no such thing as a typical American: if there has been one, it was Harry Truman. Attlee, singing the Red Flag without zest or conviction, was the prototype of an upper-middle-class Englishman. Neither of them could ever have been bosom friends of Churchill, though he enjoyed playing poker with Truman and respected Attlee's integrity, if not his capacity to inspire.

These two men were faced with even more intractable problems than the victors of 1918 at Versailles, for in 1918 there had remained no conceivable aspirant to wear the discarded imperial cloaks of Germany and Austria-Hungary. Now there was such an aspirant, who was also temporarily basking in the adulation of the English-speaking peoples. Should conflict arise, Stalin had but to give the order and under the eye of the political commissars his men would march. The British and American troops, war-weary and longing to be home, might have come close to mutiny. The pass had been irredeemably sold.

Truman and Churchill overlapped in power twice: for three months in 1945 and for just over a year from October 1951. Between these two periods came the realistic Truman doctrine, designed to combat the Russian imperialist threat in the eastern Mediterranean, and Churchill's historic Iron Curtain speech. Invited by Truman to accompany him in the Presidential train (where the poker was played), Churchill visited his host's modest home-town in Missouri and used Westminster College, Fulton, as the platform for a speech which resounded in every continent. Their earlier acquaintance had been solely confined to the Potsdam Conference, where they shared the deadly secret of the atom bomb but had no time to lay the foundations of intimacy. Now, after the short expedition to Fulton, they discovered that their thoughts on world affairs had much in common.

In October 1951 Churchill was Prime Minister again, determined to create a relationship with Truman such as he had enjoyed with Roosevelt. He did not succeed, for Truman had wary counsellors who were fearful of the effect the giant from across the Atlantic might have on their vivacious but basically small-town leader. Churchill hoped he was approaching his goal when he took part in amiable and harmonious discussions about NATO commands and other matters of joint interest at the White House in January 1952. He found Truman surrounded not only by new men who had grown to stature since he left office in 1945, but also by old friends of wartime days, Generals Marshall and Bradley, Averell Harriman and Eisenhower's former Chief of Staff, Bedell Smith, with whom he had formerly had a fruitful association. He was elated, too, when Truman agreed to a joint Anglo-American initiative to eject the tearful Mossadecq from his temporary seat of nationalist power in Tehran.

It was not to last. Churchill and Truman never exchanged an angry or even a frosty word. On one occasion at the British Embassy in Washington, Churchill, interrupting his own spirited but unsuccessful effort to convince Marshall, Bradley and Harriman of the merits of Zionism, shepherded the assembled guests to the piano where Truman played old-time songs and Churchill sang them. Truman played better than Churchill sang and afterwards he claimed that had all else failed he could have earned a living in second-class music halls. It was a convivial evening, but all the same the Americans were on guard. The British were their best friends, but the White House had been burned down once already, the President having to leave his breakfast on the table as he fled before the advancing red-coats. Whether Democrats or Republicans, the Presidential advisers were not sure that Churchill might not also have a touch of the pyromaniac in him. Anyhow, Truman's unexpectedly long reign was drawing to its close and in November 1952 there would be a Presidential election.

Churchill went to the Capitol and addressed both Houses of Congress with no less eloquence then he had displayed to them in the war years. They rose in their seats when the speech was over, and it seemed that the applause would never stop. He was just as well received when, wittily and with flattering indiscretion, he answered questions after a luncheon given in his honour by the Washington Press Club. They honoured, as he knew they would, their tradition that the words spoken were not for publication. He left Washington with the sure knowledge that whatever reservations the Administration might have, in the eyes of Congress and the press Winston Churchill was still a formidable and deeply loved statesman of much more than purely British significance.

For the rest of his active political life his opposite number in Washington was Dwight Eisenhower. They were old comrades, but Ike was no longer the Supreme Allied Commander, accustomed to drop into 10 Downing Street for strategic discussions and to receive Churchill with a broad smile and explosive greetings at his military headquarters. Different responsibilities now weighed on his shoulders and when, as quite often happened, the old ties of friendship seemed drawn too tight, there was John Foster Dulles standing in the background like a disapproving governess.

There were millions who liked Ike. Churchill was in the front rank, despite his unaltered belief that his friend had lost the opportunities of a whole generation in March and April 1945. In a telegram to Roosevelt he had praised Ike's 'shining qualities of character and personality', and he took pleasure in giving a large dinner party in the retiring general's honour when he passed through London on relinquishing his command of the NATO forces in order to present himself as a Presidential candidate at home. On that occasion Ike said that if he were elected, he would be too busily occupied to travel abroad (for this was before the days of the jet air-liners), but he would make one exception. He would visit London.

Eisenhower won the election in November 1952 and Churchill did not wait for him to be formally inaugurated. He at once crossed to New York where, prior to entering the White House, the President-elect had established his headquarters at the Commodore Hotel. He was received with warmth and acclaim. He said he had come to preach the vital importance of a common Anglo-American front 'from Korea to Kikuyu and from Kikuyu to Calais'. He also said, to me, that now Eisenhower had won the Presidency, he must omit part of what he had intended to include in Volume VI of his War History. He could no longer tell in full the story of how the United States, to please the Russians, gave away vast tracts of territory they had occupied and how suspicious they were of his pleas for caution.

Churchill was comfortably ensconced in Baruch's apartment when Eisenhower arrived, amid the flashing of camera bulbs, and greeted him with: 'Well, the one thing I have so far learned in this damned game of yours is that you have just *got* to have a sense of humour.' He stayed for dinner during which Churchill dilated on one of his favourite themes, the protoplasm. It was, he said, sexless. Then it divided itself into two sexes which in due course united again in a different way to their common benefit and gratification. This should also be the story of Britain and America. Eisenhower did not dissent, but in his own diary he made it clear that fond though he was of Churchill he did not intend to attach himself to the old magician's coat-tails. There were many areas in the world where alignment with the British would be to America's advantage, and he was 'quite ready to communicate with him personally, on our old basis of intimate friendship'; but he had been convinced that the United States administration would be well advised to treat, at any rate publicly, every country as a sovereign equal. He felt that with Russia using the spirit of nationalism to cause world-wide dissension, the two strongest Western powers, America and Britain, must not be regarded as a combination united to maintain the *status quo*.

Churchill thought this attitude was inspired by Foster Dulles. He persevered with his plans for the conversion of Eisenhower. I was despatched several times to the Commodore Hotel with memoranda and even Cabinet papers which I was to show and explain to Eisenhower. The comment I made in my diary after one of these visits was: 'He was very genial and talked a great deal. He has a bee in his bonnet about collusion with us: he is all in favour of it clandestinely but not overtly. Dulles said little, but what he did say was on our side. Ike struck me as forceful but a trifle naïve.'

On a number of occasions in the past Churchill had told me that in the relationship between Britain and America he thought the Democrats were more congenial bed-fellows than the Republicans. Had any Republican candidate other than Eisenhower been chosen in 1952, it is likely that Churchill would have held this view more strongly still. One evening at Baruch's apartment, Governor Dewey dined with Churchill, Baruch, Christopher Soames and myself. We were joined afterwards by John Foster Dulles. They succeeded in igniting Churchill's anger in its most tempestuous form, Dewey in relation to some Anglo-American differences in the Pacific and Dulles because he said that if Churchill were associated with forthcoming economic discussion in Washington, the fears of Congress and the American people that he could cast a spell on all American statesmen would be aroused to such an extent that the success of the talks would be endangered. In due course Christopher Soames and I accompanied them out and did our best to explain that a sharp debate was Churchill's idea of a pleasant evening and that he only spoke thus to men whom he trusted and looked upon as friends. It was not, unfortunately, true, for when we returned we were subjected to a tirade against the Republican party and against Dulles, with his 'great slab of a face', in particular.

The next meeting of Churchill and Eisenhower was due to take place at the end of June 1953, a few weeks after the coronation of the Queen. The largest British battleship, *Vanguard*, was waiting at Portsmouth to take us to Bermuda for the conference. A few days before our intended departure, Churchill had the stroke which incapacitated him for several weeks. So the conference was postponed till December. Eisenhower, terrified of publicizing the special relationship that Churchill so ardently wished to see confirmed, insisted on inviting the French too, so as to include the war in Indo-China on the agenda. They would not have been present had the meeting taken place in June, for they were then in the not infrequent position of having no Government.

Stalin had died and two comparatively unknown men, Malenkov and Beria, had taken power in the Kremlin. They were, in the event, transitory tyrants, for Beria was soon executed and Malenkov's reign was short. Nobody foresaw this, and Churchill was enthused by the possibility of bringing the cold war to an end once Stalin's icy fingers had lost their grip. It is ironical that Churchill, the man who had given stern warning of the Russian menace, was now challenged in his policy of 'easement' by Eisenhower, the man who had done as much as anybody to yield to Soviet ambitions at the end of the war. Two compasses had swung the best part of 180° in opposite directions.

When Eisenhower arrived in Bermuda, the Prime Minister whisked him away to the Mid-Ocean Golf Club where they lunched together. This caused consternation in the breasts of Dulles and Anthony Eden, neither of whom trusted their chiefs alone. Eisenhower broached with Churchill what did, in fact, become the principal topic at the meeting: the American belief that if the truce in the Korean War broke down, they should feel free to use an atomic bomb. This apocalyptic threat had, on American insistence, to be hidden from the French, whose tendency to leak secrets had been proved by experience. So the Eisenhower-Dulles creed that all sovereign states must be treated with equality began to look shaky. I thought it shakier still when, during an hour or so of relaxation, I strolled down to the beach with Dulles. The presence of the French, he said, and the constant need for interpretation, had greatly hampered the conference. He then plunged in to bathe. 'The surf was heavy on the beach,' I wrote, 'and Dulles was twice capsized.'

Churchill worked hard to moderate the American proposal to declare their atomic intentions. He persuaded the President to substitute the words 'reserving the right to use the atomic bomb' for 'free to use the atom bomb'; but the difference between the American and the British view was made clear to me when I took Eisenhower a message from the Prime Minister on the subject. This is how I described the scene:

Eisenhower was in his sitting-room, cross-legged in an arm chair, going through his speech [to the United Nations]. He was friendly, but I noticed that he never smiled: a change from the Ike of war days or even, indeed of last January in New York. He said that whereas Winston looked on the atomic bomb as something entirely new and terrible, he looked upon it as just the latest improvement in military weapons. There was no distinction between conventional weapons and atomic weapons: all weapons in due course became conventional.

I could hardly believe my ears. If this was the well-digested view of the President of the United States, then it reflected a basic difference of opinion between Britain and America. Fortunately the arrangements for the truce in Korea did not break down.

These atomic discussions took some attention away from the topic that interested Churchill: the Cold War with Russia. At one plenary session of the conference, however, he launched into a powerful discussion on his theory, which he called 'double dealing', that the West should combine strength towards the Soviet Union with holding out the hand of friendship. There should be as many commercial, social and cultural contacts as could be arranged, but we must be united and resolute in our strength. This theme was not well received. Anthony Eden and the Foreign Office officials disapproved, the French Foreign Minister, Monsieur Bidault, made an intransigently anti-Russian speech, and Eisenhower followed with a statement coarser in tone and even in language than is usual at international conferences. He said that as regards the Prime Minister's belief that there might be a New Look in Soviet policy since Stalin's death, Russia was in his view a woman of the streets and whether her dress was new, or just the old one patched, there was the same whore underneath it. America intended to drive her off her present 'beat' into the back streets. To his fury the French delegation lived up to their reputation by leaking his remarks, some of them verbatim, to the press.

Churchill was undismayed. His correspondence with Eisenhower was genial, but there were many differences of opinion between London and Washington over South East Asia, the admission of Germany to NATO (which Britain wanted and America did not), the Middle East and atomic policy. So in June 1954 he went to Washington again, taking Anthony Eden and Lord Cherwell with him and staying as Eisenhower's guest at the White House. Most of the outstanding difficulties were amicably resolved, and so, for a brief period, it seemed that Churchill's primary objective might also be. He had scarcely settled himself into the White House when Eisenhower unexpectedly agreed to the holding of talks with the Russians. There was also agreement

about atomic matters, a decision in principle on a common policy
for European defence and good progress on the vexed problems
of South East Asia, of Egypt and the Canal zone. There was to
be a meeting with the Russians in London. The French and the
Germans would be invited too, and the President himself would
attend the opening. It was Eisenhower's own suggestion: he was,
so it seemed, brimming over with enthusiasm and good-will.
Russia no longer needed to be driven off her 'beat' into the back
streets.

Dulles and the State Department were horrified. They descended on the President like a swarm of flies, and on the following
day he modified his proposal. America would not take an active
part in the proposed meeting but Eisenhower gave an assurance
that no objections would be raised to a British initiative. There
followed what the British Ambassador called a riotous dinner
party, at which the President and the Prime Minister joined forces
against the united front of their respective Foreign Secretaries and
declared forcefully in favour of allowing Germany to re-arm.
There was a temporary breach in the Ike-Winston axis when the
former described the French as 'a hopeless, helpless mass of protoplasm'. That was a formula Churchill, always at heart a Franco-
phile, could not accept. However, the two leaders were firm friends
and mutual admirers again: the smiles, the quips, the anecdotes
and the laughter were reminiscent of times that had seemed long
past. Churchill eventually sailed away home, delighted with his
visit and resolved to go to Moscow. He little knew what deep-
rooted opposition he would soon meet, less from Eisenhower than
from his own Foreign Secretary and his colleagues in the Cabinet.

One of Churchill's last political exchanges with Eisenhower
came two years later when he was no longer Prime Minister. The
Suez episode in November 1956 caused deep bitterness in the
White House. The Americans were themselves partly to blame,
for Dulles had led the British and French far up the garden path
before deciding that the United States would give no support.
Indeed, some months later, Selwyn Lloyd could not believe his
ears when Dulles asked him why the British had not gone through
with the Suez operation. Nevertheless, Eisenhower was infuriated
by the choice of the very day of the Presidential election, when
he was standing for his second term of office, as that on which

the Anglo-French assault on Egypt was delivered. In the storm that followed, the United States supported the demand for sanctions against Britain and France at the United Nations. Never in living memory had Anglo-American relations sunk to such a depth.

I had by then become a merchant banker, but I still saw much of Churchill and at a time when the crisis was at its worst I lunched alone with him in London at 28 Hyde Park Gate. 'Had you still been Prime Minister,' I asked, 'would you have done this?' 'I should never have dared,' he replied, 'but if I had dared I should never have dared stop.' We went on to discuss the dangerous and tragic effect of the affair on relations with America. I said that he was the only Englishman to whom Eisenhower would now listen, and that it would be valuable to remind the President that, however great his present indignation, in the long run the British were and always would be America's most trustworthy ally. He asked me to draft a letter for him to send to Eisenhower. I did so, using expressions that were essentially Churchillian and suggesting that if misunderstanding and frustration were allowed to develop, the skies would darken and it would be the Soviet Union that rode the storm. Churchill signed the letter and dispatched it through the American Embassy, refusing to allow a copy to be sent to the Foreign Office.

Eisenhower was affected. Immediately on receiving the letter, he made a friendly public reference to Britain and declared that we should not be allowed to suffer as far as oil supplies were concerned. He wrote Churchill a long and moving reply, admitting that the Suez issue was small by comparison with Anglo-American solidarity in the face of Soviet Russia. He had, he said, been deeply offended by Anthony Eden's failure even to inform him of his intentions. So Churchill's long struggle to keep open the personal line of communication was proved fruitful even when his active political life was over.

America and Great Britain are not as united, politically and economically, as Churchill in his heart desired. However, successive presidents and prime ministers, from Harold Macmillan to the present day, have maintained a special relationship and have refrained from attacking each other's policies, whether or not they approved them. This tradition was established by Roosevelt and Churchill and maintained, against all discouragement, by Truman and Eisenhower. Churchill would have preferred it to be more exclusive, but Eisenhower and Dulles were right in judging that as he approached his eightieth birthday he was tending to look back too nostalgically at past glories and to assume the continued existence of opportunities that no longer offered.

CHAPTER SEVEN

The Ladies

Having no sisters, and a mother whom he placed on a plane above that of ordinary mortals, Churchill was slow in learning to understand the other sex, much as he admired female beauty if chance brought him within range of it. I do not think he was a man with strong sexual desires and those he had were in due course concentrated in his love for his wife. When he was a young Member of Parliament, regarded with interest, but more often with aversion by his contemporaries as much as by his elders, he found ordinary social courtesies tedious. On one occasion, a dinner party at Chesterfield House, he thought the girls on each side of him so uninteresting that he left the table, without a word to his hostess, and retired to the library to write letters until the time came for the men to remain alone in the dining-room and drink port. Invited to Crewe House for a dinner at which King Edward VII and Queen Alexandra were present, he asked Lady Crewe to make changes in the *placement* because his intended neighbours struck him as dull. Lady Crewe, Rosebery's intelligent daughter, was a formidable person, not easily cajoled. But on this occasion, surprisingly enough, she did as Winston wished, altering the table plan only a few minutes before the King and Queen arrived. Many years later I asked her why. She replied that she had never found it possible to refuse Winston's demands. Even when, also at Crewe House, he met Miss Clementine Hozier for the first time, and arranged to be introduced to her, he merely stared at her in rapt admiration and spoke not a word. It is not surprising that he acquired a reputation for bad manners.

All the same, the girls were more tolerant of him than the young men, and some found his attentions irresistible; for if he thought

them interesting the brilliance, charm and originality of his conversation was a weapon he was adept at using. When he chose
to make himself agreeable, preconceived dislike vanished and resistance crumbled.

Before he set eyes on Clementine Hozier he fell head over heels
in love with Pamela Plowden. For her no trouble was too great
or too time-consuming. He proposed to her in a punt on the river
while they were both staying at Warwick Castle. She refused, and
instead of becoming Mrs Winston Churchill she married Lord
Lytton, son of a Viceroy of India and himself a future Governor
of Bengal. Gentle in manner but quick of wit, and still beautiful
in her old age, she remained on affectionate terms with her former
suitor and one of his most favoured guests. Clementine Churchill,
by no means predisposed to like or approve of her husband's
friends, whether male or female, made an enthusiastic exception
in the case of Lady Lytton, whose presence she always welcomed.
She did, however, admit to feeling just a touch of jealousy when
she saw Winston and Pamela together, although she knew well
that in her husband's eyes no woman came within distant range
of her.

Another woman who had been in love with Churchill before
he married, though he was never physically in love with her, was
Violet, daughter of the Liberal Prime Minister, Herbert Henry
Asquith. She had her father's intellectual gifts and was hard to
match as a public speaker. She was an eager conversationalist:
some thought too eager, for she tended to feel so strongly in the
cause she happened to be advocating that she would advance on
her prey unrelentingly and drive him or her back into the fire-
place. I myself once had the back of my trouser-legs badly singed.
There were those who thought that in his early days as a Cabinet
Minister Churchill used her affection somewhat unscrupulously
in order to maintain access to her father, the current fount of
power. No doubt Churchill did find the association useful but he
was genuinely enthused by the vigour of Violet's mind, even
though, at any rate in later years, he seldom agreed with her views.
Nobody interested in politics could fail to find her fascinating.
Churchill saw much of her towards the end of his life and the
friendship which had begun in early youth endured untainted
until extreme old age. Nor has a more truthful and perceptive book

been written about him than *Winston Churchill As I Knew Him* by Lady Violet Bonham Carter.

A woman of a different kind and character was Lady Desborough, known to her friends as Ettie. She was the epitome of a good listener. Young and old blossomed in her presence, for she brought out the best in them by concentrating earnestly on what they had to say and goading them on, in such a way that they were scarcely aware of it, by occasional comments or questions that struck them as entirely pertinent to their theme. She may not have had as warm a heart or charitable a nature as Lady Lytton and Lady Violet; but she seemed to combine wisdom with benevolence and there was no more beguiling hostess. If a guest at Panshanger or Taplow, where the Churchills used to stay before both World Wars, wrote a good 'Collins' (as Lady Desborough's generation called a letter of thanks, echoing *Pride and Prejudice*), she would send a long and thoughtful reply, so that what started as a normal civility developed into a full-scale correspondence.

Lady Desborough was a leading member of the Souls, a set of rich, noble and prominent intellectuals who had a vocabulary of their own and looked with pity on those of their friends and relations who had not read contemporary poetry, constructively criticized the newest artist or revelled in the latest Russian ballet. They were mostly in politics or on its fringes, and A. J. Balfour, Prime Minister until the Conservatives were defeated in 1905, was Lady Desborough's male counterpart. They were alleged to be lovers, as well as congenial companions: they were certainly intimate friends who shared aesthetic enthusiasms. Winston Churchill was in those days well but not widely grounded in English literature. He did not pretend to be an intellectual, so that while in the course of his social and political activities he came into contact with many of the Souls, he was not one of them. Lady Desborough and his Private Secretary, Eddie Marsh, were his principal links with that élite and eclectic world. Thus, at Taplow, he consorted with Maurice Baring, G. K. Chesterton and other literary figures of the period; and Eddie Marsh brought him into touch with Rupert Brooke. He never failed to find Ettie Desborough a well-informed listener (a quality he greatly approved) and a stimulating friend.

There were two of his wife's cousins of whom Churchill

saw a great deal. They were the Stanleys of Alderley, who inherited
the acutely sharp intelligence that family possessed. They had
been educated at home in Cheshire with the painstaking induction
of literary, artistic and linguistic knowledge that was the hallmark
of the governess-taught daughters of many well-to-do families in
Victorian times, especially those of Whig descent.

The Stanleys of Alderley had eccentric religious convictions,
embracing atheism, Buddhism, Muhammadanism, Roman Cath-
olicism and the Church of England. One of them, Venetia, varied
the theme by marrying a professing Jew, Edwin Montagu, son
of Lord Swaythling. A prominent Liberal politician, who held
office under Asquith and Lloyd George, he was joint author of
the Montagu-Chelmsford reforms which were the first step in
bringing self-determination to India. Venetia was unusually
quick-witted, even by Stanley standards. Mr Asquith fell in love
with her and composed indiscreet letters while he was nominally
presiding at Cabinet meetings, his mind being occupied with
thoughts of her rather than with the tedious Cabinet papers before
him. When she announced her engagement to his colleague he was
distraught by the news. Churchill, for his part, was wary of Edwin,
but he found Venetia stimulating.

Venetia's fidelity to her husband was generally doubted. When
he died she had him buried in the garden and entertained agree-
ably at Beccles, his country house in Norfolk. There she attracted
men and women of intelligence and renown, including Churchill,
who was never seduced by her physical charms (though she was
not slow to offer them), but valued her other gifts, admired her
conversational facility and enjoyed painting the rooms in her
house. In the war she was a frequent visitor to the Churchills,
the relationship being strengthened by the friendship of her
daughter Judy and Mary Churchill who made a simultaneous
entry into the ATS.

A Stanley of a different kind, of far greater sterling worth, of
less social ambition, but of equal mental agility and educational
attainment, was Venetia's sister, Sylvia Henley. She lived to be
ninety-eight, dying in 1980. Honest to the extent of thinking it
wrong to hide her thoughts or feelings, she could seem waspish
to those whose actions or sentiments she disapproved, but no wasp
ever had a less vicious sting. Her hair was the purest white. She

held herself straight as a ramrod so that even in extreme old age her carriage was superb. In her eighties she still had the figure of a young woman. One night, dining with Lady Churchill, she arrived in a beautiful evening gown which fitted her perfectly. It had been made by Paquin in 1913, and by 1975 the design was fashionable once again. She worked hard in peace and war for the welfare of others and when she was not engaged in contributing to the common weal, or working assiduously on tapestry, she spent much of her time with her cousin Clementine, with whom she was far from diffident, and Winston, with whom she surprisingly was. She looked up to him with so much respect and admiration that the barbed comments she might otherwise let fly, always from honesty and never with malice, were muted in his presence. In his old age she was attentive to his wants and would spend hours playing six-pack bézique with him long after his skill at the game and his powers of concentration had faded. Sometimes she played his hand as well as her own. Except to those who knew her well, the tartness of her remarks tended to disguise a little too effectively the selflessness of her nature. She was sufficiently feminine to like admiration; but she was modest about her achievements and those of her family, even when one of her daughters, a chemist of distinction, was elected a Fellow of the Royal Society at an early age.

The catalogue of Churchill's women friends is not a long one. He retained his friendship for Lady Helen Vincent, later Lady D'Abernon, a woman of exceptional and long-lasting beauty. There were younger ones, too, such as Lady Cranborne and Lady Dorothea Head, with whom he was more than happy to while away a few leisure hours and whose conversation greatly contented him. As he was susceptible to good looks and to wit there were many who flitted across his path and if, like Claire Luce, they were at the same time well informed and highly geared, that was a gratefully received bonus. In the South of France he used to frequent, harmlessly enough, the villa of the rich, beautiful and wicked Mrs Reggie Fellowes, renowned for breaking up happy marriages whenever she had the chance. At the Ritz in Paris she once made a fruitless attempt to seduce him from his deep-rooted conjugal fidelity. He did not hold that against her; nor, surprisingly enough, did Clementine.

One who was well informed and highly geared, but a long-term friend and by no means a 'flitter across the path', was Lady Diana Cooper. Duff Cooper, who resigned from Chamberlain's Government at Munich, and was an only moderately successful Minister of Information in 1940, was a man in whose company Churchill delighted. His spontaneity and quickness of repartee, his cultivated but never precious conversation, left him with few rivals as a companion. Since his wife was perhaps the most beautiful Englishwoman of her own generation, with an interest in politics only second to her love of the arts, Churchill was a submissive subject to her intelligent attentions. Duff Cooper crowned his career as one of the best of ambassadors to the French, but Churchill was not sure that he could maintain for long the concentration and energy required by an effective Minister of the Crown. He did, however, think that Lady Diana made up for any deficiencies.

One night at Marrakech, in January 1944, Lady Diana sat next to Churchill at dinner. Her words, and no doubt her looks, held him enthralled. Instead of dominating the conversation himself, as was his wont, he listened and conversed with her as though nobody else was present in the dining-room. 'There', said Lord Moran, Churchill's doctor, 'you have the historic spectacle of a professional siren vamping an elder statesman.' This was a little unfair: Lady Diana was unmistakably a siren, but she was not a professional one.

A woman of quite a different kind was Sybil, sister of Churchill's frequent host at Lympne, Sir Philip Sassoon, and married to Lord Cholmondeley, whom many considered the most handsome man in England. Lady Cholmondeley has both the taste and the brains of the Sassoons. She also has a passion for playing cards. She thus offered all the essentials required to stimulate Churchill; and she did so.

He was devoted to Nonie, the pretty and vivacious wife of his last Private Secretary, Anthony Montague Browne. As he grew old, and there were long periods of silence, she revitalized him by her conversation, making no unwelcome demands on his attention but giving her all in usually successful efforts to please and entertain. He came to my own wedding and he fell for the bride. Her vivacity, slim figure and strikingly good features captivated him: they laughed together, they gossiped together and whenever he possibly could he put her next to him at dinner, sometimes to the displeasure of ladies who thought they had a higher claim to precedence than the Private Secretary's wife. Churchill never failed to take trouble with the young of either sex. He encouraged the boys and he flirted, very mildly, with the girls provided they were both good-looking and forthcoming.

The notorious Mrs Fellowes was indirectly responsible for a wild-goose chase, or rather wild-cricket chase, in which my wife and I were bemused participants. Late in September 1954 we were staying alone with Churchill at La Capponcina, Lord Beaverbrook's house at Cap d'Ail, when he said that Mrs Fellowes, before leaving her sumptuous villa to return to Paris, had told him of a remarkable crustacean called a sea-cricket. It was to be found and, if desired, eaten in a quay-side restaurant at San Remo which was lined with glass tanks filled with lobsters, langoustes and crabs. In a tank of its own sat the sea-cricket. 'Let us,' said Churchill, 'dine there tonight and see, but not eat, this remarkable beast.'

Lord Beaverbrook, in all other respects a generous host, had left at Churchill's disposal a small black car, wearied with age, which held two in comfort in front and two in grave discomfort behind. We piled into it. The detective drove and Churchill sat beside him. My wife and I crouched behind. One of the windows had jammed open so that a cold, damp blast struck the passengers in the back seat.

However, the Prime Minister of Great Britain was travelling into Italy. France and Italy felt bound to show the respect and honour due to him. As we drove out of La Capponcina a shiny black police car took station ahead, motor-cyclists fell in alongside and another police car brought up the rear. With police bells ringing we dashed through Monte Carlo and quickly reached the Italian frontier. The barrier had been raised in anticipation of our arrival and Italian soldiers presented arms as our wretched little car, so grandly escorted, thundered past. By this time the off-side door was unhinged and evidently about to fall off. The detective clutched it with one hand and steered with the other. My wife began to sneeze and the rain began to fall.

We reached the restaurant. It was a bedraggled quay-side eating house. The tables were of bare wood, doubtfully clean, and the place was empty, damp and fusty. Churchill was dismayed. He insisted that Mrs Fellowes must have had another restaurant in mind. He was assured she had not. 'Well, then,' he said to the astonished patron, 'show me the sea-cuckoo.' 'Sea-*cricket*,' my wife murmured gently.

There was no sea-cricket, not even a langouste. The weather had been so rough that the fishing boats had been storm bound in harbour for several days. We ate some spaghetti; we drank some Rufino. Churchill was disappointed and morose, and after an almost discourteously short stay we departed with our large cavalcade.

On the way back, the car door finally disintegrated and my wife woke up next morning with a high temperature. Churchill declared that he must return to London and would leave us behind so that my wife could recuperate. 'It would,' he said, 'have been agreeable to see the sea-cuckoo; but I must prepare my speech for the Party Conference. Good-bye, children; Max's chef will take care of you.'

Women with achievements in their own right seldom crossed Churchill's path or impressed him when they did. There were exceptions. Lady Lavery spent hours teaching him to paint, and he was grateful for that. He enjoyed the company of Rhoda Birley, Oswald Birley's wife, herself a painter. When Helen Keller, stone-deaf and blind, who had learned to communicate by sheer will-power, came to Downing Street, Churchill was so astonished by her personality (which, he said, made him feel humble) that he kept her there three times longer than intended. Yet the famous women of his times, such as Virginia Woolf, Vita Sackville-West and Laura Knight were not among his friends, for although he liked intelligent people, he did not equate the intelligent with the intellectual and would have wilted in the hot-houses of Bloomsbury. He knew few of the great actresses, but he was entranced by Vivien Leigh and did, very late in life, strike up a South of France acquaintance with Greta Garbo.

There were, of course, the women who sat in the House of Commons. None of them made a deep impression on him, though he was fond of Thelma Cazalet and attracted by Priscilla Tweedsmuir. He and Lady Astor bickered like spoilt children and saw as little as possible of each other 'out of school'. On one occasion he interrupted her rudely in a debate, declaring that she was an

Churchill at army manœuvres with F.E. Smith, 1913.

Left to right Winston Churchill, Anthony Eden, Jack Churchill and Mrs Churchill in 1941.

Left Lord Cherwell, 'the Prof'.

Below Brendan Bracken accompanies Churchill from Number 10, Downing Street to the House of Commons, June 1940.

Right Churchill with the Private Office. *Left to right* Sir John Colville, Sir Leslie Rowan, WSC, Sir John Peck, Sir John Martin, Miss Watson, Commander C.R. Thompson, Sir Anthony Bevir, Charles Barker.

T. L. Rowan. J. K. Peck. E. M. Watson. Barker

Winston S. Churchill

J. M. Martin. Anthony

C. R. Thompson

Churchill and Beaverbrook on board
HMS *Prince of Wales* during the Atlantic
Charter meeting, August 1941.

Left The American financier, Bernard
Baruch.

Winston Churchill with President Roosevelt in Quebec, September 1944.
Winston Churchill with President Eisenhower in Washington, 1954.

Left Lady Churchill with her daughter, Mary Soames, after Sir Winston's heart-attack in 1965.

Above right Mrs Roosevelt and Mrs Churchill broadcast jointly from Quebec, September 1944.

Below left Winston Churchill with The Queen and Prince Charles at Balmoral, September 1953.

Right Mrs Churchill with General Montgomery in Marrakesh, January 1944.

The directors of the war-effort on the sun-roof of *The Citadel* at Quebec, September 1944. *Front row, left to right* General Marshall, Admiral Leahy, President Roosevelt, Winston Churchill, Sir Alan Brooke, Sir John Dill. *Back row* General Hollis, General Ismay, Admiral King, Sir Charles Portal, General Arnold, Sir A.B. Cunningham.

Sir John Dill, Chief of the Imperial General Staff, with Vice-Admiral T.S.V. Phillips in Whitehall, 1940.

undesirable alien who should go back home. To this Lady Astor replied with dignity: 'As for my Right Honourable Friend, he himself is *half* alien and *wholly* undesirable.'

Churchill's day as an active politician ended long before the rise to fame of Mrs Thatcher, Mrs Golda Meir, or Mrs Gandhi. Evita Peron was a distant nuisance, to Attlee's government rather than to his, threatening British beef supplies and therefore, since he prized beef highly, an obviously undesirable woman. One of the few powerful female politicians he did meet was Madame Chiang Kai-shek and she, for all her famed charm, made little impression on him at the Cairo Conference in December 1943. A pretty ATS acquaintance of mine was halfway down a gallery of the Abdin Palace in Cairo when the doors at each end opened simultaneously. Lord Louis Mountbatten emerged from one and Madame Chiang from the other. They were the two people at the conference most famous for their charm and this was their first meeting. They advanced towards each other smiling and then they stopped, the smiles vanishing. They both knew they had met their match. Lord Louis found the story entertaining and did not deny it. Churchill, when it was repeated to him, said that it was an unequal contest: Mountbatten had much the greater charm. And what, he added irrelevantly, had China got to contribute to victory?

It might be concluded from all this that Churchill regarded women, with rare exceptions, as second-class citizens. He would have denied such an accusation. It seemed obvious to his generation that the capacities of men and women were different and that neither should seek to usurp the other's functions. The vastness of the common ground which both could tread was a new discovery for Churchill. It was one which his two younger daughters helped him to make.

As Clementine only rarely accompanied him on his foreign travels during the war, it was his practice to take either his WAAF daughter, Sarah, or his ATS daughter, Mary, as an ADC to conferences with the President or Stalin. He soon realized that they were not merely attractive adjuncts to his staff, and invaluable for entertaining foreign guests, but competent and business-like. 'Mary,' he once said, to her amusement mixed with embarrassment, 'is a highly serviceable animal.' However, it was not only at conferences that their activities impressed him. Here were young women making a positive contribution to the war effort, one an interpreter of aerial photography with the RAF, and the other an operational member of an anti-aircraft battery. Women, it seemed, were as competent as men to perform functions which only a few years previously would have been regarded as a masculine preserve; and it was in large part his daughters, emancipated in harmony with their own generation, who brought this truth to dawn on him. He concluded that women were not, as he had been tempted to believe, just decorative objects who helped to pass the social hours, bore children and provided the amenities required for a civilized existence while being all too often, in Sir Walter Scott's words, 'uncertain, coy and hard to please'.

There was one lady by whom, from 1952 onwards, Churchill was dazzled. That was the new Queen. He was not alone in having been fascinated by her mother, though his homage, on one occasion at least, took an unusual form. For Christmas in 1940 he gave her *Fowler's English Usage*, a present which somebody less easily amused than Queen Elizabeth might have taken as a slur on her mastery of the language. He was, of course, an unswerving supporter of the Crown. He might have joined the Barons in drafting Magna Carta, but he would have insisted on presenting it to King John with flawless courtesy. He would have sided with Pym and Hampden against Charles I's use of the royal prerogative, but once the Civil War broke out he would have fought for the King to the end. He might even have been tempted to find excuses for James II. He regarded England's great queens as sovereigns rather than as women and Queen Victoria, in whose splendid sunset he had grown up, was, like his mother, on a plane elevated far above that of other women.

In 1952, however, at the age of seventy-seven, he found himself Prime Minister to a young woman of twenty-five. The shock of King George VI's death, halfway through an important parliamentary debate for which he was busily preparing a fighting speech, was severe. He sat in bed, with tears streaming down his face, recalling his comradeship with the King during the war and the love he had felt for him. Seeking to reassure him, I said that he would find the new Queen charming, attractive, intelligent and immensely conscientious. 'I hardly know her,' he replied, 'and she is only a child.' In 1928 he had been to Balmoral, as Minister in

Attendance on King George V. The only other guest on that occasion was Princess Elizabeth of York, aged two. 'She has,' he had written to Clementine, 'an air of authority and reflectiveness astonishing in an infant.' That was long ago, and he had seen Princess Elizabeth only on formal occasions after she grew up.

It was soon noticeable that his weekly audiences lasted unusually long. A photograph of the Queen, smiling radiantly on her way to open her first Parliament, was framed and hung on the wall above his bed at Chartwell. He was badly caught out, to his secret admiration, when the Queen referred to a Foreign Office telegram from Baghdad which he was obliged to admit he had failed to read. He was delighted to be asked to the Royal Box for the Derby: he revelled in his visits to Windsor and Balmoral. 'She is,' he never tired of saying 'a truly remarkable person.' Bernard Baruch, in asserting that Britain faced a gloomy future, declared, 'Your country now has only two great assets, the Queen, who is the world's sweetheart, and our great historic past.' He quickly added, 'And, of course, Winston Churchill.' Churchill replied that there were a lot more assets, some tangible and some intangible, but that he concurred in placing the Queen at the top of the list.

He was an old man whose passions were spent, but there is no doubt that at a respectful distance he fell in love with the Queen. It was not a reincarnation of Queen Victoria and Lord Melbourne, for the monarchy no longer held the political powers it did in 1837. Queen Elizabeth II had had a better, less sheltered and more sophisticated upbringing than her great-great-grandmother, and she was already married to a man of experience and intelligence.

Churchill had turned down an offer of the Garter after the war, but he accepted it from the Queen. He worried because when she was on a long tour of Australia, she wrote to him in her own hand and he, who by then found writing a major effort, signed dictated letters to her. Was this polite to the Sovereign and sufficiently attentive to such an exceptional young lady? He was so eager for her return that he insisted on boarding *Britannia* to greet her at sea off the Needles. When, on his eventual resignation, she offered him a dukedom he could scarcely believe his ears; and although he was determined, if at all possible, to die in the House of Commons, he admitted to being tempted to accept simply because it was the Queen herself who made the offer 'and she looked so beautiful'.

Here then was a lady whom he respected and admired more than any man. After 1952, I noticed that he nearly always referred to women in appreciative language, though it must be admitted that he did, from time to time, continue to express doubts about his colleague in the Government, the dedicated but uninspiring Miss Florence Horsbrugh, and to be embarrassingly inattentive to worthy, middle-aged ladies next to whom he was obliged to sit at luncheon or dinner.

The most important, continuous feminine influence on him was of course his wife, some of whose qualities are described elsewhere in this book and have been far more effectively elaborated by Mary Soames in *Clementine Churchill*. Suffice to say that, while Clementine was no ardent feminist, she did believe firmly in women's rights and was angered by insensitive displays of masculine complacency and implied superiority. She provided everything that Winston Churchill thought women should provide: a well-run household, ambrosial food, five children and, above all, a loyal and loving heart. There are many marriages in which fidelity is all but unbreakable, but there can be few that excelled the Churchills'. What was notable was the way in which their qualities and defects complemented and cancelled each other. She was never for one minute afraid of her formidable husband. When she thought he was going wrong or making a mistake, she said so forthrightly. She did not always agree with his political views; she deplored his unpunctual and inconsiderate habits; she was acutely aware of any injustice or unkindness of which, almost always unconsciously, he was guilty. What he lacked, she provided.

Thus, although Clementine's views, complaints and criticisms sometimes seemed to be disregarded, in the long run the sparkling water that dripped on the stone made an impression on its surface. Clementine herself might appear to have no other ambition than to support her husband in the strife he had chosen for his career and to ease the burden by providing for all his physical wants. Even her hard labours in organizing the Red Cross Aid to Russia fund during the war can be regarded as an extension of her husband's activities. Yet, as in the poem by Arthur Clough which Churchill loved to quote:

For while the tired waves, vainly breaking,
   Seem here no painful inch to gain,
Far back through creeks and inlets making,
   Comes silent, flooding in, the main.

The main brought with it an ever growing conviction that women's rights were, as Clementine insisted, commensurate as well as compatible with their domestic and maternal duties. One day, in about 1958, Churchill held at 28 Hyde Park Gate one of the regular meetings of the Churchill College Trustees over which he presided. The trustees were eminent men: the Chairmen of Shell, ICI, Vickers and Associated Electrical Industries, the Masters of Trinity and Christ's College, Cambridge, the Provost of Kings, and some of the most famous scientists at Cambridge – Lord Adrian, Sir Alexander Todd and Sir John Cockcroft. They were all astonished when Churchill announced that he hoped the new college, intended as the national memorial to him, would admit women on equal terms with men. No college at Oxford or Cambridge had ever done any such thing.

I asked him afterwards if this had been Clementine's idea. 'Yes,' he replied, 'and I support it. When I think what women did in the war I feel sure they deserve to be treated equally.' Churchill College was the first to treat them so.

CHAPTER EIGHT

The Counsellors

Among the most disturbing episodes in the First World War was the quarrel of the politicians and the generals – of the 'frocks', so called because they wore black frock-coats, and the 'brass hats'. It happened partly because Lloyd George, for all his vigour and capacity to inspire, knew nothing about tactics or strategy, and partly because the generals held the politicians in contempt and believed they should be a law unto themselves. The King took the side of the generals and of Haig in particular; the House of Commons tended to be carried away by Lloyd George's eloquence. Churchill, part soldier and part politician, watched the unseemly wrangles with mixed feelings.

That nothing comparable happened in the Second World War was due mainly to the good fortune that Churchill, unlike Lloyd George, had himself been a soldier and had made a lifelong study of the military art. Even so the Prime Minister, who was also Minister of Defence and therefore directly in charge of the Chiefs of Staff, might well have fallen out with them on a number of important issues, had it not been for the tact, patience and skill in promoting compromise shown by one man. That man was General Sir Hastings Ismay, to whom Churchill owed more, and admitted that he owed more, than to anybody else, military or civilian, in the whole of the war.

Ismay was called Pug, because he closely resembled one. The eyes, wrinkling nose, mouth and shape of his face produced a canine effect which was entirely delightful. When he smiled his face was alight and he gave the impression that he was wagging an easily imaginable tail. On the rare occasions when he was not working – in the car or on train journeys – he loved to discourse on polo, to play backgammon, to tell strange stories of the Mad

Mullah against whom he had once fought in Somaliland or, with a gleam of bucolic contentment, describe the beauty of his herd of Jersey cows in Worcestershire. It was rare in those arduous days for him to take so much as a day off to see his family and his Jerseys; for he was incessantly in demand.

Every inch a soldier, he was admired by all the generals; and civilians found him just as congenial and understanding. Thus to his own staff in the office of the Minister of Defence, to the Prime Minister's entourage and those working in the Cabinet Office, to the Chiefs of Staff and their acolytes, and to Churchill himself, Ismay provided an aura of personal attraction and unchallenged reliability which never palled. It was an important bonus to add to his invaluable experience of years with the Committee of Imperial Defence, his capacity for unremitting hard work and his ability to delegate. All this made him, like Professor Lindemann in other spheres, an excellent interpreter, of the Chiefs of Staff to Churchill and of Churchill to the Chiefs of Staff. However diverse their opinions on a strategic problem, however imminent a breach might seem between the Prime Minister and the service chiefs, Pug Ismay could be counted on, without appeasing either side beyond what was reasonable, to pour exactly the right measure of oil on the waters, to soothe and to explain. The debt that was owed him is hard to compute: it was certainly beyond repayment.

He was not afraid to tell the truth and say what he honestly believed. He loved and venerated Churchill; he knew by heart whole passages of *The World Crisis*, Churchill's history of the First World War, and yet he would say with an air of good-tempered resignation: 'The PM can be relied on to make a century in a test match, but he is no good at all at village cricket'. It is hard to conceive a shrewder assessment of Churchill.

Ismay himself was expected to play quite a lot of village cricket. Almost every morning there would emerge from 10 Downing Street minutes and enquiries, comments on telegrams and minor complaints. These were in addition to the majestic memoranda and directives relating to military questions of grave significance. The stream of detail would have swamped a less resilient man, but Ismay kept abreast of it, not necessarily swimming with the tide, but patiently answering written enquiries, sometimes querulous, which he must often have thought irrelevant to the more pressing problems demanding his attention. A special folder, entitled 'Replies from General Ismay', was kept in the Prime Minister's frequently replenished black box. From time to time Ismay would come over to 'weed' its considerable bulk, extracting papers that were out of date or overtaken by events, but he never failed to provide an answer to the questions addressed to him.

Churchill fascinated and impressed the service chiefs, but he often exasperated them with proposals they deemed unrealistic or, at their most extravagant, sheer fantasy. Ismay provided the corrective. Questions of high strategy were debated by the Defence Committee of the Cabinet under Churchill's chairmanship. However, the implementation of decisions and matters of disputed detail sometimes gave rise to menacing clouds. Then Ismay would beg the Chiefs of Staff, of whose committee he had once been secretary and was now a full member, to leave a solution to him. More often still, they chose that he should be their intermediary. If he was convinced that the Chiefs of Staff were right, and that a proposal by Churchill was impractical, he usually ended by converting the Prime Minister. If after full reflection he believed Churchill to be right, and the Chiefs of Staff to have been dilatory, unimaginative or merely obstructive, or if he concluded that the point at issue was of no real importance anyway, he would apply his soothing skill the other way. It is surprising how often Churchill's view, initially greeted by the combined opposition of the service chiefs, was in the end proved to have been prescient and ultimately acceptable.

Sitting patiently at Churchill's bedside, while he was working through the mass of papers in his box, and frequently diverted to discuss other matters of no immediate relevance to his visit, Ismay would await the right opportunity and the right mood. He was not prepared to risk losing an argument by faulty timing and whatever the weight of the work-load in his own office, he gave no indication of being in a hurry. If necessary he would reminisce about life as a subaltern in India, or the scandalously slow progress in rearmament before the war, until he saw his chance to fulfil the purpose of his visit. Churchill was a diligent worker, but he could also be unrivalled as a time-waster, especially when he was tired.

Ismay embodied continuity. There was nobody better equipped

to handle machinery which had evolved during the ten years before the war; for during that painful period he had been at the centre of discussions and events. He had an intimate understanding of the military mind. The ways of the three service departments, especially the Air Ministry and the War Office ('that House of Shame', as he called it), were familiar to him. The wheels of the machine revolved smoothly, if not always noiselessly, because all the principal mechanics were dedicated to their tasks and, squabble though they sometimes might, they had respect and even affection for each other.

The pre-war Committee of Imperial Defence and its sub-committees had been Ismay's arena. Now it was his arduous duty to attend the Defence Committee, the Chiefs of Staff Committee and the Cabinet itself, as well as providing the secretariat for the numerous inter-Allied conferences in Washington and Moscow, in Casablanca, Tehran, Quebec, Yalta and Potsdam. His minutes and his records were short and incisive. Like Professor Lindemann he knew that economy of words and concentration of thought were both essential if the Prime Minister's attention was to be captured. He did not seek to advise on strategy; but readily, though with restraint, he did give advice on how to handle the Chiefs of Staff and defence matters. As he had no enemies, and had a naturally charitable disposition, he did not use the opportunities that his position presented in order to denigrate or destroy. If he thought ill of a general's performance, he would say so; but he would not speak ill of him as a man.

This was as true of the past as of the present. He was sure that grave miscalculations had been made in the years before the war, and he was the only man I personally heard say, well before the cataclysmic events of May and June 1940, that he believed the quality and morale of the French army to be lower than was generally supposed. He also believed (wrongly, I think) that we should have gone to war at the time of Munich, despite our military nakedness, because we were stronger by comparison with the Germans than was the case a year later. He told me, early on in the war, that he knew Chamberlain and his colleagues had had no thought of waiting till the British armed forces were better prepared. To avert war, not to postpone it, was their objective, and for some months they sincerely believed it had been realized. He had always admired Churchill, but had feared his impetuous nature and impatience with opposition. By the end of May 1940, after countless meetings in London and several visits with the Prime Minister to France, he knew that his fears were groundless.

Ismay would have been less effective, and certainly less efficient, if he had not had a small staff in the office of the Minister of Defence on which it would have been difficult to improve. His lieutenants were two colonels, Joe Hollis of the Royal Marines and Ian Jacob, the sapper son of a distinguished field-marshal. They were soon, with every justification, converted into brigadiers and then into major-generals.

Joe Hollis had been at the foretop of a cruiser in the Battle of Jutland. Loyal, honest and exuding common sense, he was everybody's friend. He was always smiling, alert in manner and prompt in action. Ismay appointed him his deputy and secretary of the Chiefs of Staff Committee. He relied on him implicitly and justifiably, for he ran the office of the Minister of Defence and organized its staff in such a way that there was no bickering or ill-will among them. Moreover Churchill both trusted and liked him, so that when Ismay was otherwise engaged Hollis was a wholly acceptable substitute.

I once flew with Joe Hollis over the Atlas mountains, from Tunis to Marrakech, in a much-battered Liberator bomber. The only other passengers were some twenty young WAAF cipher officers. Just as we were crossing the mountains a side panel of the aircraft blew in. Joe took command, as a major-general should. He ordered me to seize one end of the panel and himself took the other. By main force we held it in place for ten minutes against the blast of freezing air, until the crew contrived to refix it; and all the while Joe kept the terrified WAAFs calm with a flow of comforting and diverting conversation. When we reached Marrakech, Lord Beaverbrook was so impressed by what he heard of Joe's behaviour in the crisis, that he rushed him off to the souk and bought him yards of gauze as a present for his wife. He bought me, as a minor actor in the drama, an expensive leather bag to give to the girl of my choice and, during the bargaining, accepted from the Arab stall-owner saucers of highly spiced quince jam which he eschewed himself but forced the reluctant Joe and me to swallow.

More intelligent than Hollis, and at least an equal asset to Ismay, was the other major-general, Ian Jacob. He did not, at first sight, match Hollis in charisma, for he was more serious and more austere. But he was a deeper thinker, a more professional soldier and a man whom none could classify as superficial. He was full of drive and original ideas, modified by realism and an infallible sense of the impractical. He thought Churchill the only man capable of inspiring both the country and the military leaders, but he deplored what he considered his excessive attention to detail. As early as June 1940, I noted that Ismay had produced an exhilarating paper suggesting we should not sit back and await invasion, but should start planning offensive action as soon as aircraft and equipment could be made available. Germany would only be beaten when her armies were defeated and blockade alone would not suffice. I further noted that this dynamic paper was the work of Colonel Jacob. Antony Head, who worked for a time under Ismay's command, christened Jacob 'Iron Pants'. The name had a ring of truth, but it was conferred with admiration.

When Churchill again became Prime Minister and Minister of Defence in 1951, one of his first thoughts was to recruit Jacob as his Chief of Staff. Ismay had been elevated to Secretary of State for Commonwealth Relations and Churchill looked on Jacob as a worthy successor. Jacob agreed with reluctance and the experiment was short-lived, for Churchill, having no war to fight, soon relinquished the Ministry of Defence to Field-Marshal Alexander, who was just as reluctant as Ian Jacob. Thereafter he switched his penetrating intelligence into other fields and became the occasionally harassed but always competent Director-General of the BBC.

What Ismay was to Churchill on the military side of affairs, Sir Edward Bridges, Secretary to the Cabinet, was on the civil side. He was the son of Robert Bridges, famous as Poet Laureate and author of *The Testament of Beauty*. A product of Eton and Oxford who had fought as a soldier throughout the First World War and won the Military Cross, he became a civil servant when peace came and he developed into a Treasury mandarin. In 1938 the legendary Sir Maurice Hankey, the first Secretary to the Cabinet ever to be appointed, and at the same time Secretary of both the Committee of Imperial Defence and the Privy Council, retired after an epoch of faithful service. The jobs he had held were already too heavy for one man and so Ismay succeeded him on the defence side and Bridges was selected to be Secretary to the Cabinet.

Bridges had a first-class brain and, still more important in his new appointment, administrative ability to match it. His eyes, behind gold-rimmed spectacles, were penetrating, and there was nearly always a thin but friendly smile on his lips. There was still an element of the schoolboy in this hardened Treasury warrior and his usual reaction to meeting some other official in the passages was to punch him playfully in the tummy. Words of wisdom, never undigested, emerged quietly yet forcefully from his mouth. He held firmly to the convention that it was the duty of a Civil Servant to implement and not originate political decisions. It was also his duty to offer advice, but whatever his personal convictions he must act loyally in accordance with the decisions of his political masters. When Civil Servants became too powerful, as Sir Horace Wilson at No. 10, Sir Warren Fisher at the Treasury and Sir Robert Vansittart at the Foreign Office had been, Bridges held that they were acting outside their professional brief.

If an exception to this rule might occasionally be allowed, then the Secretary to the Cabinet was that exception. Bridges, appointed to the post by Neville Chamberlain, had not merely been loyal to him, as duty demanded, but had also admired his administrative skill and quiet, unflamboyant methods. Therefore, the change from Chamberlain to Churchill was not to his taste. Indeed he admitted that on the day of the change-over he could not bring himself to congratulate Churchill: so he merely offered his good wishes. Like so many others he rapidly succumbed to the inspiration which came from the new order of things and in the heady summer of 1940, when almost every Englishman felt himself a giant with strength renewed, Bridges threw off every doubt and inhibition he had had.

I can see him vividly, even now, standing outside the Cabinet Room early in July 1940, declaiming to a small audience of ministers and officials against the danger of 'looking over our shoulder'. We must understand, he said, that a new technique of war was the offensive against morale. Nothing was more helpful to Hitler than to say we should start thinking about the establishment of skeleton government departments in Canada. Incalculable harm was already being done by attacks on the Civil Service, on Neville Chamberlain, and on the new Commander-in-Chief, Home Forces, General Ironside. Here, I remember, he looked meaningfully at Sir P. J. Grigg, Permanent Under Secretary at the War Office, who had been proclaiming that Ironside was among the worst of all generals and the most incompetent of men. If, Bridges went on, enough people said that these people and these institutions were rotten, it would be widely believed and the Germans would have good cause to rub their hands. We must stand firm; we must burn our boats; we must refuse to contemplate anything but victory. His outlook had evidently become Churchillian.

This was Bridges at his declamatory best. Such bursts of feeling were usually reserved for a small audience of fellow Civil Servants. The main tasks of his office were fulfilled quietly, without seeking credit or advertisement. Churchill relied on him to answer nearly all his enquires relating to the Home Front and to the machinery of government that were not addressed to a single ministry, and though he did not find Bridges, as he did Ismay, a man with whom it was necessarily agreeable to dine, he had esteem for his judgment and put reliance on his advice. As the war years dragged on, Churchill found less and less time and energy to read Cabinet papers on subjects with which he was not immediately engaged. It was then that Bridges, like Ismay, became indispensable as an interpreter and précis-writer. In Cabinet he sat at the Prime Minister's right hand, a painstaking guide on matters Churchill found dull or confusing and a ready supplier of answers to whispered questions. When Churchill went, defeated in the 1945 election, affairs of State became more orderly and his Cabinet business was conducted with greater expedition. But Edward Bridges, one of the men most dubious of Churchill's merits when he became Prime Minister, missed him profoundly. The fun, he told me with a genial punch in the tummy, had gone out of Cabinet meetings.

It is the sadder that when Churchill returned to power six years later his relationship with Bridges was not re-established. Bridges was by then Secretary to the Treasury and head of the Civil Service. There were no disputes over official appointments, for Churchill was but little interested in departmental chiefs. There were occasional wrangles over the Honours List; but the distance which grew between the two men was due mainly to the fact that Bridges, after years of conscientious slogging in the service of his country, and one of the heaviest burdens of responsibility, was a tired man whose patience was tattered and whose acceptance of the new Government's economic and financial policy was as always loyal, but by no means wholehearted. So Churchill dealt direct with the new Chancellor of the Exchequer, R. A. Butler, whom he began to find more congenial than ever before, and I noticed that when the Chancellor came to see the Prime Minister he was not accompanied by his Permanent Secretary.

A new light was shining in Churchill's eyes. It reflected his liking and confidence in Bridges' successor as Secretary to the Cabinet, Sir Norman Brook. Brook had a less simple and straightforward personality than Bridges, but he was more adept socially and he was equally conscientious. Little by little Churchill came to rely on him in all things and to find his presence wholly agreeable. Unlike Bridges he was invited to be a member of the Other Club and he was regarded as an *ex-officio* companion every time Churchill crossed the Atlantic to confer with the Americans. Nothing was too much trouble for him and no details escaped his attention. He was wise in his advice and while appearing to fall in, at an early stage, with ideas that he privately thought wrong or extravagant, he presented the counter-arguments so skilfully and so tactfully that they were nearly always approved. He did not tread on the toes of other ministers; he remained, when Churchill retired in 1955, as welcome an adviser and father confessor to both Anthony Eden and Harold Macmillan as he had been to Churchill. Churchill and Eden were often at odds between 1951 and 1955, and feelings sometimes ran high. Norman Brook listened sympathetically to both and antagonized neither. The compromises he recommended were usually accepted.

Brook did play a more active role in Cabinet and other ministerial appointments than had Bridges, although Bridges had often been asked for his advice. Brook gave his gratuitously and he did so in private so as not to upset the delicate sensitivities of the Chief Whip, Patrick Buchan Hepburn. For instance, when I was alone with Churchill at Chartwell in June 1952, Brook joined us in the evening. The object of his journey was to suggest that Lord Woolton should abandon the chairmanship of the Home Affairs Committee and that Anthony Eden should take it over, relinquishing his portfolio as Foreign Secretary. Churchill was inclined to favour the proposal, but he remarked that Eden had become 'Foreign Officissimus' and would not be induced to change. Eden would have been even less amused than Queen Victoria if he had known what plots the Prime Minister and the Secretary to the Cabinet were hatching behind his back.

Again, in August 1953, I was alone with Churchill and Brook at Chequers. They discussed a reconstruction of the Government, with Eden becoming Leader of the House of Commons and Lord President of the Council and Lord Salisbury or Harold Macmillan being promoted to the Foreign Office. At this period Brook was a tower of strength, for Churchill had had a stroke in June, an event shrouded in secrecy, and Eden was recovering from a serious abdominal operation. Churchill had made an unexpectedly rapid recovery, but too many burdens could not be laid on his recently paralysed shoulders and there were routine matters, inseparable from his office, that could not be postponed. For three months Churchill's own secretariat were saddled with far greater responsibility than is normal, for decisions of lesser importance had sometimes to be taken in the Prime Minister's name but without his specific authority. This would have been an intolerable and, indeed, unconstitutional position had it not been for wise guidance provided by Norman Brook.

With his devotion to Parliament, Churchill thought that even junior ministers were always on a higher level than officials, even if he preferred some of the officials, such as Eddie Marsh, personally. This had not always been so, for ambassadors, of which there were only five or six at the beginning of the century, were placed on the highest pedestals and both they and the heads of the more important Civil Departments were frequently Privy Councillors. However, Churchill considered the Privy Council a politician's preserve and had always refused to recommend for that honour an ambassador or senior Civil Servant.

I was therefore surprised one morning when the Prime Minister asked me what I thought of his idea of making Norman Brook a Privy Councillor. He had never, he said, been so well and faithfully served by anyone, nor did he know a man of greater natural distinction or higher character. I replied that I thought this idea an excellent one, but he would obviously have to recommend Edward Bridges too. He was strangely recalcitrant, dwelling emphatically on the exceptional qualities of Brook. However, I reminded him of Bridges' equally estimable services in the war and he did, in the end, agree to recommend both. The coveted honour had already been bestowed on Ismay when, in 1951, he became a Secretary of State.

The list of Churchill's official advisers is a short one, for he was little responsive to advice. However, when he did have confidence in a man, it was wholeheartedly given and seldom withdrawn. He was prepared to listen to colleagues or military chiefs or his friends. Sometimes what they said would lead him to modify his immediate thoughts and change his mind. Not even Ismay or Bridges or Brook could prevail on him to alter course once a decision had been maturely considered and firmly made. His will was his own and in the last resort it was adamant. This did not mean he was impervious to argument, but because he was so strong, indeed sometimes so fierce, in his method of declaring his intention, it needed resolution and preferably wiliness to modify it. His official advisers were all resolute men and with experience they learned to be wily.

There was another class of advisers, operating still more often by telegram than by their presence in London. That was the Dominion Prime Ministers, of whom the most treasured was the Prime Minister of South Africa, Field-Marshal Jan Smuts. 'Slim Jan' they called him in his own country, for he could be more cunning than many of his compatriots liked, and on hearing him say that 'order and discipline are the first essentials of democracy', I remember noticing that liberty was not included. Churchill, however, could find no fault in Smuts, who represented so much that he approved: the chivalrous enemy of the Boer War years who had been treated generously and become an unflinching ally in two World Wars; the philosopher who would discuss earnestly what were the bounds of man's capacity and whether human nature was immutable; the statesman who had left the table of the Imperial War Cabinet in 1917 to travel to south Wales and resolve a menacing coal strike, where Lloyd George had failed, by persuading the disgruntled miners to sing before they voted;

the man who, against the odds, had induced the South African Parliament to declare war in 1939, thus maintaining the solidarity of the whole British Empire in which Smuts was as fervent a believer as Churchill.

To all this was added a string of telegrams, from Pretoria or Cairo, making suggestions on strategy and bestriding the range of world politics. In June 1940 he stressed the deadly peril facing the Middle East, Africa and ultimately India from the conquest of which Hitler could secure the resources to sustain himself. When Churchill took the risk, in the autumn of 1940, of sending the only intact British armoured division to North Africa, Smuts's advice weighed with him and in January 1941 he ended a telegram with words of praise for 'your sure-footed judgment which marches with our laboriously reached conclusions'. In the disasters that befell British arms in Greece and Crete Smuts was stalwart in his support, providing encouragement rather than consolation. So it was throughout the war. He came to London from time to time, but wherever he might be he gave counsel which was usually wise, though sometimes unrealistic. His optimism did not flag and I was not surprised to hear Churchill say to the South African High Commissioner towards the end of the war: 'Smuts and I are like two old love-birds moulting together on a perch, but still able to peck.'

Another Dominion Prime Minister, no less constant in his attitude to the war than Smuts, was Robert Menzies from Australia. In the spring and summer of 1941, when Australian forces were deploying in Egypt, he spent months in England and was, like Smuts and all visiting Dominion Premiers, invited to attend the meetings of the War Cabinet. He spent many week-ends at Chequers, mixing on equal terms with de Gaulle, Sikorski, the American visitors and the British Chiefs of Staff. No doubt he learned a lot, but he also gave a lot. So when he temporarily fell from power in Australia, and a less dynamic successor replaced him, his presence at the war centre was greatly missed. Churchill's feelings for him were shown by his taking him to Bristol, in flames after a savage air-raid, to receive an honorary degree at his hands in the shattered University Senate, where the scarlet gowns and the pageantry attending Churchill as Chancellor of the University made a strange contrast with the smoking ruins outside. He found

Menzies so agreeable that he also made him, like Smuts, a member of the Other Club.

The two other Dominion Prime Ministers, Mackenzie King of Canada and Peter Fraser of New Zealand, did not have the same personal relationship with Churchill. However, he was assiduous in sending them long telegrams describing the movement of events and he sincerely welcomed the comments they sent in reply. When they came to London every facility and all possible courtesies were offered. The Empire was far-flung, but its men were fighting with the British in all three elements and in every theatre of war. It would have been easy for discontents to emerge and misunderstandings to arise. That they rarely did so was due as much to the comprehension and collaboration of the Dominion Prime Ministers, from near or far, as it was to the trouble which Churchill always took in consulting and convincing them.

CHAPTER NINE

The Warriors

Admirals, generals and air marshals were Churchill's daily bread during the Second World War. For five years they came in scores to 10 Downing Street and Chequers, to lunch, to dine, but principally to confer, and when they were not visiting Churchill he was, as often as not, visiting them. Since much of his life's experience had been with military affairs, this connection with the men of war was for the most part harmonious; but there was only a handful of them with whom his association was other than simply professional. With that handful this chapter is principally concerned.

Churchill preferred to deal with men who expressed themselves lucidly and found it easy to converse. The few military chiefs whom he failed to understand, and in consequence tended to undervalue, were the reticent. Wavell was tongue-tied in his presence. So were A.B. Cunningham and Auchinleck. Their qualities were greater than Churchill would admit, for judgment of men was not one of his strongest points.

As Minister of Defence his first line of communication was with the Chiefs of Staff. General Ismay was the daily channel, but the heads of the three services were all in direct contact with him. In May 1940 they consisted of Sir Dudley Pound, First Sea Lord, Sir Edmund Ironside, Chief of the Imperial General Staff, and Sir Cyril Newall, Chief of the Air Staff. Only one of them, Pound, remained at his post until, late in 1943, he died in harness. The other two were replaced in the course of the year.

Sir Dudley Pound stood as high as anybody in Churchill's affection. He had once been on the staff of Admiral Lord Fisher, an eccentric and sometimes almost insane genius whom Churchill had alternately loved and hated during his years as First Lord of the Admiralty before and during the First World War. In 1939

Churchill returned to the Admiralty to find Pound already established there as First Sea Lord. His nose was long and straight; his chin was pointed, and his deep-set, observant eyes contradicted any superficial impression of lethargy. He was a naval officer of the highest worth: courageous, matter of fact in thought and word, and gifted with a fine precision of mind. He embodied the traditions of the navy and was not amused when Churchill, advised that a proposed action was not in keeping with them, asked, 'What are the traditions of the navy? Rum, sodomy and the lash!' Pound had a slow, wry sense of humour, but this was going too far.

He was ready to take great risks. When Churchill was goading the Chiefs of Staff to send through dangerous Mediterranean waters a large consignment of tanks, the loss of which we could not afford, to enable Wavell to mount an offensive in North Africa, Pound was the only one of the Chiefs of Staff to argue that the risk was acceptable. It was he, too, who was prepared to lose a great capital ship in order to shell Rommel's supply base at Tripoli. Once he had given a proposal careful, unhurried thought, he did not hesitate in its execution however dire the consequences of failure might be. But he did require time and consideration before making up his mind and Churchill, though himself obstinately refusing to be hurried in decisions of major importance, was impatient of delay by others. In August 1940, I walked along Whitehall with Churchill on the way back from a conference in the Admiralty War Room. It was proposed to send our only armoured division to Egypt at a time when invasion threatened the British Isles, and Pound was doubtful. 'He is so confoundedly cautious,' Churchill complained; and although this was his refrain on many subsequent occasions, I think that in his heart he knew the old admiral was a wholesome check on impetuosity.

There were some who thought that Pound acquiesced too readily in Churchill's interference with naval strategy. I do not believe this was so. Churchill prodded the admirals, as he did the generals and air marshals, and having twice been First Lord of the Admiralty he took an even keener interest in naval details than in those of the other services. However, in the last analysis, he seldom overrode if he failed to persuade.

It is, however, true that when Churchill left the Admiralty to become Prime Minister and Minister of Defence, Pound continued to regard him as his master rather than the new First Lord, A.V. Alexander, though he was the soul of courtesy and consideration to the head of his department. A.V. Alexander had many virtues. They did not include modesty. He annoyed Pound and others by talking about 'my navy', until one day the King pointed out that it was his. I remember, too, that after the naval attack on the Italian fleet at Taranto, he walked into my office and I congratulated him. He replied, 'Thank you, my boy. The credit is really Cunningham's but in fairness to Pound I must say that when I suggested the idea to him, he did telegraph it out to Cunningham.' In 1943, Pound lay dying. Brendan Bracken, who was no less fond of him than Churchill, called to see him and found A.V. Alexander already at his bedside. Alexander told the dying man that without him he would have had difficulty in achieving all that he had. According to Brendan, Pound turned his face to the wall and made no reply.

Until he died, and despite Churchill's complaints about his slowness and excessive caution, the two men remained faithful friends and colleagues. One night in August 1940, Pound was taking part in an after-dinner discussion at Chequers with the Prime Minister and Generals Wavell and Dill. During this conference enemy raiders were reported to be passing overhead. Churchill forthwith led the whole party out into the star-lit garden. We stumbled in the darkness. The First Sea Lord, who was a little lame, fell down a flight of steps. Having picked himself up disconsolately, he then fell down another, ending in a heap on the ground where a sentry, thinking him an intruder, threatened him with a fixed bayonet. I ran forward to explain who he was. At that moment Churchill also arrived on the scene from the rose-garden. 'This is not the place for a First Sea Lord,' said Pound. Churchill replied: 'Try to remember you are an Admiral of the Fleet and not a midshipman.' They walked happily together back into the house.

Churchill believed that Pound had the best brains in the navy. Others attributed that distinction to the Vice-Chief of the Naval Staff, Vice-Admiral Tom Phillips. He was often to be seen, during half an hour's relaxation from his duties in the Admiralty, tinkering with the engine of his car on Horse Guards Parade; but when he was summoned by the Prime Minister, or was awaiting his turn to enter the conference chamber, he could be counted on to make penetrating comments on the war situation, on land and in the air as well as at sea. As early as 18 May 1940, while the battle still raged, he was the first man I heard say that if we sent more fighter squadrons to France we should lose them. If that was allowed to happen, we should be left at the mercy of a concentrated air attack and could hardly avoid destruction. He had a pleasing touch of cynicism. In December of that year he was at Chequers where there was elation over Wavell's early victories in Cyrenaica. Phillips turned to me and said, 'If this sort of thing goes on much longer, we must be careful; or we shall suddenly find that we have got many more friends than we thought.'

Like all chair-bound sailors, Phillips longed to turn his back on the Admiralty and put to sea. At the end of 1941 he had his wish and as he steamed without air-cover off Malaysia, in a gallant but fruitless endeavour to intercept reported Japanese landings on the coast, his flagship, *Prince of Wales*, and her companion, the huge battle-cruiser *Repulse*, were sunk by enemy torpedo-bombers. Two thirds of the men were saved, but Phillips went down with his ship.

General Ismay, who thought him an officer of exceptional ability, told me that when news of the calamity reached him, his memory went back to a meeting of the Joint Planning Staff a few years before the war. The naval representative, Captain Tom Phillips RN, held forth on the invulnerability of modern capital ships to air attack. It was an Admiralty theme that infuriated the Air Ministry. It was even more frequently propounded, and was only a few degrees less ridiculous, than that voiced in some War Office quarters that tanks had frequent mechanical failures whereas cavalry horses did not. On this occasion the Air Ministry representative was Air Commodore Arthur Harris. According to Ismay he thumped the table and said, 'Phillips, you make me sick. I can tell you what is going to happen. One day we shall be at war with Japan and you will be sailing across the South China seas in one of your beautiful battleships. Out of a cloud there will come a squadron of Japanese bombers and as your great ship capsizes, you will turn to your navigating officer and say, "That was a whopping great mine we hit".' Even by December 1941 Phillips, for all his shrewdness and ability, had failed to learn the lesson about air-cover taught by many painful episodes in the preceding fifteen months. Others had been equally slow to learn, but Phillips's tragic death finally cemented in the minds of soldiers, sailors and politicians an irrefutable truth which they had known but disregarded.

When Pound died, his successor as First Sea Lord was the forceful Commander-in-Chief, Mediterranean, Sir Andrew Browne Cunningham, universally known as A.B.C. Churchill never doubted his capacity, but there was no warmth between them, and the days of chaff and challenge, of indignant reproof and unflustered justification, that had characterized his relationship with Pound were gone for ever. Cunningham at sea was a naval commander without rival in the Second World War. Cunningham ashore, as First Sea Lord, was misplaced. This was particularly so because he came into frequent contact with a Prime Minister and Minister of Defence in whom his confidence was limited. He expressed himself badly and often failed to make his point. He nursed hurt feeling engendered by signals he had received from Churchill when he was Commander-in-Chief, Mediterranean, signals which had seemed to him to cast doubt on his ardour for battle. He had not lacked that ardour, nor had Churchill thought he did; but what was intended to encourage explanation and extract justification was believed by Cunningham to convey reproof. It would have been better to leave him where he excelled – at sea.

Before the war Churchill was impressed by General Ironside, an imposing giant who had commanded the anti-Soviet expedition to Archangel in 1919 and was taken by John Buchan as the model for Richard Hannay in *The Thirty-Nine Steps*. He was not suited to be Chief of the Imperial General Staff, the appointment he received in September 1939 when his predecessor, Lord Gort, left to take command of the British Expeditionary Force. Churchill, who had been his principal sponsor, was disappointed by his performance.

So in June 1940 a soldier with as much charm and real goodness as any then living, Sir John Dill, succeeded to the post. Many had thought him the right candidate for command of the BEF, but Gort had more experience of fighting in the field of battle, had an unsurpassed record of gallantry and was acknowledged to have greater drive. As successor to Ironside, Dill was esteemed by his Secretary of State, Anthony Eden, and by Eden's successor, David Margesson. Churchill loved to discuss the background knowledge that a good general should have acquired. He told Dill that every prospective commander should follow General Gordon's advice and read Plutarch's *Lives*. He thought modern officers were admirably versed in weapon-training, but had little stimulus to use their imagination and to regard military problems on a broad view. Dill recommended the study of Stonewall Jackson as an alternative course for generals. It is not surprising that his opinions later carried weight in the United States. All the same, he was a tired man who seemed to lack the vigour expected of him. So in the autumn of 1941 he was left in Washington where his conduct as permanent British representative with the Combined Chiefs of Staff was exemplary and his last service to his country the greatest he performed.

To take Dill's place at the War Office Churchill chose a man of tougher fibre and less compromising disposition, General Sir Alan Brooke. In harness with Dill he had been one of the corps commanders in the BEF under Gort. Brooke had a better brain than either of them. He was also more personally ambitious and more prone to carp and criticize. He did so bitterly in the temporary privacy of his diary. When it came to dispensing with unsuccessful commanders, he had a ruthlessness which Dill lacked and Churchill tended to admire. Churchill did not share his love of bird-watching, but he praised his intelligence and strategic sense as well as his readiness to take decisions. He found him a bulwark when it came to resisting American plans for a premature invasion of France and, whatever their differences over matters of detail, in their broad strategic conceptions they were usually as one.

However, Brooke liked business to be conducted in an orderly fashion and Churchill, as often as not, was the reverse of orderly. Brooke wanted quick, clear-cut rulings. Churchill liked to mull over a proposal and view it from every angle. To outwit the systematic German military machine, Churchill had no doubt that it was essential to be both unorthodox and imaginative. He devised schemes for raids on the Continent, a landing in the north of Norway, the occupation of Aegean islands, an assault on Pantellaria, the seizure of Heligoland and the recapture of Rangoon. Before these schemes were rejected he required them to be examined in detail and himself to be convinced they were impractical. Many undoubtedly were, but others were adopted and proved. Brooke, usually with the support of the American Chiefs of Staff, wished to concentrate on the main strategic programme. Churchill's addiction to diversionary tactics infuriated him.

Churchill was grieved that in the event it was not in his power to give Brooke the prize he longed to receive: command of the Allied armies in Normandy. The Americans insisted that that was their preserve, and the prize was awarded to Eisenhower whose experience and decisiveness were no match for Brooke's. After the war his diaries were published too soon. They showed that while he was fond of Churchill and admitted his genius, he found his methods of work and his interventions exasperating almost beyond endurance. He considered many of his ideas an irrelevant waste of time and he resented the hours of discussion required before Churchill approved a project. When major operations were under discussion, the notoriously impetuous Prime Minister had in fact become, under the weight of responsibility, more circumspect than the Chief of the Imperial General Staff. On reading the diaries, Churchill was hurt and antagonized. Brooke was the only man on whom I ever saw him deliberately and ostentatiously turn his back.

Of all the armed services, the navy meant most to Churchill, for he had presided over its fortunes at the outbreak of both world wars. Having himself been a soldier, and a student of military campaigns from the wars of Marlborough to those of the twentieth century, the plans and the performance of the generals were also of burning interest to him. Yet it was to the newest of the services, the Royal Air Force, that in the end he paid the most attention, for he believed it was the most vital to victory. The daring exploits of the fighter pilots in the Battle of Britain aroused in him a latent schoolboy instinct of hero-worship. When I myself went off to train as a pilot, he said to me with emotion that I was joining 'the cavalry of modern war'. To him that was the highest possible recommendation.

Before describing some of the air personalities with whom he was in closest touch, it seems pertinent to dwell on his faith in what the RAF could achieve. By the end of June 1940, with the total collapse of France a tragic reality, he wrote, 'It seems to me the blockade is largely ruined, in which case the sole decisive weapon in our hands would be overwhelming air attack on

Germany.' A week later he sent this note to Beaverbrook at the Ministry of Aircraft Production:

When I look around to see how we can win the war, I see that there is only one sure path. We have no continental army which can defeat the German military power. The blockade is broken and Hitler has Asia and probably Africa to draw from. Should he be repulsed here, or not try invasion, he will recoil eastwards and we have nothing to stop him. But there is one thing that will bring him back and bring him down, and that is an absolutely devastating, exterminating attack by very heavy bombers from this country on the Nazi homeland. We must be able to overwhelm them by this means, without which I do not see a way through.

He persisted with this line of thought during the whole anxious summer of 1940. In July he said to the assembled company at the Chequers luncheon-table:

Even if that man [as he always called Hitler] were at the Caspian, and there is nothing to stop him from going there, we should bring him back to find a fire in his own back-yard and we will make Germany a desert, yes, a desert. Hitler can do what he likes where there is no salt-water to cross, but it will avail him nothing if he reaches the Great Wall of China and this island remains undefeated.

Bombing of military objectives was, as he told Lord Halifax, 'our main road home', and he listened attentively to Sir Charles Portal, the Commander-in-Chief, Bomber Command, who said that as soon as his command had the strength he planned to concentrate his attacks on small areas, first with incendiary bombs and then with high explosive. However, a few months later, in December 1940, when London was under nightly bombardment, Churchill was doubtful about 'Operation Abigail', a plan to single out a German town, as the Germans themselves had singled out Coventry, and destroy it completely. At the same time a list would have been published of other towns destined for a similar fate. Churchill and the War Cabinet had moral scruples when this proposal was put to them, even though the citizens of many British cities were clamouring for vengeance.

It was thus that the epic of the fighter pilots and the conviction that bombing was the road to victory combined to give the Royal Air Force pre-eminent importance in Churchill's eyes until the time came when we were again in a position to take the offensive on land. Whatever Beaverbrook might say about the air marshals, Churchill cultivated their friendship.

The Chief of the Air Staff whom he inherited was Sir Cyril Newall. Churchill thought he had many good points and said so to Beaverbrook, who replied caustically, 'He was an Observer in the last war and has remained an Observer ever since.' Observer was the name then used for the navigator of a bomber. At the end of 1940 Newall went away to be Governor General of New Zealand, and Sir Charles Portal took his place.

Portal was tall and slim, his streaky, dark hair untidily receding, his complexion rubicund and an aquiline nose dominating his face. He was a master of the art of reticence, disinclined to volunteer any opinion or information unless invited to do so. Every day he arrived in his large official Rolls-Royce for luncheon at the Travellers' Club in Pall Mall, marched upstairs, greeted nobody and ate a solitary meal. He accepted no invitations except obligatory ones from the Prime Minister or Secretary of State for Air. Had he been a commander in the field, out of immediate touch, it is probable that Churchill would have found him as difficult to influence as he did Wavell and Auchinleck. At home, and in perpetual contact with day-to-day affairs, he both understood Churchill's methods and sympathized with them. He was the principal exception to Churchill's inability to work with the reticent; but then he lacked nothing in skill as a communicator.

Portal dominated the RAF and the Air Ministry, with the exception of the Commander-in-Chief, Bomber Command, Sir Arthur Harris. Whatever he said at official meetings was wise and well calculated, although it did not fall to his lot to bear the brunt of the strategic discussions with Churchill and the Americans. Churchill told me that he considered Portal the ablest of the Chiefs of Staff at the end of the war and that he was the one on whose judgment he relied. The Americans were also his fervent admirers. He was a man with whom it was pleasant and indeed a privilege to be, and so Churchill elected him to the Other Club. As he practically never came, it was difficult to decide whether he was also a man with whom it was agreeable to dine. Perhaps he was not, at any rate in large and talkative company; but despite his modesty and distaste for conversation he was such a born leader that those who found him lacking in the social graces at the dinner-table would none the less have been glad to obey his commands.

These were the Chiefs of Staff, whose activities were permanently intermingled with Churchill's. He was not just a critic of their deliberations and an instigator of decisions. He would dictate 'directives' for them to consider. These were masterly documents, well thought out, original in content, clear and to the point. Like papal encyclicals they were known in central government circles by their opening words. Thus a long and detailed one which began 'Renown awaits the Commander who first ...' was in frequent demand and was simply called 'Renown Awaits'. They were the instruments by which Churchill sought to direct the conduct and strategy of the war.

Despite the harmony that reigned, Churchill did chivy the Chiefs of Staff, usually because he wanted a theme well debated. If they were adamant in opposition, he seldom insisted on his own point of view. He would, however, express disgust at their caution, probably in terms more outspoken than he really believed. One afternoon I went into his darkened bedroom with some urgent message when his usual hour's sleep was due to end. His waking remark was, 'The poor Chiefs of Staff will get very much out of breath in their desire to run away.' This was at the time of the Greek campaign in March 1941. On another occasion, Ismay reported that his Parthian shot as he left a meeting of the Defence Committee was: 'I am expected to wage modern war with antiquated weapons.' And he was never averse from justifying his own contested views. 'The Chiefs of Staff,' he said to me, 'complain that I have led them up the garden path. But at every turning I have provided them with delicious fruits and wholesome vegetables. Poor Chiefs of Staff.'

Churchill had a special relationship with three or four of the commanders in the field. The naval commanders were out of reach at sea. Many of the soldiers were subjected to long telegrams which, for Churchill, replaced the conversation and the enquiries he would have liked to make in conference or at the Chequers dining-room table. The leading airmen, however, had their headquarters within easy range of Chequers and were regular week-end guests for dinner. There were two who received special attention, Sir Hugh Dowding and Sir Arthur Harris. Neither was popular with his fellow air marshals, and both were treated badly by the Air Ministry when their tasks were completed. Churchill had great esteem for them.

Dowding's grim determination was evident when the Prime Minister, in a desperate endeavour to steady our quavering French allies, offered to send to France more fighter squadrons than could safely be spared. The War Cabinet debated the offer. In a letter he wrote to me after the war Dowding gave his account of the affair:

In the opening stages of our discussion the Prime Minister strongly resisted my view, and I got no support from Sinclair and Newall (who, of course, ought to have been the people resisting the despatch of so many squadrons to France).

Lord Beaverbrook in his account of the meeting states at a certain stage I threw down my pencil on to the table and he took this to be a threat of resignation on my part. (I should never resign on a point such as this.)

What I did do was to get out of my chair, walk round the Cabinet table, lay down in front of Churchill a graph which I had prepared in anticipation of some opportunity of using it. I said, 'This is my graph of the losses of Hurricanes during the past ten days; it shows that if losses continue at the same rate for another ten days we shall not have a single Hurricane left in France or in England.'

This did the trick and the wastage of fighters was stopped.

I know of course that Churchill was under tremendous pressure from the French, but they had already ineradicably lost the battle and it had come to a question of obliging the French or losing the war, for, make no mistake about it, the immediate threat after Dunkirk was the invasion of this country.... The primary requisite for the Germans was the defeat of the British Fighters *during daylight hours*, or at least Hitler believed this to be the case.

He ended this letter by saying, 'I am glad to hear that Churchill acknowledged the value of my action in this respect, but he never mentioned the matter to me.'

There is another aspect of the affair for an account of which I am indebted to General Sir Ian Jacob, who was present at the meetings in May and June 1940. Churchill had to make an agonizing decision between two claims on the resources of Fighter Command: the French demand for every British squadron to sustain their battered armies in what they believed to be the decisive battle of the war; and the requirements for home defence if France fell and the Germans turned their full fury on Britain. The question was how many squadrons were essential for the safety of the country, and to this Churchill and the Chiefs of Staff received conflicting answers. Churchill wanted to do his utmost to satisfy both claims and Dowding's graph emphasized the dilemma.

Like any commander-in-chief with a severe battle in prospect, Dowding naturally, and quite rightly, pressed to retain all the resources he could. It is, however, wrong to suppose that he alone saved the country from disaster. The Prime Minister, the Cabinet and the Chiefs of Staff had to listen to all the arguments and to make the decision. In fact, General Jacob records, the Secretary of State for Air and the Chief of the Air Staff backed Dowding's view in the various meetings, at some of which Dowding himself was not present. Jacob is sure that Churchill never for one moment contemplated denuding the British Isles of their vital defence in order to support the rapidly declining chances of saving the situation in France. The sole question at issue was how many squadrons could be spared without fatally lowering Britain's guard.

It seems that Dowding remained unaware how impressed Churchill was by his unwavering stand against the French demands. If Churchill never said so directly to Dowding, I thought that by his attitude to him for the rest of that summer he showed how much he valued him. Churchill was a frequent caller at Fighter Command and Dowding came time and again to Chequers to report on German tactics and his own. He described how much we owed to the curious failure of the Germans to place armour behind the engines of their aircraft. He declared there was no means of preventing indiscriminate night bombing and was sure that each side must soon race for the destruction of the other's aircraft industry, a rivalry which would be bound to involve bombing the civilian population. When he came to dine, he would stand up fearlessly to the Prime Minister and prove himself, to Churchill's approval, an antidote to any hint of complacency. They argued about the ethics of shooting enemy pilots escaping by parachute, Dowding maintaining it was necessary and Churchill saying it was as bad as shooting a shipwrecked sailor. He produced what Churchill called 'a masterly paper' about night interception, on reading which the Prof said scathingly that it was Dowding's first recognition of scientific facts which had been impressed on him for months past. All the same, Churchill maintained that it was masterly.

To show his approval of Dowding's invaluable services Churchill recommended him for a peerage. The Air Ministry were less gracious. He was never made a Marshal of the Royal Air Force, and although he was a tired man after the hectic months of the Battle of Britain, and due for retirement, he was superseded with a lack of tact that hurt him deeply. That was none of Churchill's doing.

Dowding did have an eccentric side to his character. He was addicted to spiritualism and believed himself to be in touch with the souls of the pilots who had been killed. One night at Chequers he told us that the battle was going well. The only things that worried him were his dreams. The previous night he had dreamt there was only one man in England capable of operating a Bofors gun and his name was William Shakespeare. We supposed we were intended to laugh, but I looked at Dowding's face and was sure he was speaking in deadly earnest. However that may be, Churchill continued to regard 'Stuffy' Dowding as one of the prime heroes of the Second World War.

In later years a regular diner at Chequers was Air Marshal Sir Arthur Harris, who would drive over from Bomber Command Headquarters at High Wycombe. A man of ruthless drive and efficiency, who paid little attention to directives from the Chiefs of Staff, and practically none at all to the Air Ministry, he demanded the limit of endurance from his bomber crews. Their casualty rate was blood-curdling, but Harris won Churchill's esteem by his unflagging determination to reach his objectives. It fell to his lot to do what the citizens of London and a dozen other British towns had been demanding: to obliterate German cities as brutally as the Germans themselves had set about devastating those in Britain. Hamburg was left a burning wreck, the Ruhr was in ruins, Berlin, Cologne, Frankfurt, Munich and Stuttgart had scarcely a house standing. Only in the heat of war, when after a time men's sensitivities are hardened to an extent that seems incredible in later years, could such apocalyptic fury be approved. But it was approved, by all but a scanty band of humanitarians protesting to a deaf majority. Almost at the end came Dresden. At the time

it seemed just another big raid. I do not recall any special consideration being given to it in advance. The Russians, suspicious
that we were allowing enemy divisions to be diverted to the eastern
front so that the Germans could profit from a soft option in the
West, demanded that Dresden be bombed on the grounds that
armoured formations were consolidating their strength in the
city on their way to the River Oder. Both the British and the
Americans wished to calm Russian suspicions. So for thirty-six
consecutive hours RAF Bomber Command and the USAAF turned
Dresden into hell on earth. The night it ended, Harris came to
dine at Chequers. He arrived early and when I went into the Great
Hall, he was sitting there alone. 'What is the news of Dresden?' I
asked. He replied: 'There is no such place as Dresden.'

It is easy to be critical, even sanctimonious, now that it is long
over; but Harris was carrying out a policy approved in principal
by the British and American Chiefs of Staff, with the support of
their Governments, although in his enthusiasm he may sometimes
have exceeded their intentions. The early inhibition against bombing the civilian population vanished when London and Coventry,
Bristol, Plymouth, Birmingham and Liverpool went up in flames,
when thousands died in Glasgow, Swansea and Belfast. War
stimulates the finest qualities of man: courage, comradeship and
self-sacrifice. He almost learns to love his neighbours as himself and he tends to pay more attention than in peace-time to
at least some of the commandments of God. War also blinds him,
as year after year passes and hatred grows, to many of the basic
decencies. Those who did not experience these feelings should be
guarded in their condemnation.

After the war, the Air Ministry were mean in their acknowledg-
ment of Harris's services, though his surviving bomber crews
stood stalwartly behind him. Churchill saw no reason why he
should be overlooked just because many of his fellow air marshals
disliked him. So the first thing he did on returning to power in
1951 was to make Harris a baronet. He wanted it to be a peerage;
but the Air Ministry howled, and there was a point beyond which
he thought it indelicate to overrule them.

Only two of the soldiers commanding in the field were in the
category of Churchill's personal friends. They were Alexander and
Montgomery. As I have already stated, he had little sympathy for

Wavell, who was not at his best with him; he liked Auchinleck but felt obliged to replace him when the tide ran against us in North Africa and the morale of the Eighth Army fell with defeat; he had nothing but admiration for Slim, both as a superb commander in Burma and as CIGS after 1951, but his personal contacts with him were limited; and Mountbatten's courage and ingenuity, as Director of Combined Operations and later as Supreme Allied Commander in the Far East, were not lost on him. He put 'Alex' and 'Monty', however, on a plane above all others.

I have no doubt he thought Monty the better general in the field. The Americans considered Alexander a great strategist and Eisenhower wished to have him as his deputy for 'Operation Overlord'. In the event an airman, Air Chief Marshal Tedder, was selected for the appointment. He had won distinction in command of the desert air force in Africa, but Churchill was doubtful of his qualification to be Deputy Supreme Allied Commander. When he was sent to discuss military operations with Stalin, Churchill commented to me, 'Sending Tedder to Moscow to talk about army matters is like asking a man to paint a picture when he has only learned how to ride a bicycle'.

Those who served under Alexander loved him for his courage, his straightforwardness and his ease of communication with all ranks. Montgomery's whole life was dedicated to his profession, to the exclusion of outside interests. He did not have Alexander's striking record in action as a junior officer, but he had the better brains of the two and was versed in profound study of the military art. Just as those who served under Alex were strong in their championship, so those who served under Monty considered him a professional soldier beyond comparison. Monty shared this view.

Alex was an unmistakable aristocrat, with a natural diffidence and modesty that his birth and established position provided no inducement to discard. His courageous determination was displayed while he was still a boy. In the celebrated Fowler's Match between Eton and Harrow, when Harrow's overwhelming lead was eroded by a single Etonian bowler, Fowler, Alex went in as last man for Harrow, confronted the formidable Fowler, and all but snatched victory for his school. Many years later Sir Arthur Bryant asked him whether he felt the greater anxiety in Fowler's Match or in the desperate days of disease and defeat when he extricated the British Army from Burma in 1942. Alex replied that Fowler's Match worried him more, for he was unsure of victory, whereas in the long retreat from Rangoon he had no doubt at all that we should win in the end.

His gallantry as an Irish Guards officer in the First World War had given him a reputation of precisely the kind calculated to appeal to Churchill. This favourable impression was enhanced by his cool, unworried command of the rearguard in the Dunkirk evacuation and the equally calm confidence he showed when given Southern Command in Britain at the peak of the invasion threat. Churchill returned to London from a tour of the defences loud in praise of the dispositions Alexander had made, and on the following Sunday he invited him to Chequers to be put still further through his paces. Thenceforward Alexander was a marked man in Churchill's eyes and at a critical moment in the North African campaign he was ordered back from Burma to assume command. Churchill liked his direct approach, was susceptible to his smart physical appearance ('his easy smiling grace', as he described it) and never doubted his willingness to carry out his instructions punctually and with meticulous attention to detail. On only two occasions did Churchill doubt Alexander's initiative. The first was when two of his divisions, under the immediate command of the American General Lucas, remained static on the beach at Anzio instead of driving inland to cut the German communications. Churchill said he had believed we were going to launch a tiger-cat and all we got ashore was a stranded whale. The second was when he allowed General Mark Clark to disobey his orders in June 1944 and seize Rome instead of first destroying the retreating German army, which thus escaped to reform and to fight resolutely for almost another full year.

When the war was over Churchill placed Alexander at the centre of his Pantheon of heroes. He saw as much of him as he could and found him, as an equally gifted amateur painter, as good a companion in peace as a comrade in war. Alex had surprisingly advanced political views. He was an enemy of class distinction and said he was alarmed by it in his own Brigade of Guards. He was one of the earliest protagonists of a generous policy to defeated Germany, believing she should be invited to join NATO and be treated as an equal in the concourse of the nations. He was, in sum, a man incapable of pettiness or hatred: always calm, detached and precise, always ready to examine dispassionately another's point of view.

He was happy as Governor General of Canada, the last Briton to be chosen for that office by a Canadian Government. The Canadians, sensible of the leadership he had given their armed forces in war, were captivated by the simplicity with which he performed his duties as the King's representative. They loved both him and his wife, Margaret, who reciprocated their feelings to such an extent that at one time they planned to settle in Canada when the term of Governor Generalship ended.

In January 1952, Churchill descended on Rideau Hall, the Governor General's official residence at Ottawa. While he was there he sent for General Templer. Most favourably impressed by him and reinforced in this by Alex, whose view he had solicited, as well as by the CIGS, Slim, Churchill asked Templer to take command in Malaya where an intractable Communist revolt had foiled all attempts at suppression. Templer's subsequent mastery of the situation earned him too a secure place in Churchill's Pantheon.

During his stay at Rideau Hall Churchill made an impetuous decision. He asked Alexander to leave Canada and join his Government as Minister of Defence. No prospect could have pleased Alexander less. He did have political, or at least diplomatic skill, as his handling of many diverse national contingents during the Italian campaign proved; but he was not by temperament or inclination a domestic politician. He told me he was well aware that from the time of Cromwell onwards the British people had mistrusted generals in political office. He thought that neither Wellington nor Kitchener had been good advertisements for the opposite point of view. However, such was his love of Churchill, and so instinctive his attitude of obedience to higher command, that he did as he was asked, forsook his beloved Canada and became one of the least effective Ministers of Defence on record. The incident endorsed what was already known: Alexander was a man who invariably put duty before personal predilection. It was that as much as all his other graces and virtues which so endeared him to Churchill.

There is pleasure in contrast, especially when it embraces two subjects of exceptional merit. Montgomery was a complete contrast to Alexander in manner, method and personality. There were indeed, as far as Churchill was concerned, three distinct faces of Monty. When one of them was on display, the other two were only dimly recognizable.

First there was the general, exercising rare qualities of leadership, raising fallen morale and exuding confidence so infectious that it filled the humblest private soldier no less than the divisional commander. This was the man unwilling to contemplate anything but victory, discarding potential dead wood long before it had begun to rot, explaining his objectives in terms that were at once simple and exhilarating, a master of lucidity in his written and spoken orders. Churchill perceived his ability early in July 1940 when he visited the Third Division at Brighton and discovered that its commander shared his conviction about the method of repelling invasion. There should be no thin line of troops to defend the beaches: our best equipped surviving forces, and such armour as we could muster, would be concentrated inland, endowed with all possible means of mobility, and stand ready to counter-attack as soon as enemy beach-heads were established. When Churchill went to Brighton, the Third Division was immobile. He took immediate steps to have that remedied in keeping with Monty's ideas and his own. He commented adversely on Monty's practice of making his men go for a three-mile run every morning before breakfast: he thought the order smacked of Victorian schoolboy fetishes. In every other respect he gave high marks to this general he had never met before.

When General Hobart, an eccentric tank expert whose gifts Churchill wished to exploit, was criticized by the CIGS, Churchill replied, 'You cannot expect to have the genius type with a conventional copy-book style.' He might equally have applied the words to Monty. Nevertheless, Monty, his thoughts intent on implementing his own crystal-clear decisions, was often high-handed. It required patience and diplomacy to sort out his disputes with Eisenhower and Omar Bradley, and tolerance to disregard his tactless denigration of those who disagreed with him. He loved to impress, but instead of relying on his deeds to achieve that end, he was inclined to make remarks that were nothing short of hair-raising. The Eighth Army, he said at Marrakech on New

Year's Day 1944, would vote in the next General Election as he told them to vote; and he was certainly seeking for effect when he said on the same occasion, 'My army chaplains are of greater importance to me than my artillery'. I was not surprised when later that year a distinguished visitor, returning from Twenty-first Army Group Headquarters, said that Monty was one of nature's fascists. His style was that of the American General MacArthur, but being nearer home he was a trifle easier to control.

The least attractive of his traits was the egocentricity which often marred his conversation and led him to the heights, or depths, of exhibitionism. One of the worst examples of this, at any rate in my experience, was in January 1945 when Monty's vigorous intervention, and assumption of command on the northern salient, was a major factor in stemming the last great German offensive against the Americans in the Ardennes. That Monty should have had to be summoned to the rescue was in any case a humiliation for Eisenhower and Bradley. It would have been wise to let the course of events speak for themselves. Monty, however, chose to hold a press conference at which he spoke in such jingoistic and self-satisfied terms that Churchill felt he had no option but to send, and publish, a telegram of congratulation to General Omar Bradley on a success that would, in other circumstances, have been hard to identify.

That was the harmful side of Monty's egocentricity. It was perpetuated after the war when he set himself to diminish Eisenhower's reputation as a general. There was a less distressing, in some ways almost an endearing side. I went with Churchill to Monty's field headquarters in March 1945 to watch the crossing of the Rhine. His camp was in the middle of a pine forest, surrounding a rectangular clearing that had once been a riding-school. He had provided two caravans for the Prime Minister, one for work and one for sleep, but his own were the more fascinating. One had belonged to the defeated Italian General Berganzoli, known as 'Electric Whiskers' by the British press, and another had been captured from General Messe. A third, fitted as a map-room, was full of caged canaries. All the caravans were decorated with photographs of Monty himself, though I did count in addition three large ones of Rommel and one of Rundstedt.

He may, as Air Chief Marshal Maori Coningham once told me, have been ruthless in his demands for the destruction of French towns and villages during the Normandy campaign, demands which Coningham asserted that he sometimes refused. But he did not lightly sacrifice lives. Indeed he took every measure he could to avoid so doing, and he was the soul of chivalry to the captives and the vanquished. As a rigidly professional soldier his task was to win battles, by whatever means, not to wreak vengeance or to punish the aggressor. When it was all over, Monty's third face soon became visible, and Churchill, who had always defended him, and tolerantly forgiven the troubles he suffered from the recurring disagreements with Eisenhower, became deeply attached to him.

The third face of Monty was smiling and lovable. He would arrive at Chartwell lugging a case of plum brandy he had brought from Tito as a gift to Churchill, or a case of port from Salazar. He would play croquet with Clementine Churchill, who was expert at the game, announcing his tactics as if he were directing a battle. On one occasion, I remember, the game ended in disarray, for Monty ill-advisedly announced that all politicians were dishonest. The lightning that thereupon flashed from Clementine ('How dare you have the ill-bred impudence to say such a thing in my house!') burned the Field-Marshall to a cinder. He was soon forgiven, and whether he was CIGS under a Labour government or chairman of all the NATO commanders-in-chief at Fontainebleau and Deputy Supreme Allied Commander to Eisenhower, he was a regular attendant on the Churchills.

He was evidently lonely and he felt the need to attach himself to a closely knit family circle. Sir Gerald Templer told me a story about Monty which seems to explain much. He adored his wife, who meant more to him than all other human beings combined. She was in India with him when the Quetta earthquake struck and she flung herself into the ruins to help drag out the maimed and the trapped. She overdid herself and, according to Templer, was infected by a slow-working oriental infection. Back in England she grew weaker and in 1937 died in Monty's arms, having been fatally poisoned by an insect bite. Thenceforward he looked at no other woman, he spoke to nobody of his heartbreak and, as Templer put it, 'he rolled up his sleeves and got on with the job', saying to his officers when he returned from the funeral late for a conference: 'Gentlemen, I ask you to forgive this display of human weakness'. Being sincerely religious, he sought consolation in his Christian convictions, and more than ever he became the one-track-minded, dedicated professional soldier; but deep within him there was a great loneliness.

When Churchill was again Prime Minister, Monty would come over from Fontainebleau, self-invited but always welcome, to join week-end gatherings at Chequers and Chartwell. He tried to lobby Churchill on matters of foreign policy. The Prime Minister would listen good-naturedly, but he thought it a pity Monty should express opinions about matters on which he was not an expert, and although Churchill was no lover of the Foreign Office, he did rise in its defence when Monty stated with undue emphasis that Foreign Office officials had 'a rigid, constipated mentality'. He looked across at me and said, 'I hope, for his sake, that Jock is not constipated. And I have never found him rigid.'

He would fire questions at the Prime Minister as from a machine gun, loving to act the part of Grand Inquisitor. How did Churchill define a great man? Was Hitler great? Certainly not, said Churchill; he made too many mistakes. How could Churchill maintain that Napoleon was great when he was the Hitler of the nineteenth century? He was not, Churchill replied. Surely the only really great men were the religious leaders? Churchill's reply to that interested me, for he seldom spoke of religion. He said that their greatness was undisputed, but it was of a different kind: Christ's story was unequalled and his death to save sinners unsurpassed; the Sermon on the Mount was the last word in ethics. Monty was content with this simple reply.

He had developed a liking for having his leg pulled, particularly by young people, to whom he was invariably kind and thoughtful. One evening at Chequers he was floored, and delighted, by a Spanish girl, Maria de Casa Valdes. 'You tell me,' she said, 'you don't drink and you don't smoke. What do you do that is wrong? Bite your nails?' My own daughter, aged four, was so entranced by his attentions that she said she would like to have 'Gomery' for her daddy and I could be the gardener. Monty promptly sent her a book, suitably inscribed.

It is worth recording one conversation that took place at

Chequers in August 1953. Monty was alone with the Prime Minister and me. Churchill admonished him for a series of derogatory remarks about Eisenhower, and this led to a discussion about the errors the Americans had made in the last two years of the war. Military historians may not agree, but Churchill and Monty considered that they had made four capital mistakes. The first was doing at Anzio what General Stopford did at Suvla Bay in 1915: clinging to the beaches and failing to establish positions inland. The second was insistence on 'Operation Anvil', the August 1944 landing in the south of France, thus destroying Alexander's chances of taking Trieste and Vienna. Thirdly, for internal political rather than for strategic reasons, Eisenhower had refused to let Monty concentrate the power of the push eastwards from Normandy on the left flank. The decision to make a broad advance across northern France, rather than the concentrated punch on the left that Monty strenuously advocated, had given Rundstedt his chance to counter-attack in the Ardennes and had prolonged the war. Finally, they agreed that it had been disastrous to allow the Russians to occupy Berlin, Prague and Vienna, all of which could have been entered first by the Americans. If Eisenhower had been present, he would doubtless have disputed these accusations, though judging from some of his subsequent statements, General Marshall might have agreed with several of them. They certainly represented Churchill's and Montgomery's mature reflections nearly ten years after the events.

In Monty's mellow retirement, he delighted to entertain friends for luncheon at Isington Mill, near Alton. There was always rice pudding to eat; hung on the walls were countless photographs of great men standing with Monty, all signed in full by Monty himself as well as by the great men; there were walks in the garden, where newly planted shrubs stood rigidly in line, tallest on the right and shortest on the left; there was a visit to the row of caravans that had been such a feature of Twenty-first Army Group Headquarters. There was acid criticism of politicians in general and of the government of the day in particular. But in these clinical surroundings, where a woman's taste and touch were so clearly needed, Monty was benign, and none who went there left without feeling happier, conscious that beneath their host's unbending, egotistic, austere and carping exterior there was a heart of true honesty and a yearning for human sympathy that had been too long denied.

When Churchill's powers began to fail Monty was not one to desert him. Sometimes he sought to embroil him in mischievous initiatives, as when, at the time of the Suez episode, he persuaded him to join, to the annoyance of the Chiefs of Staff, in pressing for a landing at Mersa Matruh and an armoured sweep on Cairo. Principally, however, his mission was one of companionship and comfort. His name appears twelve times in sequence in the visitor's book at Chartwell. There the two old men would sit together, Churchill mainly silent while Monty reminisced about the triumphs and the tragedies of days gone by. Monty was prone to start a sentence: 'In the evening of my life...'. It was a radiant and a peaceful evening, one in which he did much to brighten that of Winston Churchill too.

CHAPTER TEN

Anthony Eden

Anthony Eden was twenty-three years younger than Winston Churchill. When he entered Parliament, after courageous war service with the Rifle Brigade, Churchill was already a renowned, if not universally approved, statesman who had held six important ministerial offices and was about to hold a seventh, the Exchequer. It was not under Churchill's aegis that Eden served his political apprenticeship, but under that of Sir Austen Chamberlain, a man of noble character who, as Lord Birkenhead characteristically said, 'always played the game – and always lost it'. Eden was his Parliamentary Private Secretary for three years and as Chamberlain was Foreign Secretary, his indentures were served in the department which was to be his spiritual home.

He was tall and handsome, intelligent and matured by the experience of war. Holding both the Military Cross and a first-class honours degree from Oxford in oriental studies, he was the Conservative party's ideal recruit, sure to make an impact on Parliament and the public, clearly destined for early promotion. He soon attracted the attention of Stanley Baldwin, who was not one of Churchill's heroes. Indeed Churchill obstinately declined to admit the merits Baldwin had. In the early years of the war, when the crowds bayed at their former idol, believing that he more than any other man was responsible for the country's lack of preparation (a guilt that was theirs still more than Baldwin's), Churchill did take pity on him, invited him to Downing Street and showed him all the tenderness he could. Nevertheless, nothing would convince him that Baldwin and his followers had been anything but a national disaster and he described him to me as the greatest of non-statesmen, softening his verdict a little by adding that 'the climate of public opinion on people is overwhelming'.

Eden was thus one of Baldwin's men. He was Lord Privy Seal in 1934 and joined the Cabinet with a special responsibility for League of Nations affairs. In 1935, two years before Baldwin handed over to Neville Chamberlain, he became Foreign Secretary. He was quickly recognized, at home and abroad, as a clever and tireless negotiator, and as a man with high ideals. Churchill, at this time, was in the wilderness, an almost solitary figure fighting Baldwin tooth and nail over India, defence and, finally, the abdication of Edward VIII.

Times changed and Churchill's feelings for Eden changed with them. Eden was resolved to be master of foreign policy. There were two obstacles. The first was the Permanent Under-Secretary, Sir Robert Vansittart, a man of so powerful, albeit volatile, an intellect and personality that the world believed him to be the true source of all Foreign Office initiative. Eden overcame this obstacle by leaving him in his spacious room overlooking Horse Guards Parade, persuading Neville Chamberlain to appoint him Chief Diplomatic Adviser to the Government, an office with a resounding title but no power, and replacing him as Permanent Under-Secretary by Sir Alexander Cadogan who had a smaller room but greater authority.

The second obstacle proved insurmountable. Chamberlain knew little of foreign affairs but, obsessed by his determination to avoid war, he sought to conduct them from 10 Downing Street with the co-operation of Sir Horace Wilson, whose experience stemmed mainly from the Ministry of Labour and who had been appointed Chief Industrial Adviser to the Government in 1930. Sitting at No. 10, next door to the Cabinet Room, the Chief Intrial Adviser, unlike the Chief Diplomatic Adviser, had real power. He did not use it incontinently, and he did not aspire to create policy; but Chamberlain consulted him on all things, including foreign affairs, and as the views of 10 Downing Street were in some respects diametrically opposed to those of the Foreign Office, Wilson became the reddest of rags to every Foreign Office bull and to Anthony Eden in particular.

In February 1938 things came to a head. Chamberlain wanted to make friends with Mussolini by acknowledging the Italian conquest of Abyssinia, and he turned down a proposal of President Roosevelt for an international conference in Washington to discuss

outstanding problems in Spain and elsewhere. Eden, in total disagreement, exasperated by the Prime Minister's evident intention
to conduct foreign affairs in accordance with his own policy of
appeasement, resigned. He did so three weeks before Hitler seized
Austria and eight months before the Munich agreement. Lord
Halifax reigned in his stead.

Churchill had assembled a small body of Members of Parliament and public figures who were as opposed as he was to appeasing the dictators. They had looked upon Eden as the one member
of the Government who could be relied upon to be firm. His
resignation brought them anguish: Churchill, who had grown to
like and admire him, described it as physical anguish. Eden did
not overtly join the rebellious Churchill clique, but he sympathized
with them more and more as the months went by and the war-
clouds massed on the horizon. By September 1939, Chamberlain's
supporters placed him second only to Churchill among the dis-
sidents, and Churchill considered him a trusted friend and ally.

With the outbreak of war the dissident Tories had to be accom-
modated. Churchill entered the War Cabinet as First Lord of the
Admiralty and Eden became Secretary of State for the Dominions.
It was certain that when Churchill became Prime Minister, his
talents would be more fully employed, but since Churchill was
determined to form a government of reconciliation, Halifax must
remain at the Foreign Office and Eden was therefore appointed
Secretary of State for War. Apart from charming the generals and
taking an active part in the frenzied efforts to make military preparation for invasion, his scope was limited; for defence policy
was no longer a primary responsibility of the political heads of
the service departments. It is even questionable whether he was a
good Secretary of State for War: his permanent Under-Secretary,
Sir James Grigg, said loudly to all and sundry that he was not.
'The man is complete junk,' he announced to a shocked audience
of soldiers and civil servants one summer morning at No. 10.

However that might be, Churchill believed in Eden. Although
he did, in a moment of temporary hallucination, propose sending
Lloyd George to the Embassy in Washington when Lord Lothian
died, he was on reflection delighted to be able to send Lord Halifax
there, thus enabling him to restore Eden to the seat at the Foreign
Office he had vacated three years previously. There was no

question of Churchill leaving Eden an entirely free hand, for he conducted relations with America personally and he interfered as and when he chose with any aspect of foreign policy that took his fancy. But Churchill was not Chamberlain: for the duration of the war Eden, with only occasional grumbles, was content to be Churchill's lieutenant. He was serving, on terms of intimate friendship and collaboration, a man whose personality dominated the scene almost as much abroad as at home. There were times when Churchill felt Eden should have wider experience, with a view to his own future, and on several occasions he thought of moving him from the Foreign Office to become Lord President of the Council with responsibility for many aspects of policy at home. Once he seriously considered becoming Foreign Secretary himself, as well as Minister of Defence, and running the Foreign Office from No. 10, as Lord Salisbury had done in Queen Victoria's reign.

For Churchill to intervene in foreign policy was one thing, but if anybody else did so, or criticized Eden's decisions, his wrath knew no bounds. In June 1941 he stormed into No. 10 complaining that Sir Stafford Cripps, who changed his opinion every five minutes, had the impertinence to want to teach *him* how to manage foreign affairs. Again, later in the war, Beaverbrook and Brendan Bracken were closeted with the Prime Minister at midnight making an ineffectual effort to persuade him to oppose the Welfare State proposals due for discussion by the Cabinet. The telephone rang and, answering it, I was subjected to a torrent of hysterical rage by Eden about a paper from Lindemann which Churchill had sent him. This paper flatly denied certain Foreign Office assertions about the starvation facing Europe. Eden told me in tones of almost falsetto fury that he would resign if inexpert, academic opinions were sought on matters to which he, as Foreign Secretary, had given much thought. Crushed by this outburst, I was at last able to interject that he had better complain to the Prime Minister rather than to me. I went next door to tell Churchill what was happening and he picked up the telephone. While Beaverbrook and Bracken listened, Eden ranted in a way Churchill said he had never heard before. He handled his furious friend in an adept and paternal way. He would take Lindemann's paper back and go into the matter himself; Anthony should not vex himself with such matters at the end of a long, wearying day; there was only one thing Churchill would not allow, and he was sure Anthony agreed, and that was the feeding of liberated Europe at the expense of hard-rationed Britain. When it was over, Churchill turned to us and said, 'I am not quite sure what is happening to Anthony.'

Such outbursts were comparatively rare in the war and, in general, Churchill defended Eden against all comers. He was not, however, muted in private criticism. As early as July 1941, he said to me that in Oliver Lyttelton, who was *persona grata* to the Tory party and had established his reputation as Minister of State in Egypt, Eden now had a competitor for the future leadership. He was doubtful of Eden's standing in the House and in the party. However, he personally would stand by him, because he so admired his physical and moral courage. 'He would equally well charge a battery or go to the stake for his principles, though the principles might be wrongly conceived and he might charge the battery from the wrong angle.'

On another occasion, Eden sent Churchill the text of a speech he proposed to make in Glasgow. The Prime Minister spent the whole of dinner correcting it, making penetrating comments and grumbling, as he improved the English, that Eden was only half-educated and had not added to his learning by subsequent reading.

After the 1945 General Election there were many, including Clementine Churchill, who felt that Churchill should be content with what he had achieved and retire from politics. His evident successor was Eden. Now, between 1945 and 1951, Eden, one of whose shining virtues was loyalty, made no move to claim what most of his followers thought his due. He must have known there were intrigues afoot, but if Churchill chose to stay, then he would have no part at all in them.

Eden was not only loyal; he was a man of absolute personal integrity. He became Foreign Secretary again in October 1951, just when the ever weeping or fainting Prime Minister Mossadeq was stirring anti-British feelings in Persia. There was a crisis facing the Anglo-Persian Oil Company, as British Petroleum was formerly called. Eden was not a rich man. Most of his small capital had been invested for many years past in Anglo-Persian Oil shares. Should he sell them, since he was officially involved in a dispute with Persia? All his friends said it was unnecessary: his was a long-standing, long-term investment bearing no relationship to the current troubles. His conscience defied this advice: he sold all his shares at the lowest price they ever commanded. Vain he might be, and easily driven to frenzy by personal attacks in the newspapers; but nothing would induce him to veer an inch from the path of honesty.

The 1951 Government marked a steady deterioration in the relationship of Churchill and Eden. Churchill would still say that their political instincts were the same, that if they were thousands of miles apart they would reach an identical conclusion on any issue of importance that arose. But it was no longer true. By April 1952, less than six months after the new Government had been formed, there were signs of a rift over policy towards Egypt, where Colonel Neguib had dethroned and succeeded the self-indulgent King Farouk. Eden, I wrote at the time, 'is rather discredited in Winston's eyes at present'.

A few months later he married Jack Churchill's beautiful daughter Clarissa. The reception was at 10 Downing Street and Churchill was delighted; but family ties did nothing to impede mounting irritation. Eden was no longer prepared as he had been in the war to admit Prime Ministerial interference in the affairs of his department. While he was still on his honeymoon he learned that Churchill and Truman, with the approval of the Foreign Office and the oil companies, had dispatched a joint message to Mossadeq. He sent an indignant protest from Lisbon; but he was objecting to the method, not to the substance of the message. Churchill had stolen his thunder.

During the winter of 1952–3 Eden's health gave grounds for worry and in the spring of 1953 he was obliged to relinquish his duties temporarily while arrangements were made for an internal operation by a surgeon in Boston, Massachusetts. This operation took place in the very week of June that Churchill had a stroke. In the meanwhile, on 12 May, Churchill made a speech in the House of Commons that had a startling effect. It stated his own policy; it was not in accordance with Foreign Office thought, and it would not have been approved by Eden. It called for an end to the cold war and a new approach to relations with the Soviet Union.

Churchill recovered from his stroke at least as fast as Eden from his serious operation. At the end of August 1953, the Edens came to Chequers. He was thin and frail, but he displayed the courage and good manners that were natural to him. No business was transacted, but there were three underlying problems of which nobody spoke but everybody was aware. They related to the Middle East, to Russia and to the date that Churchill might surrender office to the universally accepted successor, Anthony Eden.

Eden wanted a treaty with the new Egyptian Government, of which Abdul Gamal Nasser was now the leader. In return for the establishment of British civil contractors in the Suez Canal zone, the large British garrison there would be withdrawn. Churchill did not trust Nasser and had no intention of agreeing to the withdrawal of British troops. Most of the Cabinet agreed with Eden, but a few supported Churchill who sat, like Buddha, brooding and immovable. One day Eden asked me to go and see him at the Foreign Office. He believed that I might be able to influence Churchill and that as a member of the Foreign Service it was my duty to do so. His voice was harsh and querulous. Could I not make the Prime Minister see that by means of a treaty with Egypt we could replace an expensive military presence in the Canal zone with the lasting gratitude and friendship of the Egyptian Government and people? I could not; but the explosion of the first hydrogen bomb did. Churchill concluded that this new weapon, 'as far removed from the atom bomb, as the atom bomb was from the bow and arrow' (an eloquent Churchillian exaggeration), repainted the whole strategic picture. He gave way; an Anglo-Egyptian treaty was signed; but, alas, as Eden discovered two years later, we had not won the lasting gratitude and friendship of the Egyptian Government and people.

Eden was no longer as calm as he had once been. Perhaps it was his illness; perhaps it was inability to stand up to strain. There were frequent bouts of ill temper, not with the Prime Minister, whom he continued to treat with courtesy and for whom he clearly felt a real affection, but with his officials in the Foreign Office, who did not have the same regard for him as in years past, and sometimes with his colleagues in the Government. He was uneasy, and his uneasiness was contagious.

With backward glances to Churchill's intervention on behalf of the Whites during the Russian revolution, and to his unfaltering antagonism to Communism at home and abroad, most people assumed that there was no more resolute anti-Soviet figure in the western world. I first became aware that this was not so on 22 June 1941, the day Hitler attacked Russia. That evening, after Churchill's stirring speech calling for solidarity with our new allies, there was a dinner party at Chequers. The question at issue was whether a debate in the House of Commons should be confined to the military aspects of the situation or a broader discussion be encouraged. Eden and Lord Cranborne declared that Russia's regime was in most ways as despicable as Germany's and that half the country would object to being associated with it. Churchill argued to the contrary with passion: Russia was now at war, innocent peasants were being slaughtered, we should forget about the Soviet system and the Comintern and we must give every ounce of help we could offer to fellow human beings in distress. As for those like Sir John Dill, who said that Russian resistance would crumble in six weeks before the superb German military machine he would bet that in two years' time Russia would still be fighting, and fighting victoriously. The generals should read about Napoleon and the 1812 retreat from Moscow.

The war ended with shameless rapacity on Stalin's part and the descent of the Iron Curtain. Churchill had been among the first, after the Tehran conference, to scent the danger, and a few years later, while he was Leader of the Opposition, both he and Eden were in complete accord with Ernest Bevin's confrontation with the dour, impenetrable Molotov. He startled and influenced the whole world with his Iron Curtain speech at Fulton, Missouri. All the same, when Stalin died in March 1953, Churchill thought the time had come to work for a period of 'easement': to proceed warily indeed, until the character of the new Soviet regime was better known, but not to shut all doors by a policy of persistent hostility.

Eden did not agree. He was set on retaining the painfully consolidated strength of NATO and the Western alliance, and in this he was reinforced by the advice of both the Foreign Office and the State Department in Washington. Churchill said that a negative attitude consigned us to years and years of hatred and hostility. It was anybody's guess how Malenkov, Stalin's successor, might behave, but it would be a grave responsibility not to try for a genuine *détente*.

During a visit to Washington in July 1954 there was a lively discussion about Guatemala where an aggressive Communist regime was temporarily in power. Churchill supported the American view that a tough line should be adopted against it. Eden preached caution and was out-argued by Churchill in the presence of the American leaders. As he was going to bed that night Churchill said to me, 'Anthony is sometimes very foolish. He is prepared to quarrel with the Americans over some petty Central American issue, which is much more their affair than ours, and to forget about the downtrodden millions in Poland.' As I went to my own bedroom, I reflected with sorrow that the much vaunted identity of view between Prime Minister and Foreign Secretary was wearing thin.

We returned home by sea. Churchill decided to send a telegram to Molotov proposing an exploratory meeting in Moscow, and he proposed to send it without first consulting the Cabinet. A new cold war broke out: between Churchill and Eden. It was my unhappy lot to act as the intermediary, employed on a peripatetic service between their two cabins.

Eden was the more reasonable of the two. He told me he disliked the whole thing. He had been weighing up the pros and cons. The cons included the danger of a rift with the United States, the certain antipathy of Adenauer in Western Germany, the damage to a common front so laboriously built in Europe; and the practical certainty that the expectations of the British people, excited to fever pitch by Churchill's initiative, would be disastrously disappointed. He thought the cons far outweighed the pros, but what he disliked above all was the Prime Minister's intention to send the telegram without first consulting the Cabinet.

Back I went to Churchill and was told that Eden's views were nonsense. He was only proposing to make an unofficial enquiry of Molotov. If it were accepted, that would be the time to consult the Cabinet. I interjected that he would be putting the Cabinet on the spot, for if Molotov sent a favourable reply to the unofficial enquiry, it would be impossible for the Cabinet to reject the policy. 'You are,' he said 'as bad as Anthony. It must be your Foreign Office training.' Anyhow, he would make it a question of confidence. The Cabinet – and perhaps the country – must decide between losing him and thwarting his intentions. He then said that he would first submit the draft telegram to the Cabinet provided Eden would say that he favoured it in principle. Back I went to Eden who weakly and unhappily gave way.

This was Churchill in a mood that I had seldom seen since the war. I wrote in my diary: 'I am afraid the PM has been ruthless and unscrupulous in all this, because he must know that at this moment, for both internal and international reasons, Eden cannot resign – though he told me, while all this was going on, that he had thought of it.' Churchill subsequently admitted to me that he had deliberately planned not to consult the Cabinet. They would raise objections and cause delay. The stakes were so high, and the possible benefits so crucial to our survival, that he was prepared to adopt any methods to ensure a meeting with the Russians was arranged.

Churchill was losing confidence in Eden. The next evening on board there was a dinner party in Churchill's private dining-room. All was friendly and even jovial until a telegram arrived from Washington recording that Senator Knowland had made a speech implying that the British were pressing the United States to let Red China join the United Nations. Churchill wanted to issue a denial to the effect that the matter had not been seriously discussed in Washington and there was no question of Britain's backing such a move while China was still at war with the United Nations in Korea. Eden replied that if we made any such statement it would wreck all his chances of successful talks about a Korean peace at Geneva and that we ought in any case to keep entry into the United Nations as a reward for China if she behaved well in the negotiations. Churchill looked grave. He had not realized, he said, that what Senator Knowland alleged was in fact the truth: Eden *did* contemplate the admission of China to the United Nations while a state of war still existed. Eden went red in the face with fury and there was a disagreeable scene. They both went off to bed in a combination of sorrow and anger, Churchill saying that Eden was totally incapable of distinguishing the things that mattered from those that did not.

The next day Churchill told Eden that, providing he always bore in mind the importance of not quarrelling with the Americans over

Far-Eastern questions, which affected them more than us, a way ought finally to be found of bringing China into the United Nations on terms tolerable to the United States. After this olive branch had been offered, he spent the next ten minutes quoting Pope, Shakespeare and sundry other poets, Eden following with a dissertation on the beauty of Persian and Arabic writings. Thus the voyage ended amiably, Eden having shown that he gave precedence to loyalty over personal judgment, a far cry from the day when he resigned from Neville Chamberlain's Government.

There was trouble in the Cabinet over the Molotov telegram, Lord Salisbury and another Minister threatening to resign; but the Russians saved the day by producing an unrealistic suggestion for a meeting of thirty-two powers to discuss a Russian European security plan. Churchill's intention to visit Moscow was temporarily placed in suspense.

This was an unpropitious background to the issue that loomed large in Eden's mind: Churchill's retirement. He was too loyal to press for it, too principled to intrigue for it. Yet Churchill, who in 1951 had proposed to stay in office for one year only, had extended his tenure to cover the coronation, then to await the Queen's return from a long tour of Australia and New Zealand, and then to give Eden time to recover his full strength. In March 1954 he suggested to Eden the end of the session in July. Then, his eyes set on an agreement with Russia as his last service to his country, he spoke of September. Now that plan too was changed. He told me he would not be hounded out of office merely because his second-in-command wanted the job, and he spoke with distaste of 'Anthony's hungry eyes'. Eden had far better start afresh after the next General Election.

This prevarication was partly that of an old man reluctant to abandon the authority he had held so long. But that was not the whole story. He had begun to doubt Eden's qualifications for the highest political office and, conscious of his own towering position in the country and the world, he continually drew attention to the ineffectiveness of Lord Rosebery after Gladstone and A. J. Balfour after Lord Salisbury. Might not Eden after Churchill be the same? There were some of his colleagues – Lord Swinton, Sir David Maxwell-Fyfe, Sir Walter Monckton and, to some extent, the Chancellor of the Exchequer, R. A. Butler – who also thought that the stepping-down of Churchill would open a gap hard to fill.

On 4 April 1955, the night before he finally resigned, Churchill gave a large dinner party for the Queen and the Duke of Edinburgh at 10 Downing Street. When it was all over and the guests had departed, I went upstairs with him to his bedroom. He drew back the curtains and pulled up the blind. Then, still dressed in black knee-breeches, resplendent in the Garter and the Order of Merit, he sat on the bed and gazed into the night. I said nothing, for I supposed he was reflecting on the years he had been at Downing Street, on the weary climb to the top, on war and victory, on his endeavours to control the aftermath. But I was misreading his thoughts, which were of the future, not the past. For he suddenly turned to me with a penetrating, almost frightening stare. All he said was: 'I don't believe Anthony can do it.'

CHAPTER ELEVEN

The Colleagues

Churchill's friends were almost exclusively drawn from circles with which he had professional contact. Whether politicians or Civil Servants, soldiers or sailors, they were men whom he had come to know for other than social purposes. It is natural that the majority of those whose company he enjoyed were politicians, and all but a few were Conservatives. The House of Commons was not just his platform and his stalking-ground; it was his second home and he was at his happiest talking and relaxing in its smoking-room. For Churchill, talking was relaxation. There were but few members he disliked, whatever their party and however much he wrangled with them across the floor of the House. James Maxton, fiery leader of the extreme left wing Independent Labour Party, won his golden opinions and he even had a soft spot for the solitary Communist, Willy Gallagher. In return, most Members of Parliament were well disposed to him personally, and there were some, before and during his years of greatness, who were particularly susceptible to the enchantment of his magic flute. Top of that list was the man whom Beaverbrook chose as his personal Aunt Sally, the leader of the Liberal Party, Sir Archibald Sinclair.

Sinclair had an air of distinction. With his fine features, black hair and swarthy complexion he resembled a Spanish grandee rather than the Highland chieftain that he was. His delivery as a speaker was slow. He had a stammer which attracted attention and lent emphasis. His oratory was not of the first order, but his words were carefully chosen and he had a gift for imagery and allusion. During the Norway debate leading to Neville Chamberlain's fall, his attack was notable for both its venom and its originality. He compared the policy of the Government with Macaulay's description of the British general, Lord Galway, at the battle of Almanza in 1707: 'He thought it more honourable to fail according to the rules than to succeed by innovation.' Chamberlain and Churchill tripped him up twice on points of detail, but his speech stood up well to those of other powerful parliamentarians on that historic day.

He was more a nineteenth-century Whig, like Churchill himself, than a twentieth-century Liberal. Starting his career in the fashionable Second Life Guards, he became in due course second-in-command of the battalion of the Royal Scots Fusiliers that Churchill commanded in the trenches during the winter of 1915–16. For both of them this brotherhood in arms, short though it was in time, was an unbreakable link, forged in war but maintained in peace. Sinclair followed Churchill first to the War Office and then to the Colonial Office as his military Private Secretary in the years following the Armistice of 1918. He accompanied him on his travels to the Arab countries and elsewhere. Then he went into politics himself. The two friends were briefly of the same party, for Sinclair was elected Liberal MP for his own county of Caithness in 1922; but Churchill soon crossed the floor, back to the Conservative benches where his parliamentary career had begun. They parted at political crossways, their personal relationship remaining undisturbed.

In 1940 Sinclair had been leader of the Liberals for nine years, but his sole experience of office had been short, as Secretary of State for Scotland in Ramsay MacDonald's National Government of 1931. Only the formation of a coalition could bring him back into power, and that was an opportunity for which he could scarcely hope. The opportunity did come in 1940 and Churchill was delighted to welcome him as a colleague. The strength of the Liberal party was insufficient to warrant a place in the War Cabinet, but he bestowed on his friend the Air Ministry, considering the charge of a service department to be the most illustrious he could confer. Sinclair might know nothing about aeroplanes, but he was by training a fighting man and at that time most of the senior officers in the RAF had begun their careers as soldiers.

He had been an impassioned opponent of the Munich settlement. In the wake of it he became consumed with animosity against Neville Chamberlain whom he was accustomed to belabour in unmeasured terms. His conviction that only Churchill could save the country fuelled the fire of his antagonism to the men of Munich. During the first nine months of the war his criticisms revealed inside information which gave rise to suspicions on security grounds. His patriotism was undoubted, but his knowldege was suspect. So his telephone was tapped and Chamberlain was foolish enough to confront him with a transcript which was in itself comparatively harmless, but which contained remarks that Chamberlain thought should not have been made on a public telephone. Sinclair was indignant and did not mince his words. He threatened to expose the incident in the House of Commons, and it required Churchill's authority to dissuade him; but on the day Chamberlain fell, Sinclair had the courtesy to apologize to him for any insolence he had shown. His good manners always triumphed over his indignation.

Under Churchill's leadership, he accepted blame or criticism with exemplary grace. He sometimes received more than his due, for though Churchill would always defend him in the last resort, he admired his personal qualities more than his ministerial competence; and Beaverbrook's unremitting assaults on him and his ministry, addressed to the Prime Minister, did not fail to ricochet on to the ultimate target. He did not complain: he carried out his duties of administration, he visited all the RAF stations, he was polite to the air marshals and with the Chief of the Air Staff beside him he conscientiously attended the meetings at which the interests of the RAF were under discussion. In operational decisions he took no part at all. Perhaps his least fine hour was when, incited by the Air Council, he called for the resignation of Sir Hugh Dowding from Fighter Command in such a way as to hurt Dowding's feelings beyond repair.

When Churchill was away, Sinclair was sometimes a prey to attacks from Brendan Bracken, perhaps instigated by Beaverbrook. Thus in October 1944, when Churchill was in Moscow, I found myself the pig in the middle between Sinclair and Bracken, neither of whom would negotiate with the other direct. The point at issue was whether, as Sinclair wished, control of civil aviation should remain with the Air Ministry for the rest of the war. Bracken was determined it should not, but he demanded a ruling from No. 10. As there happened to be nobody at No. 10 that afternoon but me, this was awkward. The indirect battle consumed several hours, while other urgent work accumulated; but it seems that in the end the victory was mine, for I was able to write in my diary: 'Finally I produced for publication a document which, like the Second Prayerbook of King Edward VI, satisfied both parties'.

If Sinclair was at the top of Churchill's list of political friends on personal grounds (leaving aside, of course, Birkenhead, Bracken and Beaverbrook), it would be invidious to give any priority to the remainder of his favourites. One of them was Oliver Lyttelton, later Viscount Chandos. The son of an eminent late Victorian, Alfred Lyttelton, and of an almost equally eminent mother, he broke with the family tradition of cricket, politics and the Church and, after gallant war service in the Grenadier Guards, went into the City. There he became associated with the Bolivian Patino family and dabbled in tin. Nobody would have accused Lyttelton of being anything but an honourable man; but he did acquire a reputation in the City for being a trifle nimble, though his drive and ingenuity were widely noticed by Lord Beaverbrook and Brendan Bracken among others. His merits were brought to Churchill's attention. Remembering Alfred Lyttelton and impressed by his son, he decided that this was precisely the kind of talent which he could use.

Lyttelton was found a seat in the Commons. He was a lamentable speaker, but that was of little account in a House overburdened with good ones. He won praise as President of the Board of Trade and then he was elevated to membership of the War Cabinet and sent off to Cairo as Minister of State in the Middle East. He understood how to handle the generals and was firm with the ill-tempered pretensions of General de Gaulle. He came home with a reputation so well established that at one moment Churchill, forgetting his inadequacy as an orator, thought of him as a future Prime Minister. His reputation was still further enhanced when the Tories were in opposition after the war, and so in 1951 Churchill, who had developed an ill-judged liking for departmental overlords, contemplated an appointment which would have given him authority over R. A. Butler, the Chancellor of the Exchequer. In the event he was made Secretary of State for the Colonies, an office benighted by the Mau-Mau rebellion in Kenya, and remained there until the call of the City led him back to a dismal fate as Chairman of the rapidly declining company, Associated Electrical Industries.

Oliver Lyttelton was successful as a minister, and he was also a good companion. He was critical without being malevolent, so that when he suggested 'a little whisky and soda treason' before dinner, the ensuing conversation was exhilarating. Churchill was invigorated by his company, for apart from his quick wit, he wrote with scholarly ease and had a fund of information, literary as well as political, a love of the arts (which led him to be Chairman of the National Theatre) and a capacity for dissipating gloom by an optimism that he invariably contrived to make credible.

Lord Cranborne was known by that title during the war. By 1951, when he had a still greater part to play in Churchill's affairs, he was the fifth Marquess of Salisbury; but it is convenient to call him Cranborne to distinguish him from his father, one of the Tory king-makers who antagonized Beaverbrook by contributing to the choice of Stanley Baldwin as Prime Minister, and from his grandfather, the third Marquess, who was Prime Minister in Queen Victoria's reign and who, amongst other things, outwitted Lord Randolph Churchill, bringing his political career to its end. Churchill could never quite make up his mind whether to admire the House of Cecil or to resent it on his father's posthumous behalf. Two of its members he did consider close friends, with scarcely a backward glance. One was his best man, Lord Hugh Cecil, and the other was Lord Hugh's nephew, Cranborne. Since he was also amused by Cranborne's wife Betty, whom he greatly admired, the wind blew fair.

Entering the House of Commons in 1929, Cranborne followed the star of a man whose integrity he recognized and whose opinions he shared, Anthony Eden. He was Parliamentary Under-Secretary at the Foreign Office when Eden was Secretary of State and he had no hesitation in resigning with Eden in February 1938. He was a man adamant in his principles and appeasement of the dictators offended them.

He made all with whom he talked feel worth-while and important. On the closest of terms with the King and Queen, as well as with the Churchills, he took as much trouble, and was as genuinely interested, if he was conversing with the housemaid. He was calmly dispassionate. When Lloyd George went to see

Hitler, he was mesmerized by his charm. Other distinguished Englishmen were as easily deluded. Cranborne found the formidable Führer commonplace and irritatingly self-satisfied, though he detected a dangerous fanaticism in his eyes.

He was sincerely religious and he thought that even if, in this world, marquesses and knights of the Garter had certain privileges that were quite possibly ordained by God, every individual should be treated with courteous dignity. In consequence he had political opponents, for he was a High Tory, but no personal enemies and, apart from Beaverbrook, few consistent detractors.

In the wartime Coalition Cranborne spent most of the time as Secretary of State for the Dominions. He was as zealous as Churchill in keeping the Dominions fully informed and the sympathetic address, which endeared him to his Sovereign and his Prime Minister, was no less efficacious with Dominion Ministers and High Commissioners. When occasional difficulties arose, he smoothed ruffled feathers with a mixture of common sense, transparent honesty and a bedside manner that any doctor would have envied. In the Cabinet he said exactly what he thought, whether or not his views were likely to coincide with those of either the Foreign Secretary or the Prime Minister.

The time came when Churchill decided that Eden had been too long at the Foreign Office. If he were ever to be Prime Minister he must learn about home affairs and devote more time to the House of Commons. So in March 1944 Churchill thought of becoming Foreign Secretary himself, as well as Prime Minister and Minister of Defence. It was a curious fancy, induced, I believe, by the fact that one of the few high offices he had never held was Secretary of State for Foreign Affairs. He told me of this bizarre proposal when I was driving with him to Chequers. Realizing that it was a fantasy which would never be allowed to become fact by the King, Mrs Churchill or the Cabinet, I enquired why, if Eden was to be put out to pasture in new fields, he did not give the Foreign Office to Cranborne, whom he liked and respected so much. 'Cecils,' he replied, 'are always ill or resigning.'

However, a fortnight later, in April 1944, he did produce a list on which Cranborne's name appeared as Foreign Secretary. The Chief Whip warmly approved; so did the Secretary to the Cabinet. But he postponed the decision week after week,

declaring that when Cranborne was not ill he would be obstinate:
it would be a fortnight's illness alternating with a fortnight's
obstinacy. So the scheme was dropped and Eden stayed at the
Foreign Office while Beaverbrook pursued his vendetta against
Cranborne in the *Daily Express* and the *Evening Standard*.

After 1951 Cranborne, Leader of the House of Lords and
holder of a series of Cabinet appointments, was powerful in the
Tory party. When both Churchill and Eden were stricken with
illness, he was made acting Foreign Secretary and went on a mission
to Washington. He returned thence in August 1953, and told
Churchill, who was recovering in the sunshine at Chequers, that
Eisenhower had become violently Russophobe, even more so than
Dulles. He believed Eisenhower to be personally responsible for
the policy of useless pinpricks and harassing tactics that the United
States were pursuing against Russia in Europe and the Far East.
It sounded as if Cranborne might be more amenable to the policy
of 'easement' on which Churchill had set his heart than was
Anthony Eden.

So a few days later the idea of moving Eden from the Foreign
Office to the Lord Presidency of the Council was revived. Churchill decided that the choice of his successor rested between Cranborne and Harold Macmillan. The latter would be less obstinate,
and less of a martyr to rigid principles; but for the conduct of
business and foreign travel there was much to be said for a Foreign
Secretary in the House of Lords. The proposal was firmly declined
by Eden. He was expecting Churchill to resign any day and he
saw no point in a change for so short a time, although that was
not the reason he gave. If he had known he would have to wait a
further eighteen months he might have decided differently.

When the crisis broke in July 1954, over Churchill's desire
to meet the Russians, Cranborne was in both obstinate and
resigning mood. Lord Swinton represented to him that this was
the end of a voyage with Churchill and also that his resignation
would harm Anglo-American relations. Senator Knowland would
proclaim that Cranborne was leading a revolt against an anti-
American move by Churchill and Eden; and Eden himself would
be embarrassed. Cranborne was unmoved, and for a few days there
was the alarming prospect of Churchill himself resigning and telling the country why. There was brinkmanship on both sides.

When the Russians themselves inadvertently resolved this internal crisis, it remained none the less true that Cranborne was the only man for many years who had openly challenged Churchill in Cabinet and induced him to consider resignation. It was typical of both Churchill and Cranborne that for the rest of their lives their relationship and that of their wives was unimpaired; for they placed political quarrels in a compartment entirely separate from personal friendship.

In a different category altogether was Captain David Margesson, whom Churchill inherited from Neville Chamberlain as Chief Whip. A handsome man, with a winning personality and outgiving manner, he was at the same time a strict disciplinarian before whom recalcitrant Tory MPs quailed. He excelled as an organizer, but laid no claim to creative talent. Baldwin found him indispensable; so did Chamberlain; and so, to his own surprise, did Churchill. He had, as was his duty, opposed Churchill's moves before the war, regarding them as contrary to discipline and good order. He had done all he could to deter Conservative back-benchers from rallying to him. Churchill often spoke disparagingly of the Men of Munich but he respected their sincerity and had a greater distaste for the Labour and Liberal propagandists who had preached pacifism and then poured scorn on appeasement. Once Churchill was Prime Minister Margesson's course seemed clear to him: to honour his leader, obey instructions and, when invited, advise on suitable candidates for office. His orderly instincts did rebel against Churchill's constant changes of mind, for he failed to understand his habit of thinking aloud and was inclined to interpret gestatory remarks as if they were final decisions. He sometimes sighed for Neville Chamberlain's clarity of thought, and in September 1940, he said that the inclusion of Sir John Anderson in the War Cabinet would be the only hope for restoring administrative sanity.

Churchill liked him and relied on him. Margesson had a stifled ambition to be Ambassador in Washington, but he modestly said that he knew he did not carry big enough guns. A few days later, when Eden left the War Office to become Foreign Secretary, Churchill decided to make Margesson Secretary of State for War. He wanted to decline because he did not think himself adequate; but Churchill refused to take no for an answer. The Prime

Minister was reinforced in his choice when, a few days before he made the offer, Attlee said at Chequers that in all his dealings with the Labour party since 1931 David Margesson had never been anything but absolutely straight.

He was no mere cipher as Secretary of State for War. He disliked the project for an expedition to Greece in support of the heroic Greek army. He thought the British strategic position dangerous and when Eden, who with Wavell had strongly endorsed the plan, telegraphed to say, 'This is as tough a proposition as ever I have known', Margesson told me he thought the whole concept a disaster. He realized the Prime Minister's unwillingness to desert an ally we were pledged to support, but he did not believe we should allow ourselves to be diverted from our main North African strategy. After listening to him I wrote in my diary: 'The danger of another Norway, Dunkirk and Dakar all rolled into one looms threateningly before us.' We were trying to do too much with too little, and in consequence we gave Rommel his opening.

In February 1942 Singapore fell, a few weeks after Hong Kong and the whole of Malaya. The *Prince of Wales* and the *Repulse* had been uselessly sacrificed, and the British Government was subjected to a storm of criticism. The Dominions were stalwartly in support of Churchill and so were the United States. But in Parliament the Government were likely to find themselves at bay. Churchill judged that it was necessary to throw a morsel to the yapping hounds, and that morsel must be the Secretary of State for War. Margesson was sufficiently hardened a politician to accept and even to approve; but he was hurt by the method employed.

His Permanent Under-Secretary was Sir James Grigg, always known as P.J., the most outspoken of all Civil Servants and also one of the cleverest. He seemed to approve of Margesson, which was a relief, for only a few days before his appointment on my way back from lunch at the Travellers, I met P.J. who, 'after running down his Secretary of State [Eden] as usual, said that the only time he had any real power was when he was Private Secretary to Winston as Chancellor'. This statement had just a small element of truth, for at the Exchequer between 1924 and 1929 P.J., with his sharp brain and dominating will-power, did wield influence over Churchill. Clementine Churchill asserted that he bullied her husband. I am sure he was capable of being a bully, but I find it hard to believe that anyone ever succeeded in bullying Churchill. However that may be, Churchill retained vivid memories of his shrewdness, and since he harboured suspicions that his colleague Leopold Amery, Secretary of State for India, might hatch plots with the Viceroy, Lord Linlithgow, he appointed P.J. his Indian watch-dog. He was to receive all the India Office telegrams, digest them and report to Churchill. By February 1942 this had become a standard routine.

After Margesson had dutifully agreed to be the Singapore scapegoat, he was sitting at his desk in the War Office on a Sunday morning when P.J. put his head round the door to report that he had been summoned to Chequers. He had the file of India Office telegrams in his hand. Margesson commented that he would assuredly hear who his successor was to be. Late that evening P.J. reappeared. 'Well, who is to be?' asked Margesson. 'Me,' replied P.J. In the flurry of events Churchill had forgotten to let Margesson know that he was being replaced by his own senior Civil Servant. With his sense of discipline he took the blow and did not complain; but he was wounded.

Margesson was not forgotten. He was continually consulted by his successor as Chief Whip, James Stuart, and in 1944 Churchill tried unavailingly to persuade him to be Chairman of the Conservative party. James Stuart, with equal lack of success, ran Duncan Sandys as a rival candidate because he wanted the Government to be rid of him. He misjudged both Churchill and Duncan Sandys. As for P.J., he remained placidly at the War Office for the rest of the war, out of his depth in the House of Commons, an administrative asset to the war machine, but neither offering nor invited to contribute to strategic or political discussions. He ended as Chairman of Bass, competent to the last, still astringent in his comments, but forgotten by Churchill.

In the days at the Treasury to which P.J. looked back with nostalgia, Churchill's Parliamentary Private Secretary was Robert Boothby, and a little later he employed as a Private Secretary Patrick Buchan Hepburn. Boothby, quick of brain, fertile in ideas and a dynamic orator, was tipped as a future Prime Minister. He was ardent in his support of the anti-Munich group which Churchill led. He might, and indeed should, have gone far, but he became embroiled in a scandal relating to Czechoslovak gold and though he rigorously protested his innocence of any irregular conduct, the House of Commons raged angrily against him. Churchill, always sensitive to the misfortunes of those who had served him, deprecated the heat that was generated, calmed the Lord Chancellor, who was out for Boothby's blood without paying due heed to the arguments in his defence, and declared that there was nothing he disliked so much as a man-hunt. However, Boothby's prospects of high office did not revive and his gifts were never used to fruitful political ends.

It was otherwise with Patrick Buchan Hepburn, who was Chief Whip for the whole of Churchill's second administration. Tall and good-looking, with a crop of wavy fair hair, he was a painter of more than amateur status. He was finicky, highly strung, and prone to outbursts of ungovernable passion if his sensitive, artistic temperament was disturbed. Yet few found fault with him as Chief Whip and Churchill repaid his conscientious labours with confidence as well as affection. He became Minister of Works, for which his good taste made him an appropriate choice, and finally, as Governor-General of the short-lived Federation of the West Indies, he strove valiantly to make a reality of what in the event turned out to be an insubstantial pageant.

Nobody disliked Sir Walter Monckton. His mere entry into a room reaped a harvest of smiles. His company brought instantaneous conviction that all was for the best in a reasonable and benevolent world. He and General Alexander played in Fowler's Match in the same team and remained lifelong friends. That of itself was a recommendation in Churchill's eyes; but he also had memories of Monckton acting loyally for Edward VIII while retaining Baldwin's confidence, and Brendan Bracken praised him for his wartime services at the Ministry of Information. He was an eminent barrister, ambitious to succeed Lord Goddard as Lord Chief Justice; but Churchill conscripted him and turned him into an only semi-willing politician. The trouble with Monckton, almost the only trouble, was that he could not bear to make anybody unhappy. He was thus a natural appeaser and it has to be admitted that by 1951, when he was appointed Minister of Labour, Churchill was on the way to becoming one too. There was a threat of a rail strike which would have dislocated the Christmas holidays. Monckton was advised by his ministry to stand firm, though the thought of an unhappy Christmas for many who had hoped to visit their aged parents filled him with distress. Churchill was a prey to similarly sloppy sentiments. He sent for Monckton and conjured him to avert the strike by whatever measures were required. Monckton did as he was told: the railwaymen were given what they demanded; and poor Monckton earned a reputation as the architect of slippery slopes.

He and his wife, Biddy, who had a vivid personality, were welcomed with joy by both Winston and Clementine Churchill. Monckton supported Churchill in the Cabinet, judging with expert touch when to calm Eden, who was much in his debt over the handling of his private affairs, and when to employ his quiet, persuasive talents with Churchill. He rose high in favour and was offered the Home Office. He may perhaps have hoped that Churchill would influence Lord Goddard, whose anecdotal company was relished at Chequers, to retire in his favour. The difficulty was that Sir Hartley Shawcross, former Socialist Attorney General, wanted to be Lord Chief Justice too, and he was also a man with whom Churchill found it agreeable to dine. The solution was provided by Lord Goddard who grew older and older, and progressively harsher in his judicial sentences, without showing any inclination to resign whatever. So Monckton, after serving Eden as Minister of Defence, and being unable to make up his mind about the rights and wrongs of Suez, became Chairman of the Midland Bank; and Shawcross directed his clear brain to a long, multifarious career in the City and industry. It may be that Lord Goddard did them both a good turn.

In 1951 two young service ministers became more than just colleagues. The Secretary of State for Air was Lord De Lisle, a chartered accountant turned banker turned Grenadier turned politician. He lives in the glorious medieval palace at Penshurst, not far from Chartwell. Apart from being a neighbour, he was married to the daughter of Lord Gort, VC, a general whom Churchill considered an outstanding hero of both wars, however ungraciously Sir Alan Brooke and Sir John Dill might belittle his faultless handling of the British Expeditionary Force in the retreat to Dunkirk, De Lisle followed in his father-in-law's footsteps and himself won the Victoria Cross at Anzio. Churchill had labelled the Anzio expedition 'a stranded whale', but he well knew that it had given opportunities for exceptional gallantry. De Lisle's personality pleased him; his conduct of the Air Ministry satisfied him. He was proud to have him as a member of his Government.

The other was Antony Head, Secretary of State for War. He was a bosom friend of General Sir Robert Laycock, who succeeded Mountbatten as Chief of Combined Operations during the war and won Churchill's unqualified approval in a testing assignment. Head and Laycock had sailed together before the mast in one of the great full-rigged ships which carried grain round the Cape of Good Hope from Australia. Afterwards, as reasonably affluent young officers in the Household Cavalry, they found a fashionable life in London tedious. So being both energetic and enterprising, and quite possibly influenced by *The Pirates of Penzance*, they embarked on a career of burglary. They stole valuable possessions from well-stocked country houses and broke in again a week or so later to replace them. It was long before they were caught and even then a few days of extra duty as Orderly Officer was the maximum penalty appropriate.

Both had brave war records and Head, after winning a Military Cross, spent some time working under General Ismay in the office of the Minister of Defence. In that capacity he was brought to Churchill's favourable attention, and in 1945 he was elected to Parliament. He was completely unsuccessful in trying to hide an acute brain beneath a P. G. Wodehouse manner. The manner entertained, but the intelligence emerged, crisp and matter-of-fact. He had the additional advantage of being married to a skilful portrait painter, Lady Dorothea Ashley-Cooper. She painted Churchill and he painted her. Their sense of fun was the same, their opinion of people and events seldom differed. 'The Heads are coming, hurray,' was a cry I well remember hearing. Head succeeded Monckton as Eden's Minister of Defence and then he and his wife went far away. He was the first British High Commissioner in Nigeria. She painted the leading African statesmen and both were invited into Nigerian houses where no other white people had penetrated. They went from Lagos to Malaysia and were equally loved. No couple was better suited to represent Britain among the coloured inhabitants of African or Asian Commonwealth countries.

There are two men who served in all Churchill's administrations who were of greater stature than any of those hitherto described in this chapter. They stand forth in their own right and therefore, concerned though they were with Churchill's career, they can scarcely be called Churchillians. One is Richard Austen Butler, universally known as 'Rab'; the other is Harold Macmillan. Churchillians or not, they must certainly find a place in this attempt to depict Churchill's colleagues.

Some of the Butlers, like the Lindemanns, have 'beautiful brains'. Rab is counted among them. At thirty he was a junior minister and as his upbringing was against an Indian background, it was appropriate that he should spend five years as Parliamentary Under-Secretary in the India Office. In that capacity he was subjected to the blast of Churchill's assault on the Government of India bill and it was not surprising that he viewed the begetter of the controversy with disapproval aggravated by suspicion. When Cranborne resigned with Eden, Rab took his place at the Foreign Office. He was a zealous disciple of Chamberlain and Halifax, a staunch defender of the Munich Settlement. He was thus pre-eminent among the anti-Churchillians.

He did his best to persuade Halifax to fight for the succession to Chamberlain. When it was clear that his champion declined to take up the challenge, he lamented that the good, clean tradition of William Pitt had been sold to the greatest adventurer of modern political history with all the vices of Charles James Fox. Churchill decreed a truce between the factions, and as Halifax stayed at the Foreign Office, so too did Rab. He was not the only man in Britain whose judgment went sharply into reverse during the next few months. In March 1941 I walked round St James's Park with him and he confessed that he had been utterly wrong in his assessment of Churchill. He was not unique, I said. Early in 1943, in a speech in Glasgow, his taste for historical parallel induced him to compare Churchill with Chatham. By then he was President of the Board of Education and a star in the Churchillian constellation.

Butler's Education Act of 1944 was the charter of the nation's schools for a new age. It has been amended, it has been improved; but it has remained the basis of the British educational system. Churchill recognized its significance in a way I shall always remember. At a crucial moment in the bill's passage through the House of Commons, his Parliamentary Private Secretary, George Harvie Watt, misguidedly chose the wrong moment to have a bath. A division was called by opponents of a vital clause. The government lost by one vote and when Harvie Watt arrived on the scene, spotlessly clean but red in the face, it was too late. Churchill was busy, but he cast everything else aside and spent the evening and half the night in preparing a monumental oration designed to make the House change its mind. A three-line Whip was issued for the following day and he delivered his well-prepared admonishment. The bill was saved and its importance, as well as its author's virtue, were imprinted on Churchill's mind.

After the war Butler's labours at the Conservative Central Office, and in unending committee meetings, revolutionized the thought and the policies of the Conservative party. He was hailed as a new Disraeli, a modern Solon. The party recognized his achievement and so did its leader. Churchill, who seven or eight years earlier had looked on Rab with as much distaste as Rab felt for him, and had only kept him in office because it was his declared policy to forget past animosities, was becoming fond of him. He already acknowledged his intelligence: now he began positively to enjoy his company. So despite the claims of Oliver Lyttelton, preferred by some of the Tory leaders, he made Rab Chancellor of the Exchequer. It was a choice strongly urged by the Chief Whip, Patrick Buchan Hepburn; for Rab had a host of followers on the Conservative benches.

Churchill's habit of working in bed on the mornings when there was no Cabinet meeting was fully recognized. Ministers, generals, and senior Civil Servants were received in his bedroom, his working papers spread before him on a large broad bed-table, a cigar continually having to be relit from a huge box of matches with blue and white tips, one of his 'young ladies' sitting patiently beside him with dictation book and pencil, his red-ink pens and blue-ink pens – and the gold pen used to sign documents – constantly lost in the debris before him. There might be a cat curled up on the blankets at his feet but, cat or no cat, there was always Toby, the budgerigar, who flew round the room making countless dry, and therefore easily removable, messes wherever he chose to alight.

It was in this scenery that the Chancellor would spend two or three hours going through the details of his budget with the Prime Minister. The young lady was dismissed and if anybody had to be admitted for some urgent reason the budget papers were quickly covered. One morning I had to go in. There was the Chancellor beside the bed. On his balding head sat Toby who had, I gathered, been there for three-quarters of an hour. Before leaving I counted fourteen messes on Rab's pate. It appealed to his sense of humour; and Churchill saw nothing at all odd in the situation.

In June 1953, when Churchill and Eden were stricken at almost the identical moment, it fell to Rab to preside over the Cabinet. An ambitious, unscrupulous man might have sought to take advantage of this opportunity. Rab did not. He made frequent journeys to Chartwell in Churchill's convalescence to keep him informed of events and to cheer him with diverting conversation. It was clear that he was subordinating his own ambitions to the loyalty due to his chief.

Twice in later years he was disappointed of the highest office at times when all the omens seemed favourable. He accepted these perverse strokes of fate with philosophical resignation. Perhaps he was in reality fortunate, for he was spared exhausting responsibilities. It may be that the Mastership of Trinity College, Cambridge, brought him greater contentment than he would have found at 10 Downing Street.

Harold Macmillan had the Churchillian credentials that Rab lacked. His early political career was of the kind that appealed to Churchill. He was a radical and a rebel. The appeasers and all their works were anathema to him. In the years immediately before the war he was one of that rebellious Conservative band who were unmoved by David Margesson's displeasure or that of Margesson's deputy, Macmillan's own brother-in-law, James Stuart. His speeches in the House needled the Government, and they were cleverly enough conceived to cause alarm in ministerial breasts. It was obvious that Chamberlain would never give him office; it was equally obvious that Churchill would.

Yet Churchill and Macmillan were not intimate in the war years. As Under-Secretary at the Ministry of Supply and in the Colonial Office he was hidden from view, and in 1942 he was sent far away to be resident minister with the Allied forces in North Africa.

He had an influential part to play in the Mediterranean scene and when the affairs of Italy or Greece were to the fore, his advice was studied with care. But he was nowhere near the seat of power, and he was not directly involved in the main stream of policy which flowed through London, Washington and Moscow.

He returned to the centre of events as Secretary of State for Air in Churchill's short Conservative administration that preceded the General Election of 1945. There followed six years of opposition in which Macmillan first made his mark from the front benches. By 1951 he was clearly destined for high office, and as the Conservatives had laid stress on their ability to overcome the housing shortage, he was given that challenging portfolio. He exceeded, beyond all expectations, the high target set and he became a hero. He was not close to Churchill, not frequently to be be seen at Chequers or Chartwell; but Churchill recognized that he was one of the most formidable members of his team. He seriously thought of moving him to the Foreign Office.

Harold Macmillan has his own place in the catalogue of British statesmen. He was a craftier politician than Churchill, as decisive but less impetuous, and more ruthless in attaining his ends. He was as ready to recognize that consistency does not mean hostility to change, but rather a readiness to adapt to new circumstances while, as Churchill put it, 'retaining the same dominating purpose'. Like Churchill, he had a profound knowledge and vivid sense of history which stimulated his imagination and lifted him high above the commonplace. He does not rank with Churchill, for he did not have the same capacity to move men's hearts and stir their souls. Nor did it fall to him to stand as Churchill did, like Leonidas at the pass of Thermopylae, against a torrent that threatened civilization. Nevertheless it is significant that in January 1957, when Anthony Eden stepped down and the Queen sought advice about his successor, Churchill, who thought so well of Rab Butler, gave his in favour of Harold Macmillan. I asked him why. 'Harold,' he replied, 'is more decisive.'

CHAPTER TWELVE

Lord Moran

When Churchill first became Prime Minister he had seldom been ill. He was smitten with appendicitis at the start of an election in 1922 and, as he put it, lost both his seat and his appendix. He was run over by a taxi in New York in 1931 and seriously but not permanently injured. Professor Lindemann informed him by telegram that the impact of the taxi was equal to six thousand foot-pounds of energy and that his body had been moved with a strength of eight thousand horse-power. Apart from these interruptions to an active life, he had scarcely spent an obligatory day in bed since childhood and suffered from nothing more alarming than occasional indigestion. It transpired, from enquiry, that the well-known physician Lord Horder was assumed to be his doctor, but it was long since any ministrations had been required.

The pace was hot and fast in the first year of the war. Churchill was not visibly wilting: indeed he seemed to go from strength to strength. He smoked and drank more than would be good for most men and took no regular exercise. Yet when he set off on a tour of inspection, younger and apparently fitter men found it difficult to keep up with him. All the same he had anxious friends, including Lord Beaverbrook and Brendan Bracken. They decided, and persuaded Clementine Churchill, that a doctor must be appointed to keep close watch and pay regular visits. In May 1940 they selected one in whom Beaverbrook had trust, Sir Charles Wilson, President of the Royal College of Physicians.

Churchill was too busy to remonstrate, though he began by declaring that nothing would induce him to take the fellow with him when he travelled. He did not include him in his entourage in HMS *Prince of Wales* when, in August 1941, he sailed to meet President Roosevelt off Newfoundland for their first wartime conference. This did not suit Beaverbrook or Bracken, who thought a doctor in attendance an essential precaution; nor did it suit Sir Charles Wilson who was determined not to be left out of things and was aware that although Churchill was polite to him on his routine visits, he was not welcomed with enthusiasm. Thus for more than two years of war, including the whole period when Britain stood alone and the strain was greatest, Churchill neither received nor required medical attention.

There was a change after December 1941. Churchill went to Washington at the first opportunity after Pearl Harbor and he was induced to take Sir Charles. On the day after Christmas he had a minor heart disturbance in his bedroom at the White House. It affected him little, but thereafter Charles Wilson accompanied him on his longer journeys abroad.

It is a convention generally accepted that professional men do not write about their clients and customers any more than priests reveal the secrets of the confessional. Charles Wilson, created Lord Moran on Churchill's recommendation in 1943, broke this convention and thereby provoked the indignation of Churchill's family and friends and almost the entire medical profession. My object is not primarily to discuss that issue. The excuse Moran gave for his action seemed to me and many others false and special pleading. It was that Churchill's declining health had a decisive effect on the outcome of the war and its aftermath. The fact rather than the fantasy is that it was Roosevelt, not Churchill, whose physical collapse led to consequences of immense significance. It is an interesting question whether Moran's diaries contribute, at any rate as far as their main theme is concerned, to the truth in historical research; but the object of this short study is rather to describe his relationship with Churchill and his gifted, unusual and sometimes contorted personality.

He expressed himself lucidly in speech and in writing. His style was invigorating and his words well chosen. He had the makings of a philosopher and he was endowed with the perceptiveness essential to a good physician. Thus he noticed moods and motives of which others might be oblivious. When he did so, he expounded his discoveries freely and with only the smallest regard for discretion. Being obsessed by the importance of morale to fighting men and of psychology in handling troops, he published a short and challenging book, called *The Anatomy of Courage*, so well written and so simply explained that it was as interesting to the layman as to the psychologist. It did not, however, impress Churchill who said, with brutal frankness, that he thought it was largely rubbish: it overlooked the greater importance to victory of the maximum number of men deployed in the front line than the maintenance of thousands in the rearward services employed to increase comfort and administer psychology.

Moran's diaries, published under the title *Winston Churchill, the Struggle for Survival*, were also written with style; and to many who did not know Churchill they were convincing. Extracts purporting to have been written on the day of the event may perhaps have been interpolated or expanded later. It is, for instance, improbable that anybody crossing the Atlantic with the Prime Minister in the Cunard liner *Queen Mary* would, if actually writing on board, have described a passage in the *Queen Elizabeth*. When allowance is made for a number of such inaccuracies, and for the insertion of arguments about Churchill's health intended as a justification for writing the book at all, it can be acclaimed as a work of no mean literary merit.

He made incisive comments that were often memorable. What, I asked him at Carthage in December 1943, would be the effect of the new drug penicillin? 'One of its effects,' he replied, 'will be to make lust safe for democracy.' Having an inquisitive mind, and also a sense of history, he made a point of asking questions of all the important soldiers, sailors and airmen, diplomats and statesmen, with whom Churchill's journeys and conferences brought him into contact. He made a note of their replies, reflected on them and analysed them. He was not, of course, present when discussions of political and military importance took place; but he was often invited to luncheon afterwards and as a recorder of opinions made full use of his opportunities. It was sensible of him to do so, and it was understandable, for except when the Prime Minister was ill he had nothing else with which to occupy himself except for his golf-clubs; and they, for one reason or another, always seemed to have been lost or left behind.

Moran's critical faculties were well developed, perhaps over developed. I do not think he was malevolent, but he did appear malicious, for whenever he spoke of statesmen or soldiers he almost invariably emphasized their defects. On pressure being applied he would then speak of their merits, but his first reaction to a man, or indeed to a proposal, was to stress the darker side. It was a habit more pronounced in speech than in writing, but perhaps he softened his words for publication. There were a few exceptions: those like General Marshall on whom he lavished nothing but praise; but I often heard him launch into an attack on men whom I knew that in reality he esteemed. His comments were shrewd, but he evidently thought the negative more note-worthy than the positive and he would seize on comparatively minor episodes to use as a text for demolishing his victim. Thus his belief that Anthony Eden had mishandled a Turkish delegation in Cairo led him to dissect Eden, and he told me that he had seen the real, cleverly hidden face of Ismay when the latter spoke sharply to a marine messenger during a visit to Moscow. He was the only man I ever heard speak ill of Ismay.

He was equally critical of plans and policies. At one dinner party on the *Queen Mary* he held the table for ten minutes criticizing unfavourably the entire military strategy in Europe. Churchill listened patiently to this catalogue of the follies he and others had committed. Then he said quietly: 'Well, Charles what do *you* propose?' Moran had no reply to give.

One of his themes was the poor use being made of Britain's scientific brains and resources during the war. With Watson Watt, Barnes Wallis, R.V. Jones and scores of others fighting and winning the technological war, and with British physicists playing a large part in the development of nuclear power, this was a strange obsession, and it was one that irritated Professor Lindemann. The explanation may have been that Moran, justly convinced of the vital contribution that science of all kinds, including medicine, must make in the changing world, had at least one subject on which he could dilate with authority when surrounded by experts of another kind, military, diplomatic and political, to whose circle he only had social access. Another theme, perhaps with the same basis and perhaps borrowed from his former patient, Beaverbrook, was the superiority of self-made men. He was not self-made, but he had certainly risen to the height of the medical profession by his own efforts. He gave me, and others, many lectures on the evils of privilege and I was, therefore, amused when he let fall that he would like the Prime Minister to submit his name for a Crown appointment as Provost of Eton, a school to which, incidently, he sent both his sons. I said that Churchill could not display his Harrovian bias as blatantly as that; but he was not amused.

Moran deserves credit for the scrupulous care with which he watched over Churchill's ailments in the last eighteen months of the war and in the twenty years thereafter. No doubt he underestimated his patient's strength, for as early as September 1944 he told me that he did not give him a long life and thought he would die, perhaps before the war ended, from a stroke or a heart attack. Churchill's great physical strength, and his determination to complete his mission, were the vital elements in the survival of a man who passed his three score years and ten while the battles still raged; but the attentions Moran himself provided played their part. So did his comprehensive knowledge of the medical profession which enabled him to summon the foremost experts in their field, men such as Doctors Bedford, Whitby and Braine, when the symptoms demanded special treatment. His skill in diagnosis and the unhesitating speed with which he found the right men at the right time were the greatest services he rendered.

It is not easy to assess Churchill's personal attitude to Moran. It was not always the same. On the one hand he became accustomed to him (and for Churchill that was always half the battle), he trusted him, he spoke freely to him and he relied on him. Indeed, I am sure that he was fond of him. On the other hand, he disliked Moran's continual criticism of people, even though he paid no attention at all to his criticism of policies, regarding Moran's comments on them as superficial and inexpert. He was grateful to him, as he had every reason to be, but he never fully recovered from Moran's direct and importunate demand that, in return for all he had done, Churchill should make him Minister of Health. To imagine that such a proposal would be well received showed how little Moran, for all the value he set on psychology, understood the psychology of his own patient.

As with the advance of age Churchill's maladies, great and small, increased in number and in frequency, Moran's visits became more regular and more welcome. The Prime Ministerial journeys ended and the chances of quizzing the mighty were over;

but Moran was attentive as ever and his skill had not diminished. Churchill had not listed him high among those with whom it was agreeable to dine, but in the late 1950s Moran asked outright to be elected a member of the Other Club. Churchill, though surprised at such a forthright request, had no wish to hurt his feelings by refusing. It is a sad epilogue to the story that when Moran published his diaries, which he had prepared in readiness for Churchill's death, the members of the club, almost all personal friends of Churchill, asked him to resign. It is almost equally sad that he saw no reason for doing so.

CHAPTER THIRTEEN

De Gaulle

Charles de Gaulle was no more a Churchillian than Churchill was a Gaullist; but it may be said without undue exaggeration that Churchill created de Gaulle, though certainly not in his own image, and with still less fear of contradiction that had it not been for Churchill, de Gaulle would in all probability have been discarded at an early stage in the war.

The interaction of the two men had its effect on the future of France and, in years to come, of Europe as a whole. Twenty years later it had its effect on Britain, too, and perhaps indirectly on the United States whose soldiers faced disaster in the swamps and jungles of the former French colony of Indo-China and whose Government and people were subjected to the enduring dislike and, whenever he could show it, the disdain of President de Gaulle. This was not what Churchill would have wished. It was, at any rate in part, de Gaulle's revenge on President Roosevelt.

When France fell in the early summer of 1940, de Gaulle was a junior brigadier who had fought and won a minor tank battle near Abbeville, one of the few engagements the French did win in May 1940. He had caught the eye of the French Prime Minister, Paul Reynaud, who had thereupon appointed him Under-Secretary in the Ministry of Defence. In those hectic days of the French collapse, he also caught the eye of Winston Churchill. During a hurried conference at Briare on 11 June, Churchill sat next to him at dinner and noted that while Pétain, Weygand and the other French generals were impregnated with defeatism and in the grip of apparently irreparable despondency, de Gaulle was filled with a spirit of resistance.

Two days later Churchill was back in France at Tours, using all his eloquence to revive the sinking morale of the French

Government and General Staff. Once again it was de Gaulle who seemed to be keeping a solitary flame alight in the thickening gloom and it was clear that Weygand, whom events were to prove deceitful as well as defeatist, strongly disapproved of the brigadier. 'The man of destiny,' Churchill murmured as he said good-bye to de Gaulle on leaving Tours.

When de Gaulle flew to London on 17 June to escape arrest by Weygand's orders, it was neither his nor Churchill's expectation that he would lead a Free French movement in England. He was junior, he was far from eloquent and he was repeatedly rebuffed by the numerous French soldiers rescued from Dunkirk and marooned on British soil. They were invited to decide whether to stay and fight or to go home. The vast majority elected to go home.

Churchill was looking for a well-known politician to raise the French standard in England once it became clear that the high hopes of persuading the French Government to carry on the struggle from North Africa had collapsed and that the French generals in the Colonies stood behind Marshal Pétain and General Weygand in their resolve to make peace at almost any price with the victorious Nazis. He hoped to persuade the brilliant Jewish politician, Georges Mandel, Clemenceau's secretary and trusted adviser in the First World War, to lead the new movement; but Mandel, who was the bravest of the brave, refused to leave France precisely because he was a Jew. He believed that to fly before the advancing Gestapo would show cowardice and that in any case a Jewish standard-bearer would be unacceptable to many of his compatriots. He died because of that belief.

There was no other available politician of comparable renown and experience. The lot therefore fell on Charles de Gaulle. He was a single-minded man with one supreme obsession: the honour and glory of France. Scrupulously honest and unselfseeking where his personal interests were concerned, he was devious and offensive when he thought the interests of his country were at stake. For him any means whatever justified his only end, which was to restore the greatness of France.

Churchill, who was no less a patriot than de Gaulle, realized this. In a way he admired his defiant and frequently crude demeanour, making allowance for rudeness and constant ingratitude.

He realized that only thus could the General (as he had now become) convince himself and his small band of followers that he was maintaining the dignity of his country. What Churchill could not entirely forgive were his ineradicable suspicions. The British never for one moment contemplated the seizure of any part of the French Empire. It did not cross their minds that Syria, the Lebanon, Indo-China or any of the French African Colonies might one day be plums ripe to pick. Yet de Gaulle, who distrusted Anglo-Saxons on principle, was sure the British had greedy designs on French territories.

Historic rivalries die hard. In the face of danger from across the Rhine, Britain and France were linked closer than ever before from the Entente Cordiale of 1904 to the outbreak of the Second World War, but this political association was not reflected in popular sentiment on either side of the Channel. Men of letters, artists and scientists of the two nations had long cross-fertilized each other. English philosophers such as Hobbes and Locke influenced a whole generation of French thinkers: Rousseau, Voltaire and Descartes made a profound impression in Britain. English and still more Scottish schoolchildren were taught to admire the achievements of the French revolution and to regard Napoleon as a genius. Deep down, however, there was rivalry and antipathy going back as far as the Hundred Years War and stoked by almost incessant conflict thereafter.

In June 1940, this ancient river of antipathy burst its banks. The French blamed insufficient British support on land, although there were in May 1940 four hundred thousand British troops on French soil, two hundred and fifty thousand of them actively fighting. The British saw that the almost unopposed German penetration of the French armies, and the total collapse of morale among French Staff officers, had brought the British Expeditionary Force within an ace of destruction. The French air force, weakened by the policy of the Front Populaire before the war, proved worthless. The fleet, trusting in undertakings given by a German regime which had never kept its word, refused to sail to neutral ports or to the French colony of Martinique. Four hundred German pilots shot down by the RAF were released to take part in the aerial assault on Britain. Even those who had always loved France lost their faith.

Early in July Anthony Eden said at Chequers that France's shame was so great that she could never rise again. Lord Gort and Sir Hugh Dowding asserted that the fighting value of one Pole was that of ten Frenchmen. Almost the only obstacle to the surge of anti-French feeling in government circles was Winston Churchill. He contradicted Eden: France would certainly rise again. She was humiliated by the paralysis and ignominy of Pétain, Weygand and Laval, but her spirit would revive, as it always did in adversity. The man to keep the flame alight, even if for the moment it was only flickering, was Charles de Gaulle; and in him he intended to put his trust.

Confidence in him sagged in many quarters when 'Operation Menace', an expedition to capture Dakar for the Free French, turned out a dismal failure in September 1940. The operation was mounted by the British, with the support of Free French troops and many warships. It was hoped, among other benefits, to take possession of the new French battleship *Richelieu* which would have been a serious threat in German hands. Defective intelligence about the attitude of the French garrison, a possible (though disputed) leakage of information from Free French quarters in England and the descent of thick fog on the crucial morning contributed to make an ignominious retreat necessary. De Gaulle lost much face, but put a brave expression on what remained of it and was defended valiantly by Churchill. The British Chiefs of Staff could afford to make no comment: they had ordered the abandonment of the proposed adventure, but had been overruled by Churchill after the receipt of urgent and emphatic telegrams in its favour from Sir Edward Spears.

The Free French movement did not have an easy start, for however much material aid the British might provide, supporters were slow in flocking to the Cross of Lorraine. It was important to find an admiral to balance the general. This was difficult, because the French had always been jealous of the Royal Navy and the sinking of their fleet at Oran on 3 July, justifiable though it was, had not endeared Britain to French sailors. It was therefore fortunate that Admiral Muselier rallied to the cause.

On New Year's Day 1941, Desmond Morton arrived with the news that Muselier and several of his staff were traitors. They were undercover agents of the French collaborators at Vichy.

They had betrayed the intentions of the Free French and British forces in the recent expedition to Dakar. There were documents to prove it. On being shown the evidence Churchill gave instructions that the miscreants be arrested that very night and de Gaulle informed by special messenger.

Desmond Morton passed the order to MI5. Muselier was arrested together with another Frenchman and two ladies. One of the latter was apprehended in bed with a doctor attached to the Free French forces; when the house belonging to the other was searched the discoveries included a Second Secretary of the Brazilian Embassy stark naked. It was, we were told, through the Brazilian Embassy that information was passed to Vichy.

A week or so later it was proved that the documents incriminating Muselier had been forged by two disgruntled officers of the Free French forces. The Admiral, who had been lodged in the Tower of London, was not a spy but an Officer and a Gentleman. The amorous activities of the Free French ladies were their own affair. The record of the Brazilian Embassy was untarnished. So Churchill sent his own car and chauffeur to escort the Admiral wherever he wished to go. This turned out to be a dubious address in Hampstead. 'All the same,' the Admiral was reported as saying, 'after ten days in the Bastille. . . .'

De Gaulle behaved with dignity. Churchill was greatly pleased because when told of this painful episode the General was not at all cantankerous and said his only interest was to see that honour and justice were satisfied. 'Of course,' said Desmond Morton pensively, 'he doesn't like Muselier.'

From the beginning President Roosevelt and the American State Department regarded de Gaulle with doubt verging on disfavour. When Marshal Pétain's Government signed an armistice with the Nazis, despite a solemn treaty binding France not to make a separate peace, the United States sensibly decided to keep a diplomatic mission at Vichy; for it was important to retain a listening-post in occupied Europe. Churchill raised no objection to this, nor to Roosevelt sending such a distinguished ambassador as Admiral Leahy; but de Gaulle saw the decision as a challenge to his own position as representative of French independence and the guardian of his country's honour.

The American Government's mistrust was amplified by their

belief that de Gaulle had neither the weight nor the prestige to lead a Free French movement. His only pillar of strength was Churchill, and he therefore risked his whole future by displaying bad temper and even worse manners every time his demands were questioned or declined. Nothing would have contented him, small though his resources were and flimsy his support in French territory, but to be treated as an equal by Roosevelt, Churchill and, later, Stalin. His exclusion from Anglo-American conferences seemed to him an insult to France.

At times even Churchill was tempted to throw him overboard, an action which the Americans would have welcomed. In March 1943 he did briefly favour an American proposal to replace de Gaulle by a triumvirate consisting of General Giraud, Camille Chautemps and Alexis Léger, former head of the Quai d'Orsay. This idea was opposed by Anthony Eden, who was normally less favourable to de Gaulle than Churchill, for he realized that it would alienate the increasing numbers in France itself who, largely thanks to the BBC, had by then accepted de Gaulle as the leader of resistance. So Churchill changed his mind, but there were many distasteful incidents of which a few may usefully be recalled.

The first occurred much earlier, in July 1941, when de Gaulle was dissatisfied with the British handling of the campaign against Vichy in Syria, even though he had himself signed an agreement to the effect that after the war Syria should be free to govern itself. He behaved like an angry bear to Oliver Lyttelton, the British Minister of State in the Middle East, and he quarrelled with General Wavell. He even went so far as to say that he could not care less whether or not Britain won the war. All that mattered was that France should be saved. And this was at a time when Britain had several million men under arms while de Gaulle controlled but a few thousand. Churchill, by no means the most patient of men, was gentle in his handling of the irascible Frenchman and in the end he received an apology.

It is notable, particularly in his relationship with de Gaulle, how often Churchill's initial fury, and his expressed determination to take strong action, even to withdraw his support altogether, was calmed and transformed when a few days or even hours had passed. Before acting on impulse he nearly always allowed time for reflection. However, over the years de Gaulle's curmudgeonly behaviour did leave a bitter taste behind and in 1944 I heard Churchill say, with sadness in his voice: 'My illusions about the French have been greatly corroded.'

Another occasion of Gaullist pettiness was at the Casablanca meeting of the President and the Prime Minister in January 1943. De Gaulle was invited to attend, but declined. He then arrived on the scene and was courteously treated, even by Roosevelt, but he showed no willingness to collaborate or compromise with the French General Giraud whom the Americans had wished to see as head of the Free French Government. His attitude on this score was understandable: his demeanour was not. Indeed Churchill described his behaviour as preposterous, although he continued to admire his attitude of proud defiance. 'I knew he was no friend of England,' Churchill wrote, 'but I always recognized in him the spirit and conception which, across the pages of history, the word France would ever proclaim.'

A year later, after the Tehran and Cairo conferences, Churchill spent three weeks at Marrakech recovering from a dangerous attack of pneumonia. Visitors, military and political, came and went. Among those whom Churchill thought it polite to ask was the French General de Lattre de Tassigny, much praised by the British in Algiers. He was astonished to receive a message that de Gaulle had forbidden de Lattre to accept, informing all concerned that such a visit 'would not be opportune'. Morocco was French soil and nobody might ask French generals to stay without de Gaulle's permission. No doubt his suspicious temperament led him to suspect that a plot was afoot. It would not have occurred to him that Churchill was only seeking to be hospitable and to meet an Allied commander of whom he had received a favourable account.

Churchill exploded with wrath and was adamant that when, a few days later, de Gaulle was due to visit Marrakech, he would refuse to receive him. The British representative at Algiers, Duff Cooper, came to stay, bringing the beautiful and persuasive Lady Diana. Between them they mollified Churchill, and when de Gaulle did arrive he was greeted with unalloyed good-will. For once even the General seemed pleased to bask and relax in the unexpected sunshine. He had doubtless foreseen nothing but thunder-clouds.

The last occasion that de Gaulle tried Churchill sorely was on the eve of 'Operation Overlord', the Allied landings in Normandy of 6 June 1944. As this was to be the start of liberating the soil of metropolitan France, Churchill thought it polite to summon de Gaulle from Algiers and explain the plan. He only arrived at the Prime Minister's special train, stationary at Portsmouth, on the eve of the embarkation. For four years the Free French had shown themselves incapable of maintaining secrecy and Churchill refused de Gaulle permission to telegraph the details of the military plans, in his own Free French cipher (which the Germans could probably read), to his committee in Algiers. De Gaulle considered himself insulted, was off-hand with General Eisenhower, declined the Prime Minister's invitation to dinner on the train and was last seen walking stiffly away down the railway line. His anger simmered for two months and when Churchill went to Algiers in August 1944 de Gaulle was too busy to call on him. However, he became a little less ursine when even his self-chosen enemies, the Americans, showed sufficient tact (with perhaps a little encouragement from Churchill) to detach General Leclerc's Free French Armoured Division from the advancing allied armies and give it the appropriate task of liberating Paris.

Once a substantial area of France had been freed, Churchill advocated, against American doubts and Russian indifference, that de Gaulle's Provisional Government should be recognized and its authority in French territory established with Allied approval. It was also Churchill who at Yalta persuaded a reluctant Stalin that a French zone of occupation in conquered Germany should be carved out of the British and American zones. There was no question of the Russians contributing any part of their zone.

Despite these friendly gestures, relations again deteriorated at the end of the war. The Germans had scarcely surrendered when de Gaulle, careless of the delicate state of affairs in the Middle East, sent a cruiser loaded with troops to Syria, providing no information about his intentions and risking a clash with the Syrians and even, perhaps, with British troops stationed in the Levant. Meanwhile in the Val d'Aosta he had ordered his troops to pay no attention to instructions received from the supreme Allied commander, Eisenhower. Fortunately the general rejoicing was sufficient to enable de Gaulle's uncouth vagaries to be ignored.

There were two close friends of Churchill whose task it was, in 1940 and 1941, to act as his personal representatives with de Gaulle. The first was Major-General Sir Edward Spears, MP for Carlisle. He spoke French as well as he spoke English, he had lived much of his early life in France and knew every French general and politician of consequence. It was he who brought de Gaulle to England on 17 June 1940, and later accompanied him to West Africa, Egypt and Syria. He was de Gaulle's mainstay in the first, difficult days of the Free French movement, and although they later quarrelled over the behaviour of the Free French in the Middle East, yet it might be supposed that de Gaulle would have retained grateful memories of those early months. Instead, when he came to power after the war he sent instructions to the French Embassy in London that whoever else might be invited within their hospitable doors, Sir Edward and Lady Spears should always be rigorously excluded.

'Louis' Spears, as he was generally called, was a man of high intelligence who made enemies almost as easily as he made friends. He was a brilliant writer with an attractive, unexpected turn of phrase. Since the years of their early childhood are often those about which people are most ignorant, I once asked Churchill in what books I could most easily unravel the tangled skein of the First World War. He forebore to recommend his own book, *The World Crisis*, but answered that I need read no more than Louis Spears's two works, *Liaison 1914* and *Prelude to Victory*. They were a true account and they contained all that it was necessary to know.

Despite his good brain, and an emotional affection he showed to those whom he liked, he had a streak of metallic ruthlessness which was not difficult to discern. He took pains to gratify his friends, and his hospitality was enjoyable because he matched his guests so well that they entertained each other without fail; but there were many who thought him devious, in business as well as in politics. In November 1940, after the fiasco at Dakar, Lord Lloyd, Secretary of State for the Colonies, told me that he fervently hoped the Prime Minister would never re-employ Spears. He was said to be inconsiderate to his wife, a gentle American authoress who wrote under her maiden name of Mary Borden and produced a widely praised novel called *Jane – Our Stranger*. In fact he loved her deeply, but that did not prevent his having a long-standing affair with his secretary, Nancy Maurice, whom he married when to his genuine sorrow his first wife died. As Chairman of Ashanti Goldfields he had a pleasant house in the Ghanaian hills at Obuasi and enjoyed an enduring love–hate relationship with President Nkrumah.

Churchill made friends with him during the First World War and never ceased to respect his intelligence. During the 1930s, when Churchill had but a handful of allies in opposing Munich and warning his countrymen of the wrath to come, Spears was counted among the most faithful. Though he was unpopular with the Foreign Office, there can be little doubt that, had France stayed in the war, Churchill would have insisted on sending him as Ambassador to Paris. In the event he had to be content with, first, a liaison appointment with de Gaulle and then residing in Beirut for three disillusioning years as the British Minister to Syria and the Lebanon.

De Gaulle's growing antagonism, and the almost equally hostile attitude of Anthony Eden and the Foreign Office, barred Spears from the more illustrious posts for which his abilities, if not his tact, would have qualified him in Algiers and, perhaps eventually in Paris. After 1945 he vanished from the political scene, but not from Churchill's esteem or from the fringes of big business. He continued to write excellent books.

The other man who was concerned with the Free French on the Prime Minister's behalf was Major Desmond Morton. He was the rare, perhaps the unique, example of a man who had been shot through the heart and survived. Indeed he had recovered sufficiently to finish the First World War as ADC to Field-Marshal Haig. Thereafter he became involved in Economic Intelligence, which was a gentlemanly form of spying, and since he lived at Edenbridge, close to Chartwell, he used to supply Churchill with a great deal of information for the speeches with which he was trying to rouse the country. It has never been clear whether or not he did so with the approval of the Government, but no doubt he reasoned that Churchill was a Privy Councillor who had been invited by the Government to attend meetings of the Committee of Imperial Defence.

When Churchill arrived at 10 Downing Street in May 1940,

Morton was one of the three advisers who arrived like Horsemen of the Apocalypse. The other two were Professor Lindemann and Brendan Bracken. Morton at first occupied the room adjacent to the Cabinet room vacated by Chamberlain's adviser, Sir Horace Wilson. He was consistently friendly and a prolific raconteur of amusing if sometimes improbable stories. 'His voice,' I wrote at the time, 'would penetrate the ramparts of a medieval castle.' His laughter echoed from the Private Secretaries' room and was the cause of insistent bell-ringing and furious remonstrance from the Prime Minister sitting in the Cabinet room. All the same, he endeared himself to all at No. 10. In the office 'mess', established by Brendan Bracken when the air-raids began, Morton was the life and soul of the party. Only Bracken could out-talk him and, like Bracken, he provided a genial antidote to the gloomiest news and the noisiest bombs.

Morton was made chairman of a special committee which was intended to consider policy towards the Free French and all the other free governments which had taken refuge on British soil – the Dutch, Belgian, Norwegian, Polish, Czech and, at a later date, the Yugoslavs and Greeks. He was also the Prime Minister's liaison officer with the intelligence services. From his room in Downing Street he had direct access to the Prime Minister. His committee infuriated both the Foreign Secretary and the Foreign Office who thought, with justification, that Morton was running his own separate Foreign Affairs institution. He made things worse by his inability, when dining out, to control his flow of conversation and exaggerated stories, so that it was soon rumoured in London that the man closest to the Prime Minister, and most influential in foreign policy, was his new star in the social constellation, Desmond Morton.

Right at the start Morton had indeed been closely concerned with the proposal for formal Anglo-French Union, an idea conceived by Monsieur Monnet and Monsieur Pleven as an emergency measure to persuade the French Government to continue fighting. Morton was excited by the idea which was sold first to Neville Chamberlain and David Margesson, then to de Gaulle, and finally, in the course of a single luncheon party, to Churchill. The French Prime Minister, Paul Reynaud, accepted the proposal with elation, but his Goverment thought it a ruse to turn France into a British Dominion and refused to support him. Reynaud resigned and France collapsed.

After these initial fireworks, Desmond Morton's personal association with the work of the office at 10 Downing Street, and with the Prime Minister personally, gradually diminished. His committee, which had so irritated the Foreign Office, faded into insignificance and in due course the Allied Governments in London, which were his principal preoccupation, had ambassadors appointed to them by the Foreign Office. His liaison with the Secret Service continued and he sometimes forwarded their reports to the Prime Minister; but the only aspect of their work in which Churchill was actively interested was the receipt of 'Ultra' or 'Boniface' signals, and those were delivered personally by 'C', Brigadier Stewart Menzies.

For the last years of the war Morton still had an office and a secretary at the Storey's Gate annexe to 10 Downing Street, but they were on the second floor, above that where the important activities took place. Churchill was fond of Morton, though his loud voice jarred a little and his sense of humour, which most of us enjoyed, was not Churchill's. Little by little, without any malice intended, he sank into the background. He was seldom asked to Chequers, even when foreign dignitaries such as de Gaulle and Sikorski went there. He became embittered, feeling that the Prime Minister had lost interest in him. This was, sadly enough, true, though Churchill had no intention of hurting his feelings and took pains to procure for him a knighthood of the Order of the Bath and to persuade Mr Attlee to appoint him British delegate to the Reparations Commission in Brussels when the war was over. He had not been as close to Churchill as Lindemann, Bracken and some of the Private Secretaries; and that, no doubt, was why he drifted unhappily away in disappointment and discontent.

It is in distant relationship to de Gaulle that Churchill's attitude to European unity may be examined, for in the last analysis, although for totally different reasons, their European convictions had something in common.

Churchill began brooding on the matter in the 1920s and '30s. In an article written for the *Saturday Evening Post* in 1930, he proclaimed: 'The conception of a United States of Europe is right. Every step taken to that end which appeases the obsolete hatreds and vanished oppressions, which makes easier the traffic and reciprocal services of Europe, which encourages its nations to lay aside their precautionary panoply, is good in itself, good for them and good for all.' But in the same article he wrote of the place Britain and the British Empire would occupy in the scheme of things: 'We are with Europe, but not of it. We are linked, but not comprised. We are interested and associated, but not absorbed.' He quoted the words of the Shunammite woman in the Old Testament, recommending that the British should echo her words: 'I dwell among mine own people.'

Churchill was in fact consistent in his thoughts, though many interpretations were given to his words. In the summer of 1940, when almost everybody except the British and de Gaulle believed that Germany had won the war, Churchill once spoke to me about the future. This is an extract from my diary for 10 August:

He said there was only one aim: to destroy Hitler. Let those who say they do not know what they are fighting for stop fighting, and they will see. France is now discovering what she was fighting for. After the last war people had done much constructive thinking and the League of Nations had been a magnificent idea. Something of the kind would have to be built up again: there would be a United States of Europe, and our island would be the link connecting this Federation with the New World and able to hold the balance between the two.

I said that this sounded to me like a new conception of the balance of power, to which Churchill retorted that it would rather be a balance of virtue.

Towards the end of December that year, de Gaulle came to Chequers and the future of Germany was discussed, the General making a far harsher judgment than the Prime Minister. Churchill silenced him by saying that Germany must remain in the European family and reminded him that 'Germany existed before the Gestapo'. The Prime Minister went on, later that same day, to outline his hopes for the future of Europe. There would be five great European nations: England, France, Italy, Spain and Prussia. He visualized the south German states forming part of a Danubian confederation, and there would be three other confederations so that Europe would never again be Balkanized. These nine powers would meet in a Council of Europe, which would have a federal judiciary and a Supreme Economic Council.

Each component state would have its own militia, because democracy must be based on a people's army, but all air forces would be internationalized. At the end of his exposition which, though extempore and at the dinner table, was long and detailed, Churchill said this: 'The English Speaking World would be apart from this, but closely connected with it, and it alone would control the seas as the reward for victory'.

There was a contradiction in Churchill's vision. Britain was to be a member of the Council of Europe and yet apart from it. It was a contradiction he never resolved, either intellectually or emotionally; but I have no doubt that when, after the war, he made his clarion calls for European unity at Zurich, The Hague and Luxemburg, his basic incentive was recognition of the misery and impoverishment caused throughout the world by centuries of European strife. Latterly it had been the rivalry of France and Germany, and repeated cries for vengeance, that had unleashed the armies. This must never happen again, but it could only be prevented by the demolition of rival armed forces, international trade disputes, exchange problems and eventually national frontiers themselves on the continent of Europe.

In the first few years after the war Britain was the sole European victor. She had suffered materially and she had been obliged to sell many of her foreign investments to pay for food, fuel and munitions before the American Congress passed the Lease-Lend legislation. All the same she was, by comparison with the other countries in Europe, still relatively rich and her commerce and industry were largely intact. So Churchill and Duncan Sandys thought it natural and right that Britain should lead Europe in the wholesome direction to which a United Europe pointed. They were enthused more by the belief that such a Grand Design would ensure lasting peace than by any other motive.

Churchill's mission, as he saw it, was to promote unity, but although Britain would be 'of Europe', she would, as he had written in 1930, not be comprised in it. Her destiny lay with the Empire and on the seas. It would be furthered and also insured by a close and special relationship with the United States. Britain, strong and independent, would certainly not be excluded from Europe: on the contrary, she would add purpose and stability to the new Continental Union. She would provide a vital link not only with the United States but, because of her vast Empire, with Asia, Africa and the Pacific basin.

When he became Prime Minister again in 1951, Churchill addressed himself to recreating the special relationship with America, to solving the multitudinous puzzles in the Middle East and, after Stalin's unregretted demise in 1953, to exploring the possibility of a rapprochement with Russia. There were also the affairs of NATO and the Austrian Peace Treaty, but he had no urgent preoccupation with European union. Nor was it regarded seriously by Anthony Eden and the Foreign Office; nor did it stimulate the thoughts of General de Gaulle, in temporary retirement at Colombey les Deux Eglises. Duncan Sandys, who had been Churchill's stalwart adjutant in his European tour and speechmaking three years earlier, was still a muted advocate of the Grand Design; but it was clear to all who paused to consider the matter that, whatever the Europeans might be planning, the Cabinet, Parliament and the British people would view any radical European proposition with a nicely balanced mixture of irritation and ridicule.

Charles de Gaulle's conception of European unity did not develop in sympathy with Churchill's, for America was his *bête noire* and nothing would obliterate in his elephantine memory the snubs he had received from the White House during the war. But France, like Britain, had an Empire and de Gaulle saw his country as a world power. He was certainly not prepared to see the French army absorbed in what Churchill described as 'a sludgy amalgam' of European armed forces. Neither of them was prone to supranational dreams, but de Gaulle did share Churchill's belief that some form of European unity was the best guarantee of peace on the continent; and such a union, already initiated by the time he returned to power, might well bring economic benefits to France and allow her to dominate Europe. De Gaulle's loyalty was still, as it always had been, to France *alone*. Churchill's, with less fanaticism and a much wider concept of human affairs, was merely to Britain *first*. De Gaulle was a nationalist as well as a patriot. Churchill was a devoted patriot, but never a nationalist.

For all their differences, temperamental as well as political, Churchill and de Gaulle admired and respected each other. The former had created the latter, and in return his hand was bitten again and again. Yet he felt no bitterness; and as for de Gaulle, his feelings are demonstrated by the fact that on the first anniversary of Winston Churchill's death his widow received just one letter: a warm, hand-written one from Charles de Gaulle, President of the French Republic.

CHAPTER FOURTEEN

The End of the Road

Harry Lauder, that 'grand old minstrel', as Churchill described him to the Canadian Parliament, competed with Gilbert and Sullivan, military marches and the Harrow School songs for supremacy in Churchill's not unduly highbrow musical repertory. When Lauder left the stage during a wartime music-hall performance and learned the grievous news that his only son had been killed in action, he returned to face the audience and sang to them 'Keep Right on to the End of the Road'. Churchill, too, was determined to keep right on to the end.

By the time Churchill was eighty some thought Harry Lauder's posthumous influence too strong. The leaders of the Tory party wanted Eden to take over and convinced themselves that Churchill was merely hanging on to office because he could not bear the thought of departure. Their diagnosis was not entirely correct, but in any case their difficulty was how to dislodge him, for they one and all loved him and so did the mass of the people. On his eightieth birthday a quarter of a million pounds, a huge sum by the values of 1954, was subscribed by great and small to give him a birthday present. Only the very old could remember a time without Churchill.

In April 1955 he went of his own volition. There was a newspaper strike in progress so that the tributes were muffled. Thereafter, it was a summer of sunshine. Chartwell, with its lakes and flawlessly maintained gardens, its ponds inhabited by huge golden orfe which swam towards him when he tapped the flagstones and called them, was a Churchillian paradise. Still a Member of Parliament, he could be excused for frequent absences because the Government majority was large. Establishing his right to the corner seat below the gangway which Lord Randolph had occupied after his fall from office, he was a silent spectator of the parliamentary scene, content to sit quietly in that House which brought back countless memories and stirred so many emotions. He had made two long speeches there, on defence and on foreign affairs, in the two months before he resigned. They had been good speeches, every word his own composition, and they had been acclaimed. The old fire still glowed; but he never made another speech in Parliament.

Sitting in the House of Commons or in the garden at Chartwell was soothing, but not enough to satisfy a mind which for all its eighty years was still active and on occasions restless. His old friends, apart from Beaverbrook, were dead or shortly to die; the younger ones were busily occupied; his children were married with their own lives to lead. So, despite the constant presence of the woman he loved more than anyone on earth, he was sometimes lonely. He could still be happy painting, though his skill was tending to weaken, but he no longer had the zest to write.

There were constituency needs to be fulfilled, there was a vast correspondence from admirers at home and abroad, there were messages to send, engagements to fulfil and visitors to receive. He also kept himself in touch with current affairs and the Foreign Office allowed him a regular distribution of official telegrams. Never before or since has a retired Prime Minister been provided with a Private Secretary by the State, but Churchill was regarded as so exceptional a figure that without a grumble from the Opposition an appointment was made. It was a singularly apt one, for he required an intelligent companion as well as a secretary, and he found both, for the rest of his life, in Anthony Montague Browne.

During the war Anthony flew Mosquitos in action against the Japanese and won the Distinguished Flying Cross for gallantry. Being a good linguist, and having an excellent brain, he was selected by the Foreign Office after the war and was sent to the Embassy in Paris. In 1952 a new junior Private Secretary was required at 10 Downing Street. The Foreign Office judged that Montague Browne was suitable for Churchill. They judged right. Well-read and quick on the uptake, he had strong personal opinions on foreign affairs that were well to the right of those held by the Foreign Office and, indeed, by Churchill himself. He did not hesitate to voice them. Churchill took no exception, for he liked those round him to have views of their own. He had not, for instance, been the least perturbed, even during the war, when I argued with him that the Munich settlement had been right. He merely announced that I was 'a filthy Munichois'. In 1952 he was glad to have this outspoken addition to his staff and when, a year after his retirement, a private secretary was to be made available, he did not hesitate in his choice. Montague Browne remained a member of the Foreign Service, but he effectively abandoned his diplomatic career, making the sacrifice without a word of complaint.

Looking after the old and attending to their whims can try patience severely. Anthony did not become impatient. On the contrary, he lavished thoughtful care on Churchill, being always at his side to deal with the official matters which pursued him after his retirement. There were speeches to be made, travels to be organized, foreign heads of Government to be blandished, residual parliamentary obligations to be fulfilled. Anthony was more of an intellectual than Churchill, with almost as good a memory for verse, though for French lyrics rather than Shakespeare, Macaulay or Kipling. However he was prepared to subordinate those of his tastes which touched no answering chord and to spend hours in attendance, bringing comfort and pleasure by his presence and his conversation.

In the aftermath of the Suez affair, there was a visit to Eisenhower in Washington. Discarding memories of his former antipathy, Churchill called on John Foster Dulles, who was dying. There was a last stay in New York, where Bernard Baruch extended his usual hospitality. There were two meetings with de Gaulle, and when Churchill went to Aachen to receive the Charlemagne Prize he had talks with Adenauer on the danger of pressing too hard for German reunification. On each occasion he spoke and acted with vigour, preparing himself carefully in advance. Anthony's assistance was invaluable, for despite his age and his retirement, Churchill still had influence he could bring to bear on the heads of foreign Governments.

After four or five years his memory began to fade and his activities were increasingly curtailed. Anthony would play game after game of bézique with him to help while away the time, would shield him from badgerers and would contrive to raise sparks in the flickering embers. Churchill lamented that he was no longer capable of original thought, but until near the end he could still surprise by the unexpected comment and the shaft of shrewd judgment. Anthony Montague Browne, for his part, proceeded after Churchill's death to use his abilities in a successful business career in the City of London and to be an energetic chairman of the Winston Churchill Memorial Trust.

During the last ten years of his life, as the light slowly dimmed, Churchill found solace in his beloved South of France where the landscapes of Cézanne fed his artistic imagination. Lord Beaverbrook's villa at Cap d'Ail was at his disposal and it was there that in 1958 his family joined him to celebrate his golden wedding, bringing a book of golden roses painted as loving tributes by artists of the stature of Augustus John, Paul Maze and André Dunoyer de Segonzac.

As time went on two new benefactors, in addition to Beaverbrook, offered him comfort and luxury on the Côte d'Azur. The first was a hospitable Hungarian, Emery Reves, whom he first learned to know and to like as the man responsible for negotiating the foreign rights and translations of his books, in particular his *History of the Second World War*. Reves had a villa near Roquebrunne hung with French impressionist pictures. Thither Churchill would go for weeks on end, to paint and to relax, unhindered by curious visitors, the recipient of generous care and delicate attentions by a host who spared no trouble to satisfy and to please.

One day I received a letter from Churchill, written in the South of France, telling me that he had met the Greek shipowner Aristotle Onassis. 'He is a man of mark,' Churchill wrote. Onassis thought the same of Churchill. They became friends, to such an extent that Churchill, to the astonishment of the members, invited Onassis to join the Other Club. He went for several cruises in the large and luxurious yacht *Christina* on which the food was ambrosial and the comfort beyond compare. He was encouraged to ask the guests of his choice to accompany him on voyages in the Mediterranean and as far afield as the West Indies. From aboard this magnificent yacht Onassis controlled his commercial empire, his fleet of tankers, and his other varied enterprises such as the Hôtel de Paris at Monte Carlo where Churchill and his guests were invited to stay at a rate entirely uneconomic for the hotel. Onassis found time, without the least appearance of being preoccupied, to sit with Churchill for hours on end, to talk to him and to conspire how best to make him feel an honoured and much wanted guest. When Churchill's faculties weakened, as his nine-tieth birthday approached, Onassis was as ready as in more lucid days to devote time and ingenuity to his self-imposed task. He was in many respects a hard and selfish man, a frightening tyrant to those who served him, a ruthless exploiter of weaker companies and less powerful men. But there was something in Churchill that stirred the emotional chords in his nature and those who saw them together were not deluded by the commonly held belief that collecting illustrious scalps was the sole motive of his attentions.

Clementine Churchill thought that her husband's least admir-able characteristic was a yearning for luxury so pronounced that he would accept hospitality from anybody able to offer the sur-roundings and the amenities he enjoyed. Lord Birkenhead had made the much quoted quip: 'Mr Churchill is easily satisfied with the best.' It was a side of him abhorrent to Clementine's principles, and there was undeniably an element of truth in her criticism. Many years before, Churchill, almost always without his wife, had revelled in annual visits to the villa in the South of France where the American actress Maxine Elliot entertained all the rich and the powerful she could induce to stay.

Churchill, whose nature it was to notice merits rather than defects, at least as far as social relationships were concerned, did not in fact stay with people he disliked. The Dukes of Westminster and Marlborough, as well as Lord Beaverbrook, were intimate friends. Lavish entertainment was a strong attraction, but it was not for that alone he found pleasure in the company of Maxine Elliot, Emery Reves and Aristotle Onassis. He drank their flowing champagne, and basked in the beautiful surroundings of their villas and yachts, without asking himself if he was accepting what they supplied for the wrong reasons. He might not feel drawn to Somerset Maugham, but if Maugham asked him to an excellent luncheon in a beautiful villa, why not accept? He was curiously innocent in such matters, and he was not influenced by what others might think. He was sorry his wife was so seldom willing to accompany him on these visits, but whether or not he fully understood her scruples, he felt no obligation to be bound by them. He himself was always pleased to gratify those he liked with all he could afford and every pleasure he could supply. He assumed that others felt as he did. His predilection for luxury was in any case but a small item to enter on the debit side of a long, favourable balance sheet.

Throughout his life a notable fact about Churchill's friends and associates is their variety. Few of them were bores, for he could not endure the solemn or the long-winded. Some, like Birkenhead, Beaverbrook and Lloyd George, like Brendan and the Prof, were endowed with the strongest armament of wit and originality. Some, like his dearly loved brother, Jack, or his Flag Commander in the Second World War, Tommy Thompson, were men whose intelligence the rest of the world did not rate high. Some, like Admiral Lord Fisher, were megalomaniacs, some were exhibitionists, some were ambitious and many were just worthily striving to do their best. The majority, especially among his official and political friends, were men who held office honourably and to the best of their varying abilities, but who also had a sense of humour, a ready tongue and the gift of good companionship. Collectively their names record the achievements and failures of Britain and the United States in the first sixty years of the twentieth century.

Index